RESIDENT EVIL

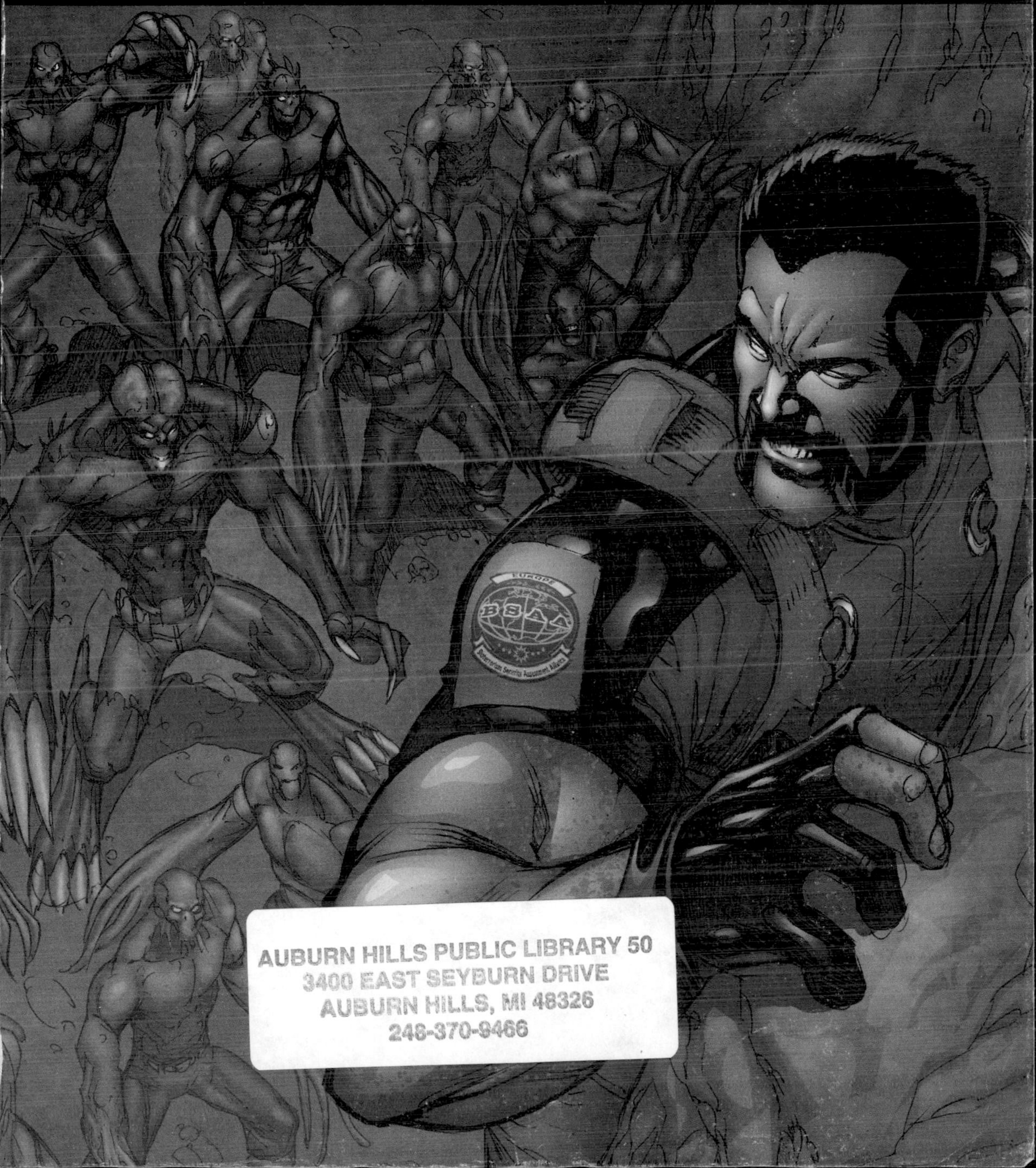
BSAA

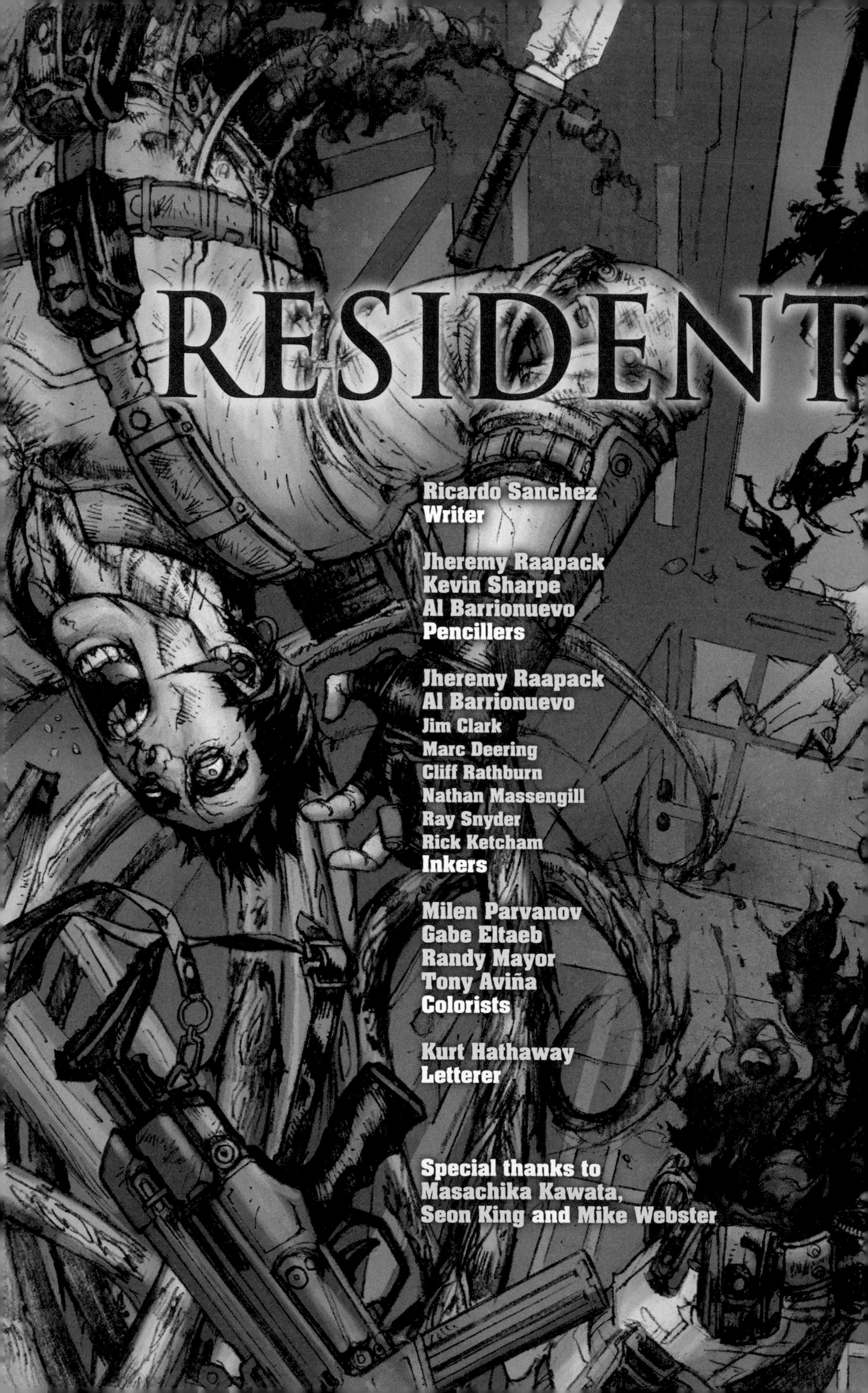

RESIDENT

Ricardo Sanchez
Writer

Jheremy Raapack
Kevin Sharpe
Al Barrionuevo
Pencillers

Jheremy Raapack
Al Barrionuevo
Jim Clark
Marc Deering
Cliff Rathburn
Nathan Massengill
Ray Snyder
Rick Ketcham
Inkers

Milen Parvanov
Gabe Eltaeb
Randy Mayor
Tony Aviña
Colorists

Kurt Hathaway
Letterer

Special thanks to
Masachika Kawata,
Seon King and Mike Webster

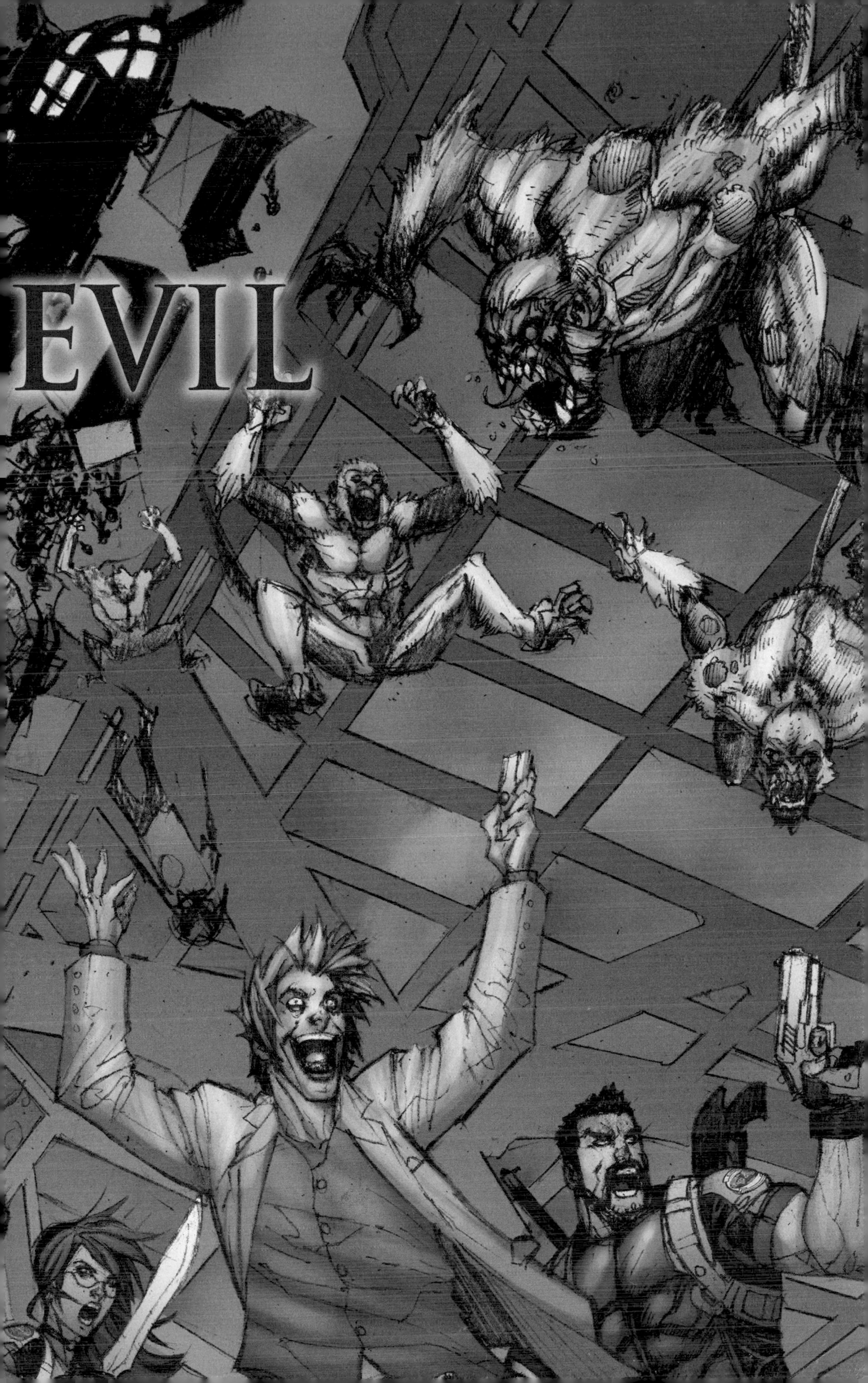
EVIL

Shannon Eric Denton
Jim Chadwick
Editors – Original Series

Michael McCalister
Kristy Quinn
Assistant Editors – Original Series

Ian Sattler
Director Editorial, Special Projects and Archival Editions

Robbin Brosterman
Design Director – Books

Eddie Berganza
Executive Editor

Bob Harras
VP – Editor in Chief

Diane Nelson
President

Dan DiDio and **Jim Lee**
Co-Publishers

Geoff Johns
Chief Creative Officer

John Rood
Executive VP – Sales, Marketing and Business Development

Amy Genkins
Senior VP – Business and Legal Affairs

Nairi Gardiner
Senior VP – Finance

Jeff Boison
VP – Publishing Operations

Mark Chiarello
VP – Art Direction and Design

John Cunningham
VP – Marketing

Terri Cunningham
VP – Talent Relations and Services

Alison Gill
Senior VP – Manufacturing and Operations

David Hyde
VP – Publicity

Hank Kanalz
Senior VP – Digital

Jay Kogan
VP – Business and Legal Affairs, Publishing

Jack Mahan
VP – Business Affairs, Talent

Nick Napolitano
VP – Manufacturing Administration

Ron Perazza
VP – Online

Sue Pohja
VP – Book Sales

Courtney Simmons
Senior VP – Publicity

Bob Wayne
Senior VP – Sales

RESIDENT EVIL: VOLUME 2

Published by DC Comics under license from CAPCOM CO. LTD.
Cover and compilation Copyright © 2011 CAPCOM CO., LTD.
All Rights Reserved.

Originally published by WildStorm Productions in single
magazine form in RESIDENT EVIL: VOLUME 2 1-6. Copyright
© 2009, 2010, 2011 CAPCOM CO. LTD. All Rights Reserved.
RESIDENT EVIL is a trademark of CAPCOM. CAPCOM is
a registered trademark of CAPCOM CO., LTD. The stories,
characters and incidents mentioned in this publication are
entirely fictional. DC Comics does not read or accept
unsolicited submissions of ideas, stories or artwork.

DC Comics, 1700 Broadway, New York, NY 10019
A Warner Bros. Entertainment Company
Printed by Quad/Graphics, Dubuque, IA. 7/15/11.
First Printing.
ISBN: 978-1-4012-2602-2

This comic is based upon an original story by WildStorm
and is not part of the officially recognized *Resident Evil*
canon as created and established by Capcom.

SUSTAINABLE
FORESTRY
INITIATIVE
Certified Chain of Custody
Promoting Sustainable
Forest Management

Fiber used in this product line meets the
sourcing requirements of the SFI program.
www.sfiprogram.org SGS-SFICOC-0130

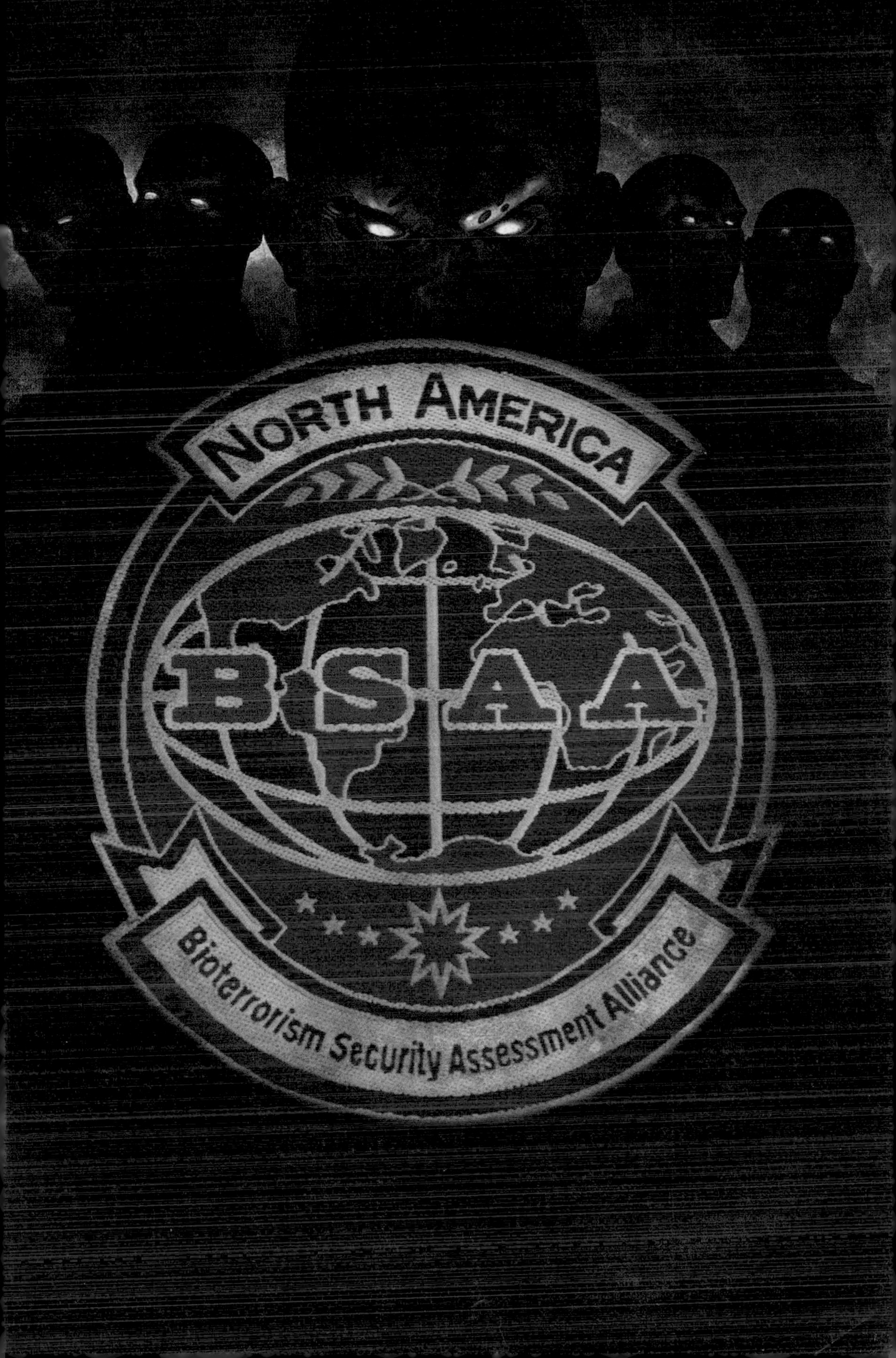
NORTH AMERICA
B.S.A.A
Bioterrorism Security Assessment Alliance

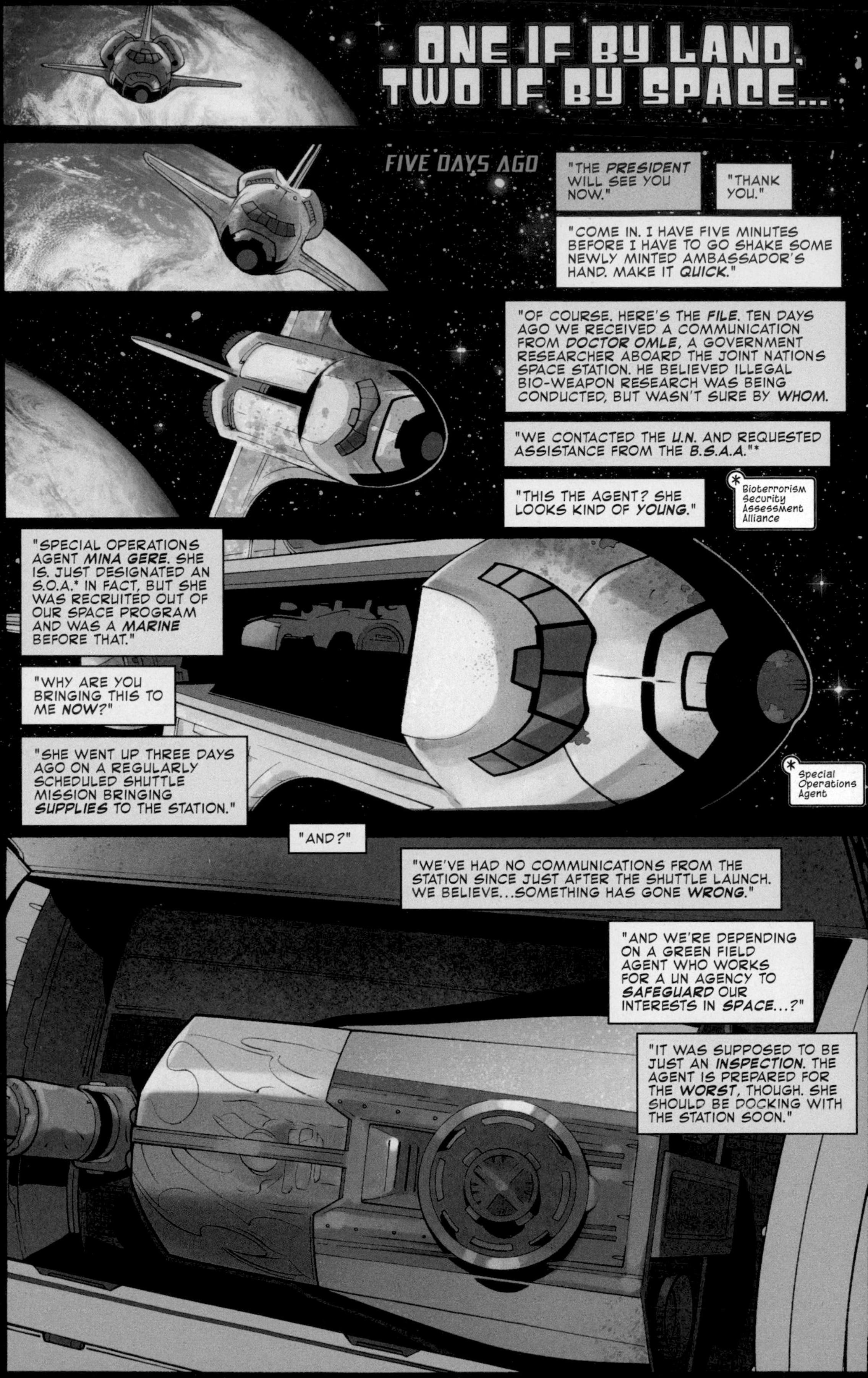
ONE IF BY LAND, TWO IF BY SPACE...
FIVE DAYS AGO
"THE PRESIDENT WILL SEE YOU NOW."
"THANK YOU."
"COME IN. I HAVE FIVE MINUTES BEFORE I HAVE TO GO SHAKE SOME NEWLY MINTED AMBASSADOR'S HAND. MAKE IT QUICK."
"OF COURSE. HERE'S THE FILE. TEN DAYS AGO WE RECEIVED A COMMUNICATION FROM DOCTOR OMLE, A GOVERNMENT RESEARCHER ABOARD THE JOINT NATIONS SPACE STATION. HE BELIEVED ILLEGAL BIO-WEAPON RESEARCH WAS BEING CONDUCTED, BUT WASN'T SURE BY WHOM.
"WE CONTACTED THE U.N. AND REQUESTED ASSISTANCE FROM THE B.S.A.A."*
"THIS THE AGENT? SHE LOOKS KIND OF YOUNG."
*Bioterrorism Security Assessment Alliance
"SPECIAL OPERATIONS AGENT MINA GERE. SHE IS. JUST DESIGNATED AN S.O.A.* IN FACT, BUT SHE WAS RECRUITED OUT OF OUR SPACE PROGRAM AND WAS A MARINE BEFORE THAT."
"WHY ARE YOU BRINGING THIS TO ME NOW?"
"SHE WENT UP THREE DAYS AGO ON A REGULARLY SCHEDULED SHUTTLE MISSION BRINGING SUPPLIES TO THE STATION."
*Special Operations Agent
"AND?"
"WE'VE HAD NO COMMUNICATIONS FROM THE STATION SINCE JUST AFTER THE SHUTTLE LAUNCH. WE BELIEVE...SOMETHING HAS GONE WRONG."
"AND WE'RE DEPENDING ON A GREEN FIELD AGENT WHO WORKS FOR A UN AGENCY TO SAFEGUARD OUR INTERESTS IN SPACE...?"
"IT WAS SUPPOSED TO BE JUST AN INSPECTION. THE AGENT IS PREPARED FOR THE WORST, THOUGH. SHE SHOULD BE DOCKING WITH THE STATION SOON."

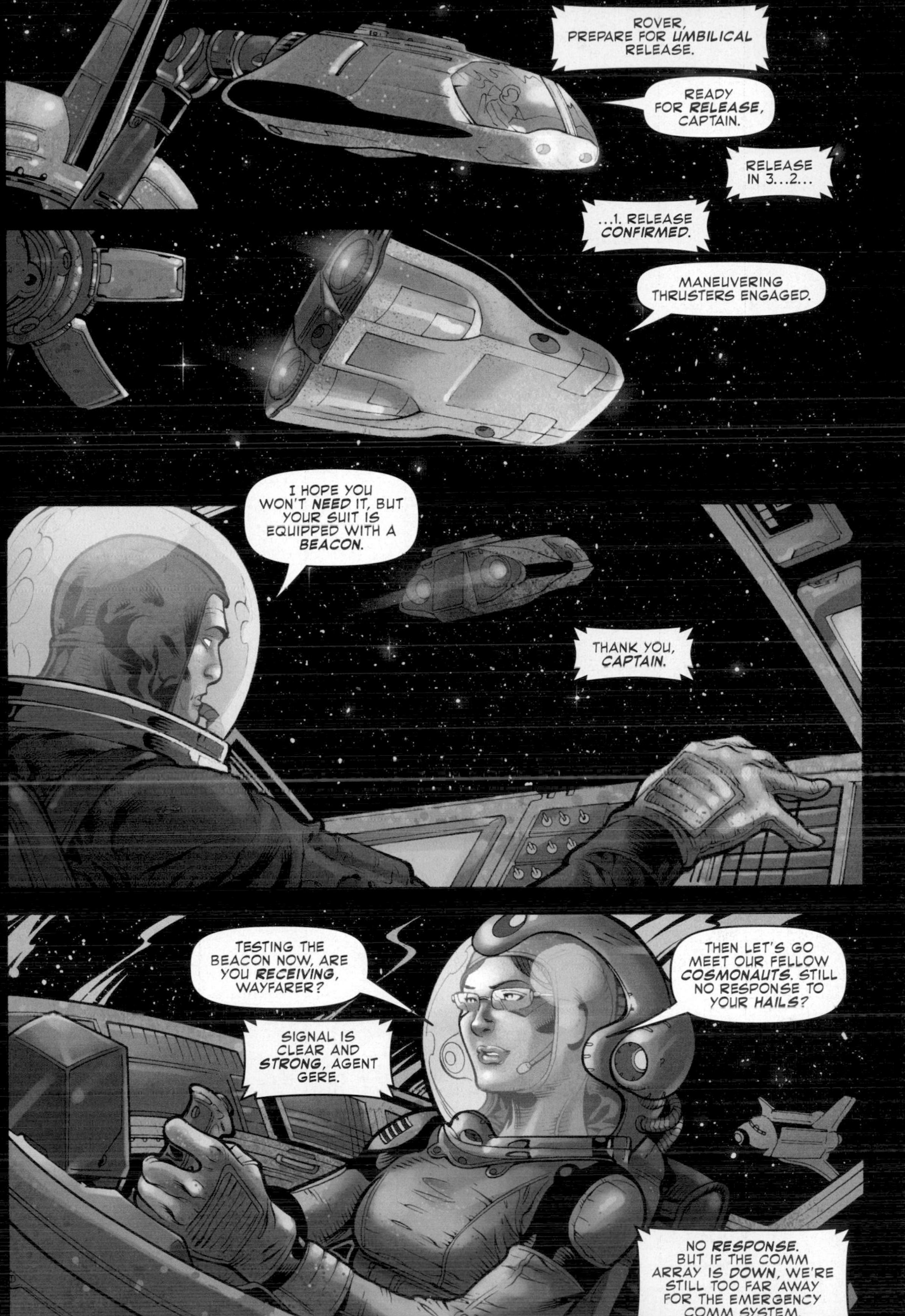
ROVER, PREPARE FOR UMBILICAL RELEASE.
READY FOR RELEASE, CAPTAIN.
RELEASE IN 3...2...
...1. RELEASE CONFIRMED.
MANEUVERING THRUSTERS ENGAGED.
I HOPE YOU WON'T NEED IT, BUT YOUR SUIT IS EQUIPPED WITH A BEACON.
THANK YOU, CAPTAIN.
TESTING THE BEACON NOW, ARE YOU RECEIVING, WAYFARER?
SIGNAL IS CLEAR AND STRONG, AGENT GERE.
THEN LET'S GO MEET OUR FELLOW COSMONAUTS. STILL NO RESPONSE TO YOUR HAILS?
NO RESPONSE. BUT IF THE COMM ARRAY IS DOWN, WE'RE STILL TOO FAR AWAY FOR THE EMERGENCY COMM SYSTEM.

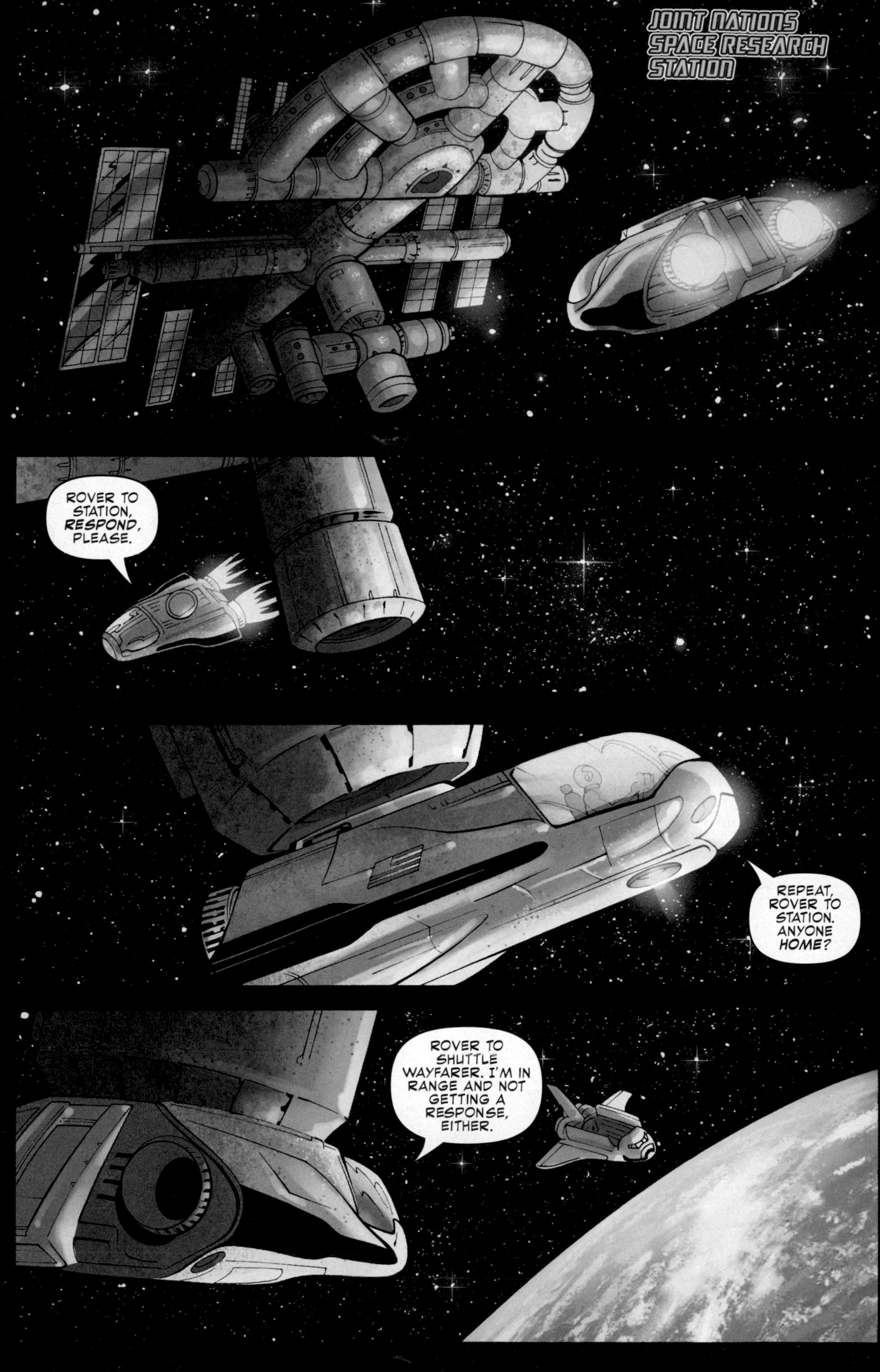
JOINT NATIONS SPACE RESEARCH STATION
ROVER TO STATION, RESPOND, PLEASE.
REPEAT, ROVER TO STATION. ANYONE HOME?
ROVER TO SHUTTLE WAYFARER. I'M IN RANGE AND NOT GETTING A RESPONSE, EITHER.

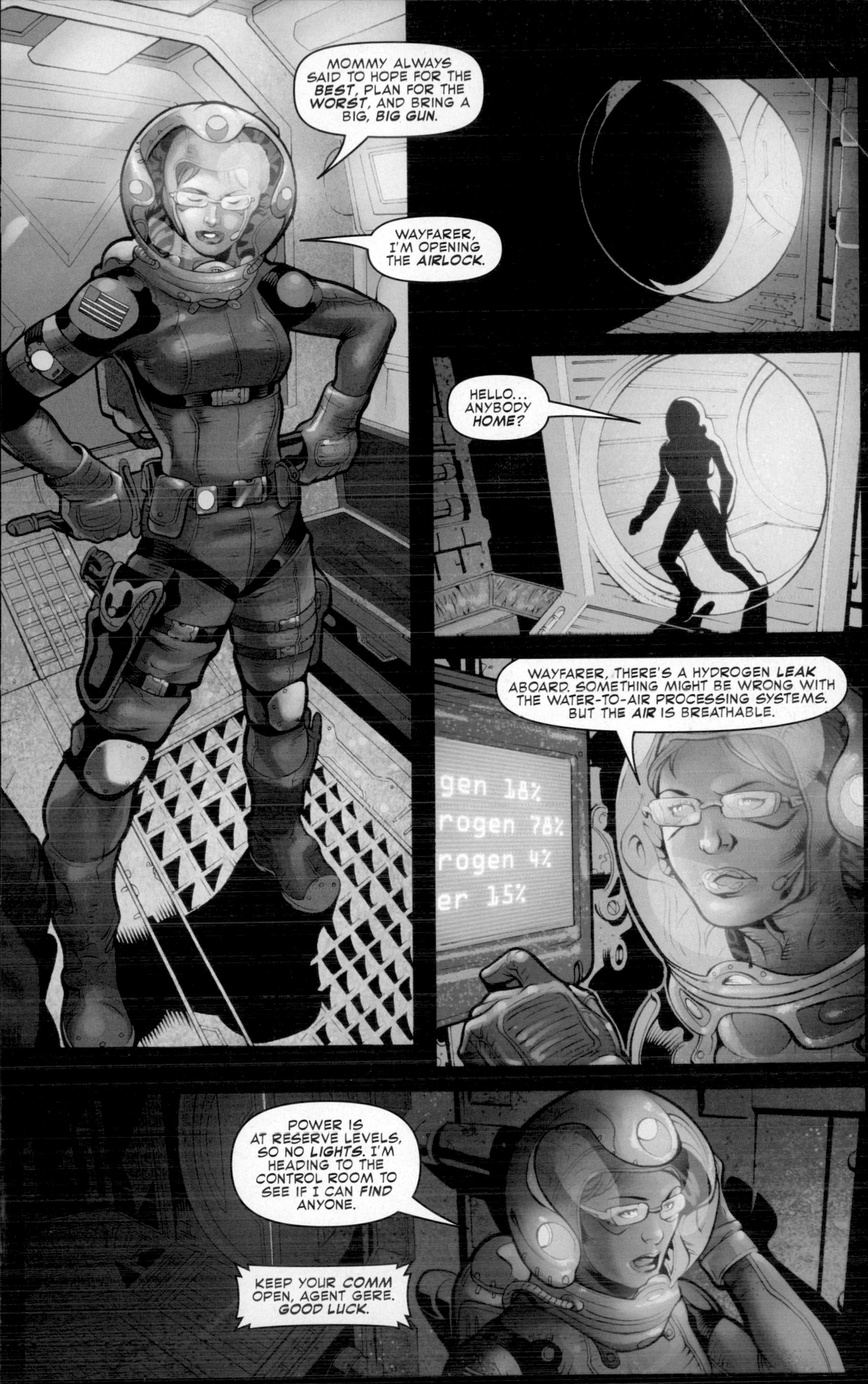
MOMMY ALWAYS SAID TO HOPE FOR THE BEST, PLAN FOR THE WORST, AND BRING A BIG, BIG GUN.
WAYFARER, I'M OPENING THE AIRLOCK.
HELLO... ANYBODY HOME?
WAYFARER, THERE'S A HYDROGEN LEAK ABOARD. SOMETHING MIGHT BE WRONG WITH THE WATER-TO-AIR PROCESSING SYSTEMS. BUT THE AIR IS BREATHABLE.
gen 18%
rogen 78%
rogen 4%
er 15%
POWER IS AT RESERVE LEVELS, SO NO LIGHTS. I'M HEADING TO THE CONTROL ROOM TO SEE IF I CAN FIND ANYONE.
KEEP YOUR COMM OPEN, AGENT GERE. GOOD LUCK.

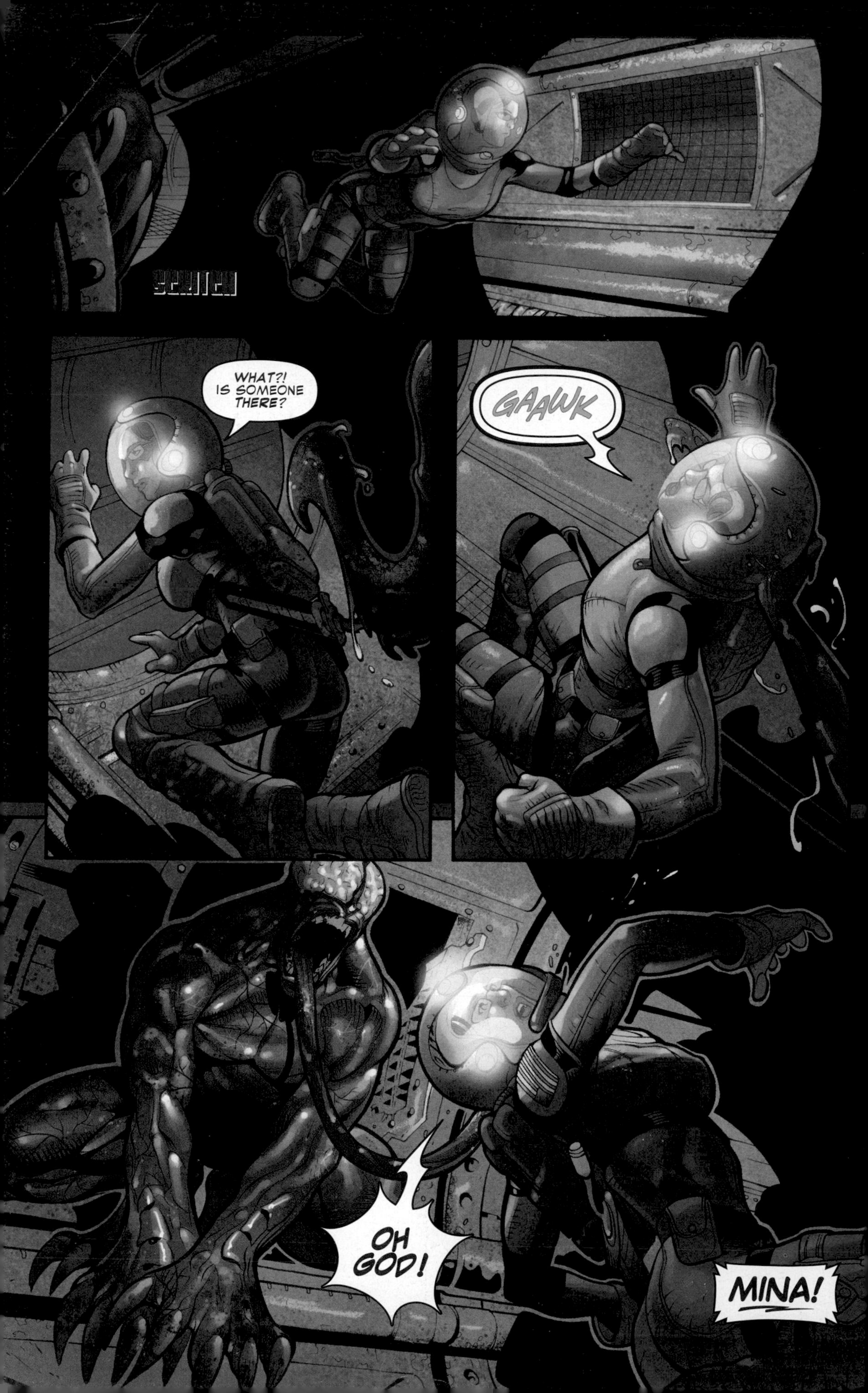
WHAT?! IS SOMEONE THERE?
GAAWK
OH GOD!
MINA!

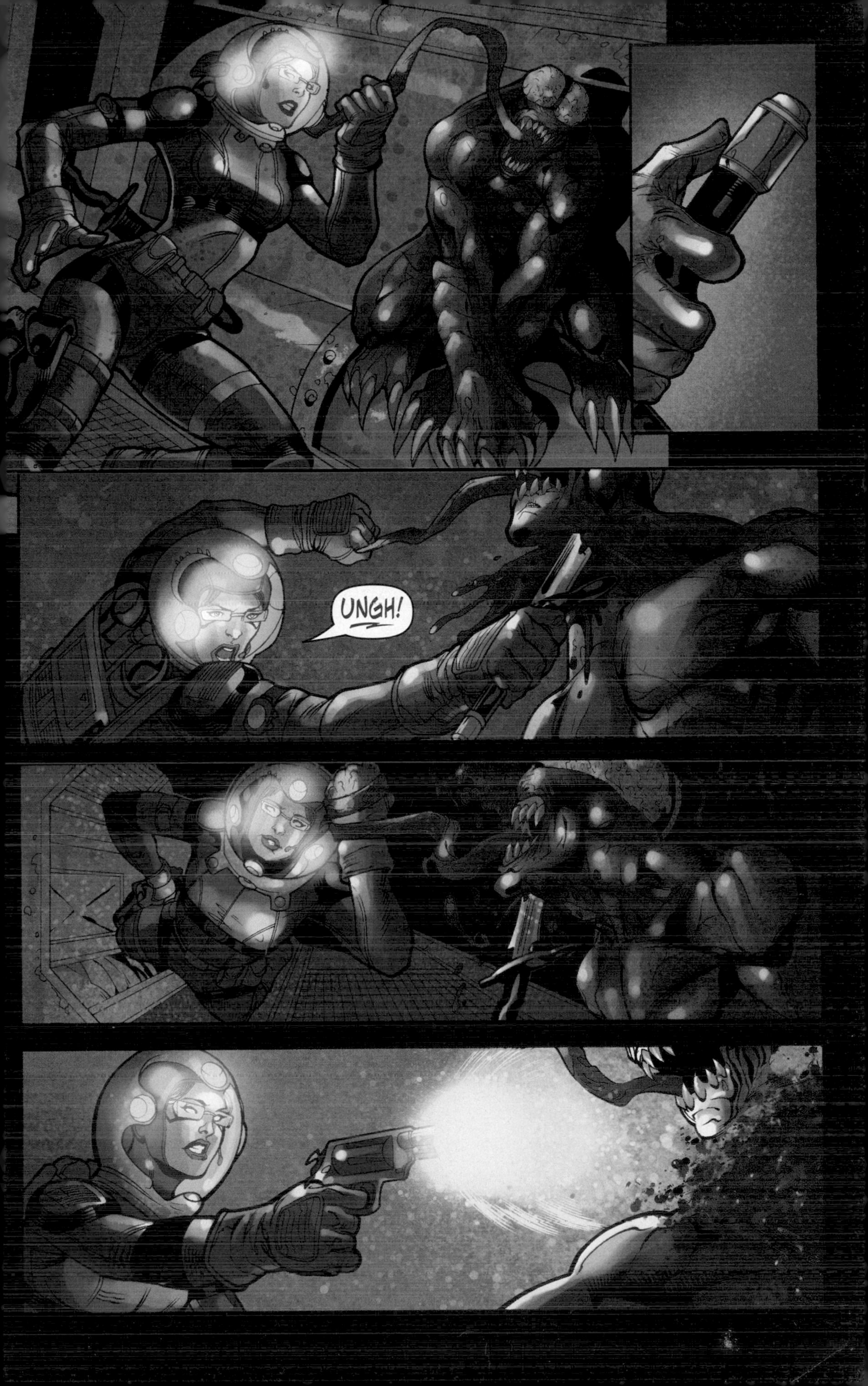
UNGH!

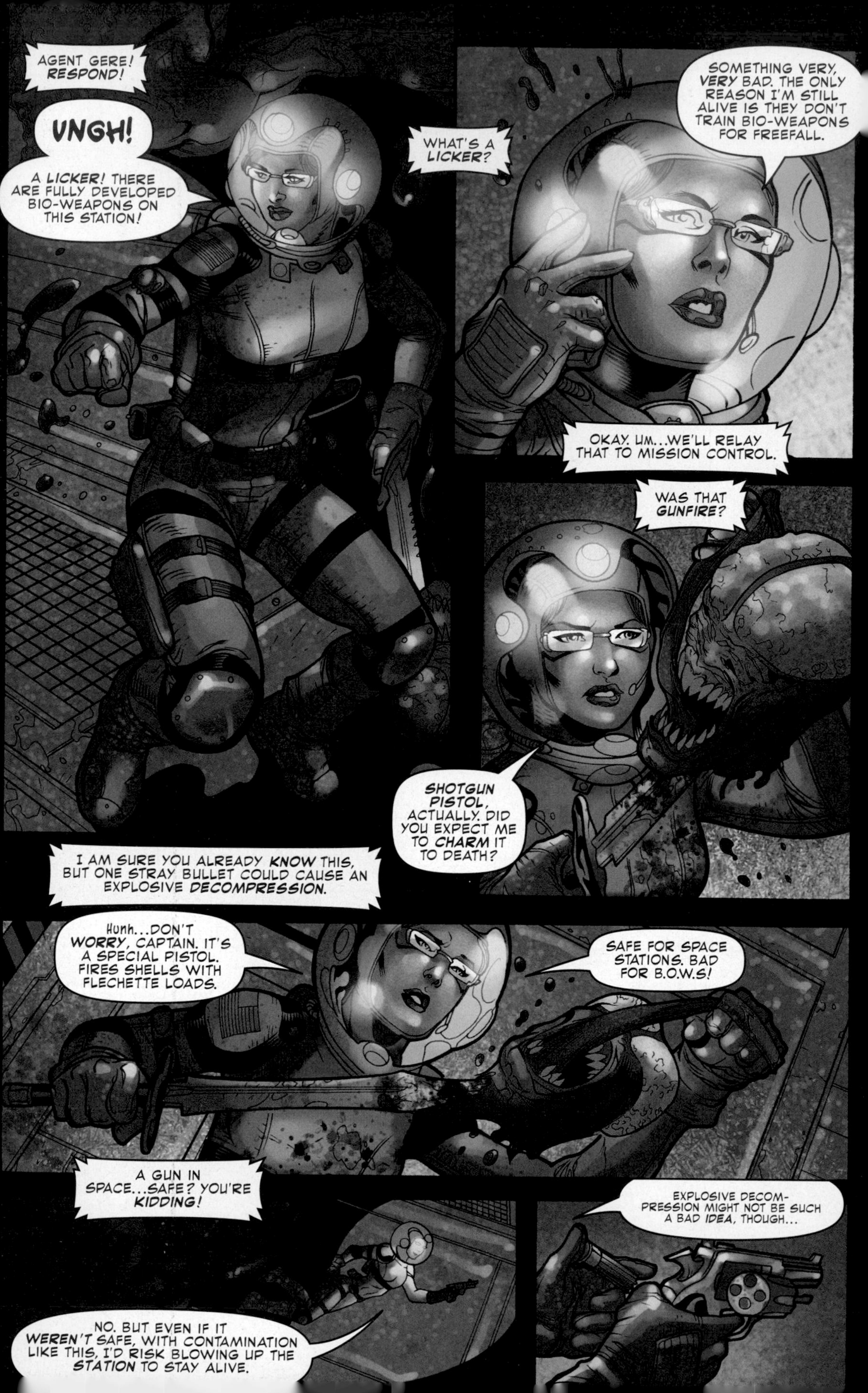
AGENT GERE! RESPOND!
UNGH!
A LICKER! THERE ARE FULLY DEVELOPED BIO-WEAPONS ON THIS STATION!
WHAT'S A LICKER?
SOMETHING VERY, VERY BAD. THE ONLY REASON I'M STILL ALIVE IS THEY DON'T TRAIN BIO-WEAPONS FOR FREEFALL.
OKAY. UM...WE'LL RELAY THAT TO MISSION CONTROL.
WAS THAT GUNFIRE?
SHOTGUN PISTOL, ACTUALLY. DID YOU EXPECT ME TO CHARM IT TO DEATH?
I AM SURE YOU ALREADY KNOW THIS, BUT ONE STRAY BULLET COULD CAUSE AN EXPLOSIVE DECOMPRESSION.
Hunh...DON'T WORRY, CAPTAIN. IT'S A SPECIAL PISTOL. FIRES SHELLS WITH FLECHETTE LOADS.
SAFE FOR SPACE STATIONS. BAD FOR B.O.W.S!
A GUN IN SPACE...SAFE? YOU'RE KIDDING!
NO. BUT EVEN IF IT WEREN'T SAFE, WITH CONTAMINATION LIKE THIS, I'D RISK BLOWING UP THE STATION TO STAY ALIVE.
EXPLOSIVE DECOM-PRESSION MIGHT NOT BE SUCH A BAD IDEA, THOUGH...

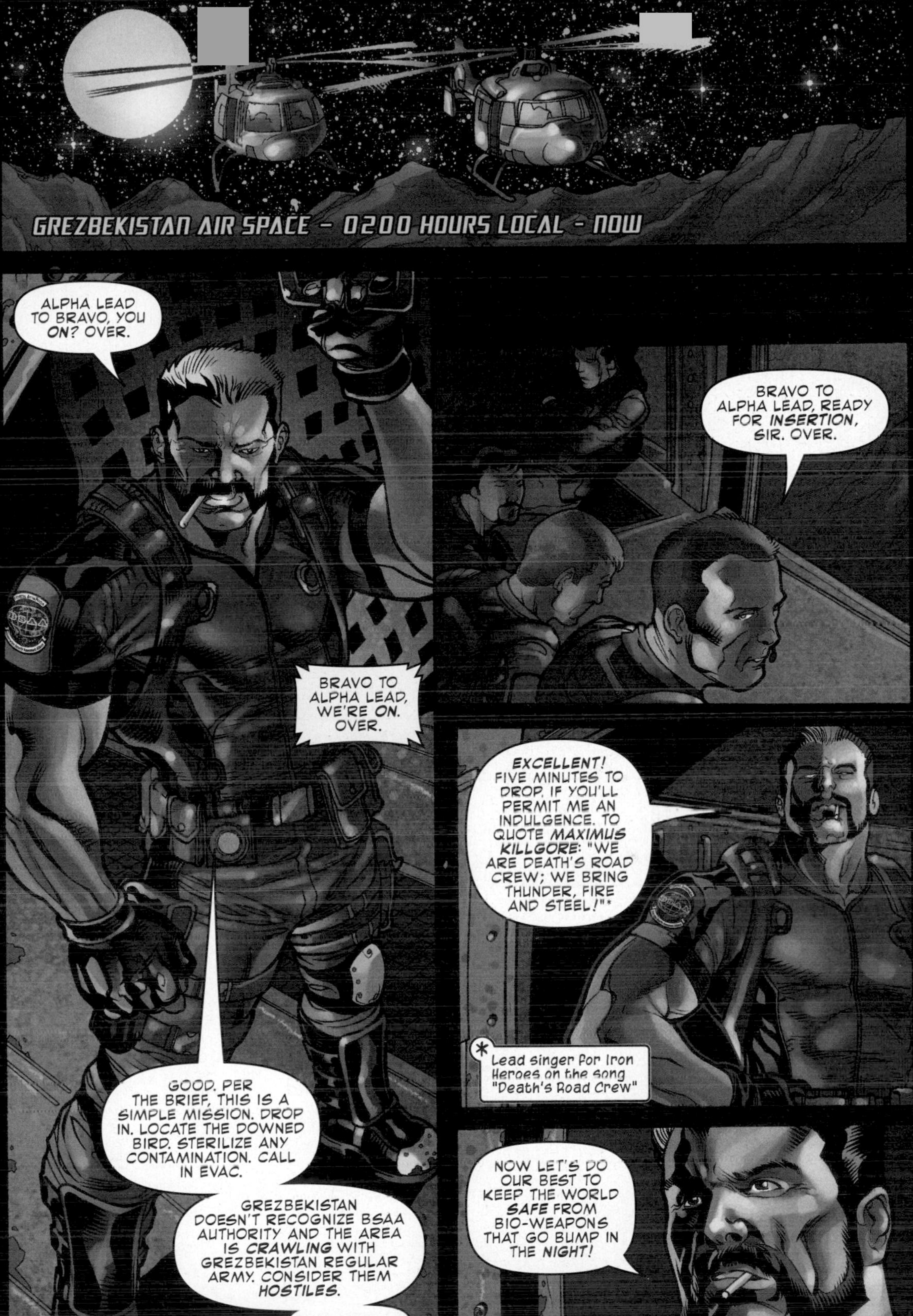
GREZBEKISTAN AIR SPACE - 0200 HOURS LOCAL - NOW
ALPHA LEAD TO BRAVO, YOU ON? OVER.
BRAVO TO ALPHA LEAD, WE'RE ON. OVER.
BRAVO TO ALPHA LEAD, READY FOR INSERTION, SIR. OVER.
GOOD. PER THE BRIEF, THIS IS A SIMPLE MISSION. DROP IN. LOCATE THE DOWNED BIRD. STERILIZE ANY CONTAMINATION. CALL IN EVAC.
GREZBEKISTAN DOESN'T RECOGNIZE BSAA AUTHORITY AND THE AREA IS CRAWLING WITH GREZBEKISTAN REGULAR ARMY. CONSIDER THEM HOSTILES.
QUESTIONS? OVER.
EXCELLENT! FIVE MINUTES TO DROP. IF YOU'LL PERMIT ME AN INDULGENCE. TO QUOTE MAXIMUS KILLGORE: "WE ARE DEATH'S ROAD CREW; WE BRING THUNDER, FIRE AND STEEL!"*
* Lead singer for Iron Heroes on the song "Death's Road Crew"
NOW LET'S DO OUR BEST TO KEEP THE WORLD SAFE FROM BIO-WEAPONS THAT GO BUMP IN THE NIGHT!

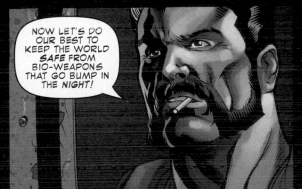

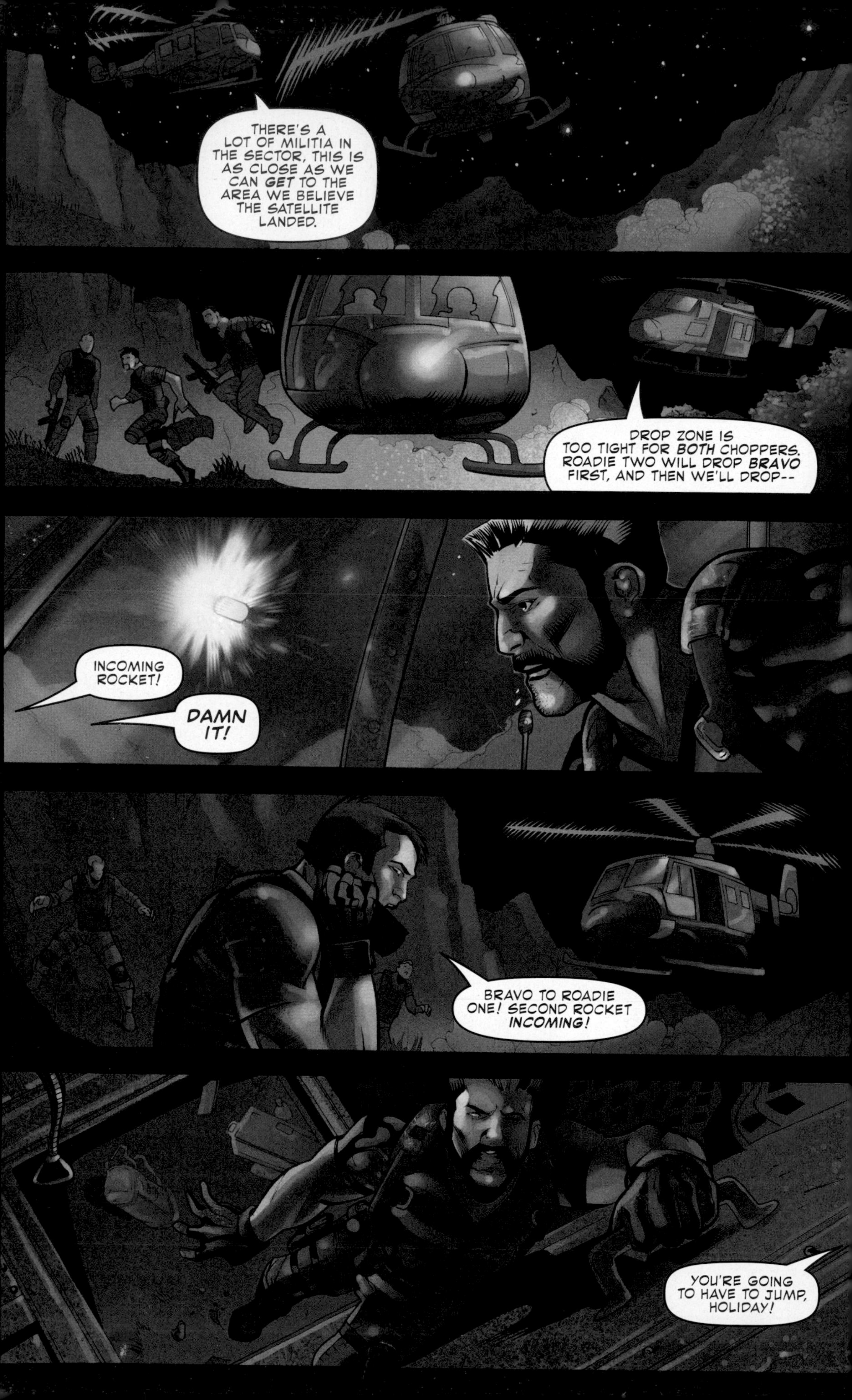
THERE'S A LOT OF MILITIA IN THE SECTOR, THIS IS AS CLOSE AS WE CAN **GET** TO THE AREA WE BELIEVE THE SATELLITE LANDED.
DROP ZONE IS TOO TIGHT FOR *BOTH* CHOPPERS. ROADIE TWO WILL DROP ***BRAVO*** FIRST, AND THEN WE'LL DROP--
INCOMING ROCKET!
DAMN IT!
BRAVO TO ROADIE ONE! SECOND ROCKET ***INCOMING!***
YOU'RE GOING TO HAVE TO JUMP, HOLIDAY!

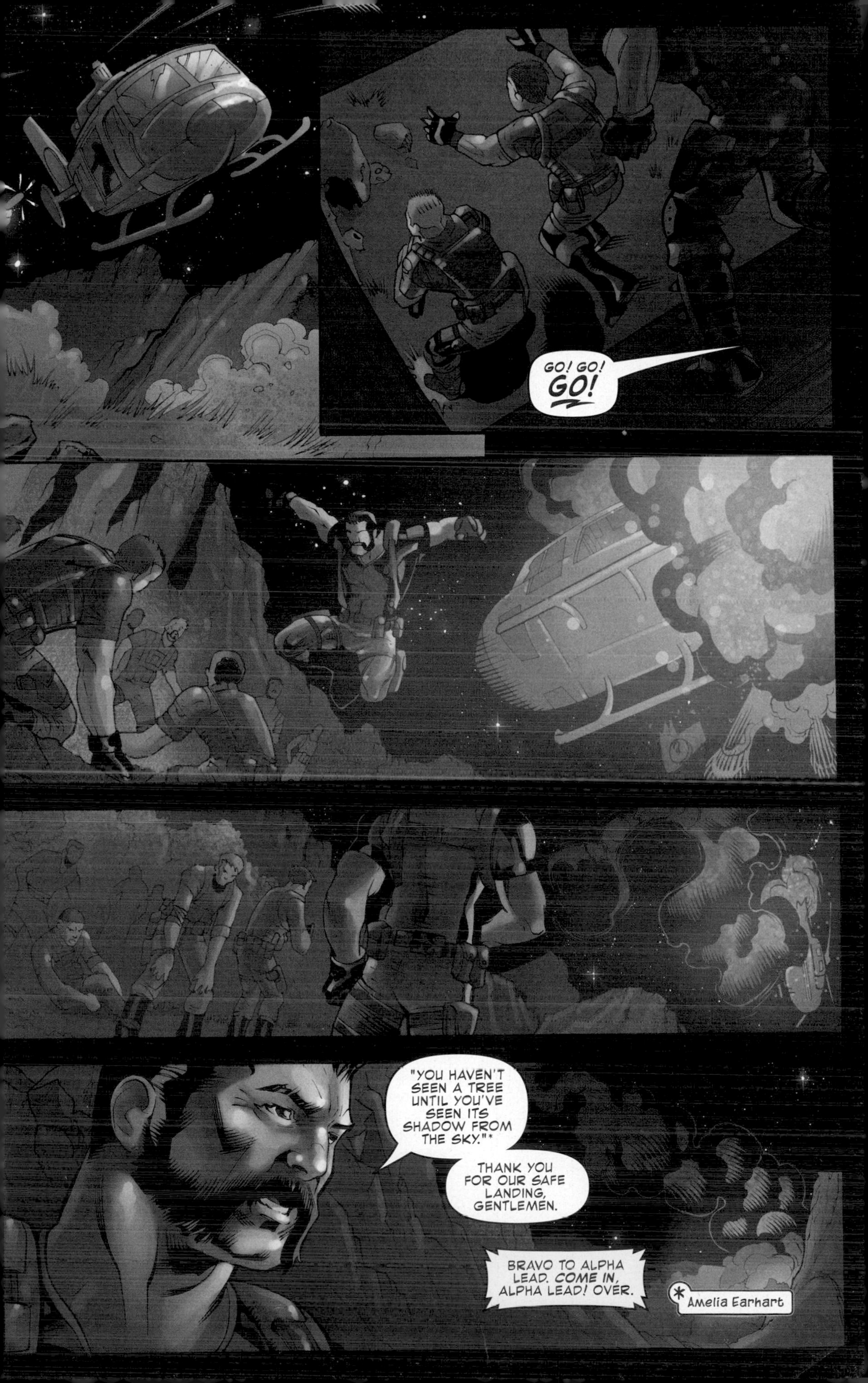
GO! GO! GO!
"YOU HAVEN'T SEEN A TREE UNTIL YOU'VE SEEN ITS SHADOW FROM THE SKY."*
THANK YOU FOR OUR SAFE LANDING, GENTLEMEN.
BRAVO TO ALPHA LEAD. COME IN, ALPHA LEAD! OVER.
*Amelia Earhart

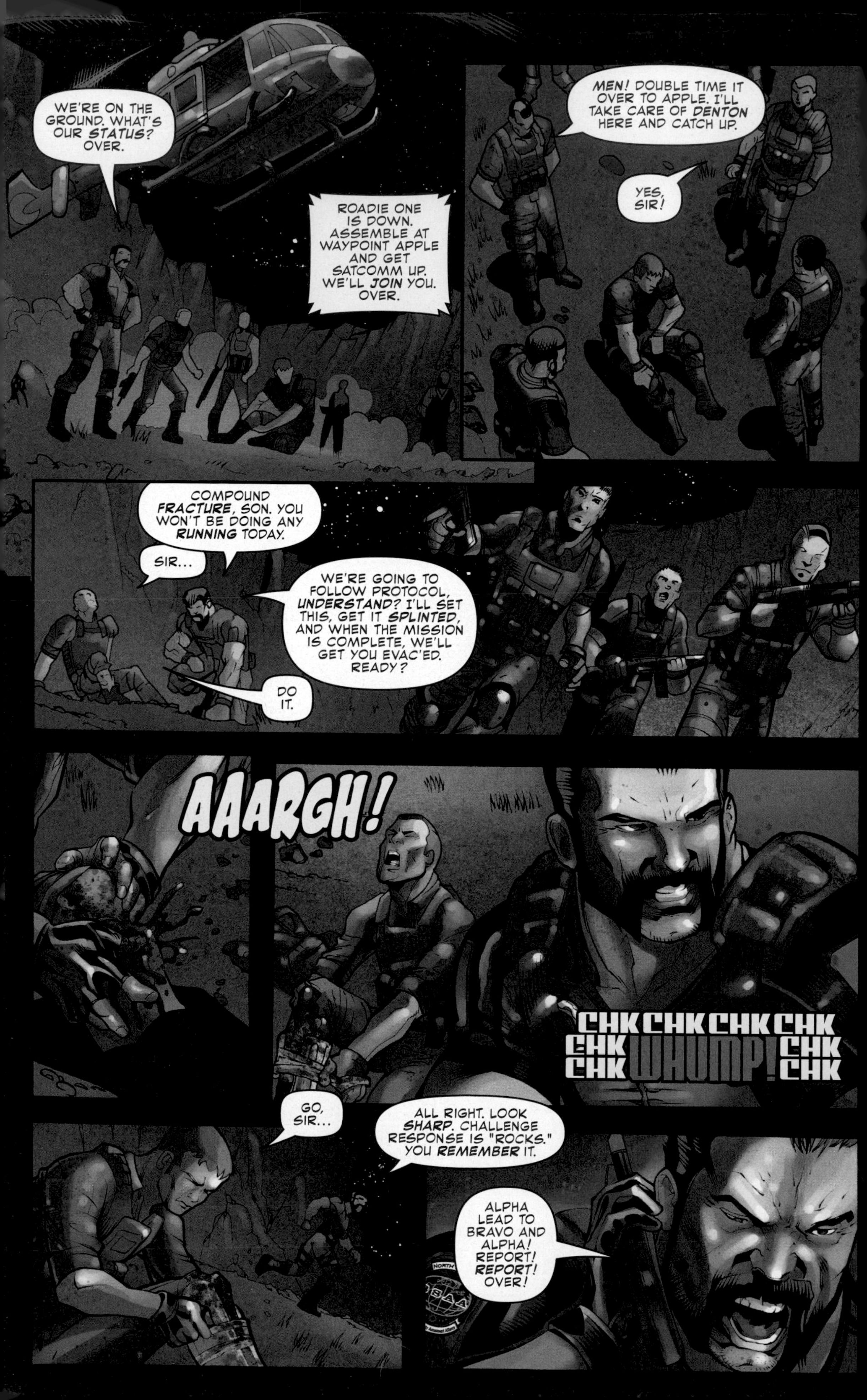
WE'RE ON THE GROUND. WHAT'S OUR STATUS? OVER.
ROADIE ONE IS DOWN. ASSEMBLE AT WAYPOINT APPLE AND GET SATCOMM UP. WE'LL JOIN YOU. OVER.
MEN! DOUBLE TIME IT OVER TO APPLE. I'LL TAKE CARE OF DENTON HERE AND CATCH UP.
YES, SIR!
COMPOUND FRACTURE, SON. YOU WON'T BE DOING ANY RUNNING TODAY.
SIR...
WE'RE GOING TO FOLLOW PROTOCOL, UNDERSTAND? I'LL SET THIS, GET IT SPLINTED, AND WHEN THE MISSION IS COMPLETE, WE'LL GET YOU EVAC'ED. READY?
DO IT.
AAARGH!
CHK CHK CHK CHK
CHK WHUMP! CHK
CHK CHK
GO, SIR...
ALL RIGHT. LOOK SHARP. CHALLENGE RESPONSE IS "ROCKS." YOU REMEMBER IT.
ALPHA LEAD TO BRAVO AND ALPHA! REPORT! REPORT! OVER!

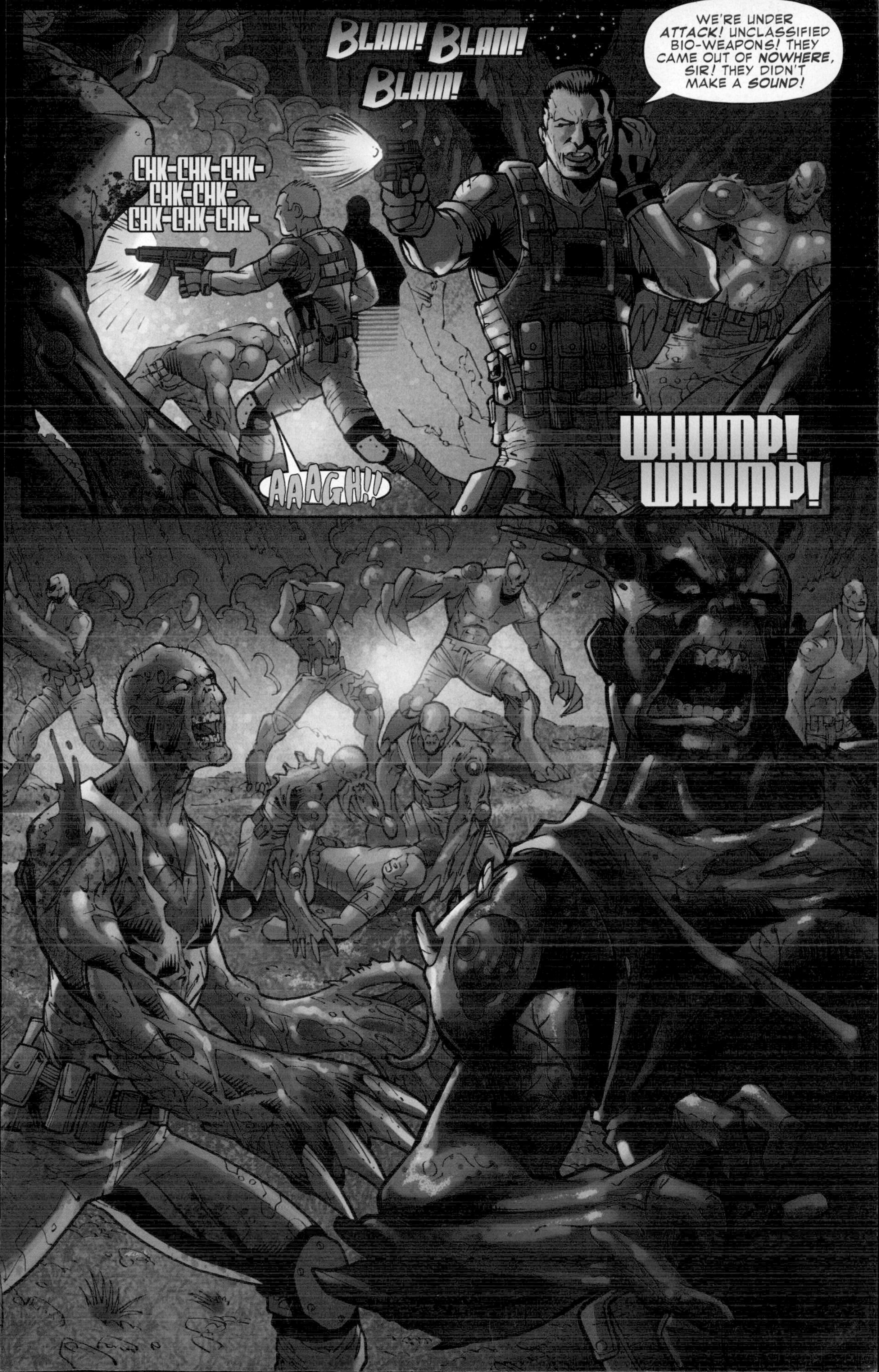
BLAM! BLAM!
BLAM!
WE'RE UNDER ATTACK! UNCLASSIFIED BIO-WEAPONS! THEY CAME OUT OF NOWHERE, SIR! THEY DIDN'T MAKE A SOUND!
CHK-CHK-CHK-CHK-CHK-CHK-CHK-CHK-
AAAGH!!
WHUMP! WHUMP!

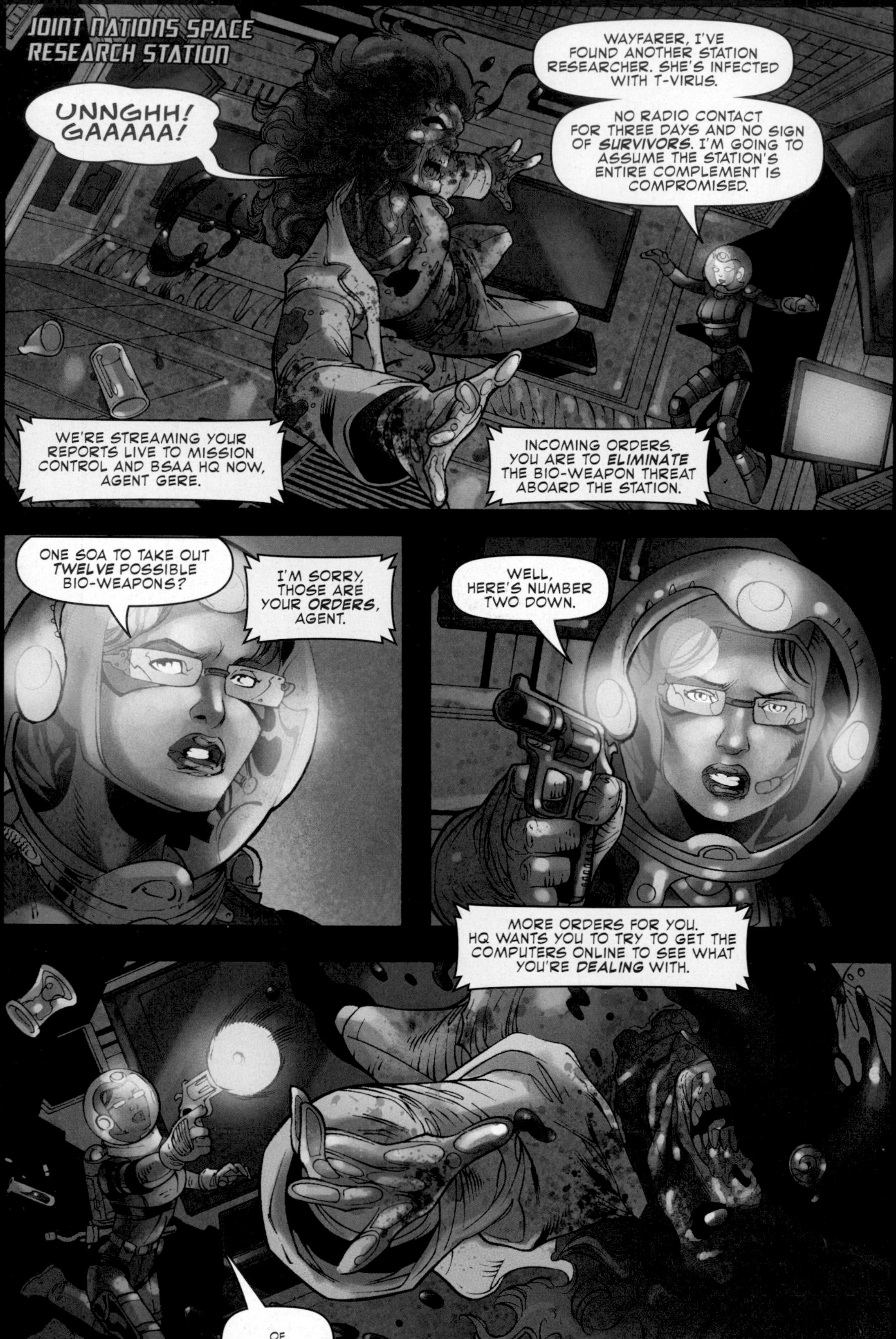
JOINT NATIONS SPACE RESEARCH STATION
UNNGHH! GAAAAA!
WAYFARER, I'VE FOUND ANOTHER STATION RESEARCHER. SHE'S INFECTED WITH T-VIRUS.
NO RADIO CONTACT FOR THREE DAYS AND NO SIGN OF SURVIVORS. I'M GOING TO ASSUME THE STATION'S ENTIRE COMPLEMENT IS COMPROMISED.
WE'RE STREAMING YOUR REPORTS LIVE TO MISSION CONTROL AND BSAA HQ NOW, AGENT GERE.
INCOMING ORDERS. YOU ARE TO ELIMINATE THE BIO-WEAPON THREAT ABOARD THE STATION.
ONE SOA TO TAKE OUT TWELVE POSSIBLE BIO-WEAPONS?
I'M SORRY, THOSE ARE YOUR ORDERS, AGENT.
WELL, HERE'S NUMBER TWO DOWN.
MORE ORDERS FOR YOU. HQ WANTS YOU TO TRY TO GET THE COMPUTERS ONLINE TO SEE WHAT YOU'RE DEALING WITH.
OF COURSE THEY DO.

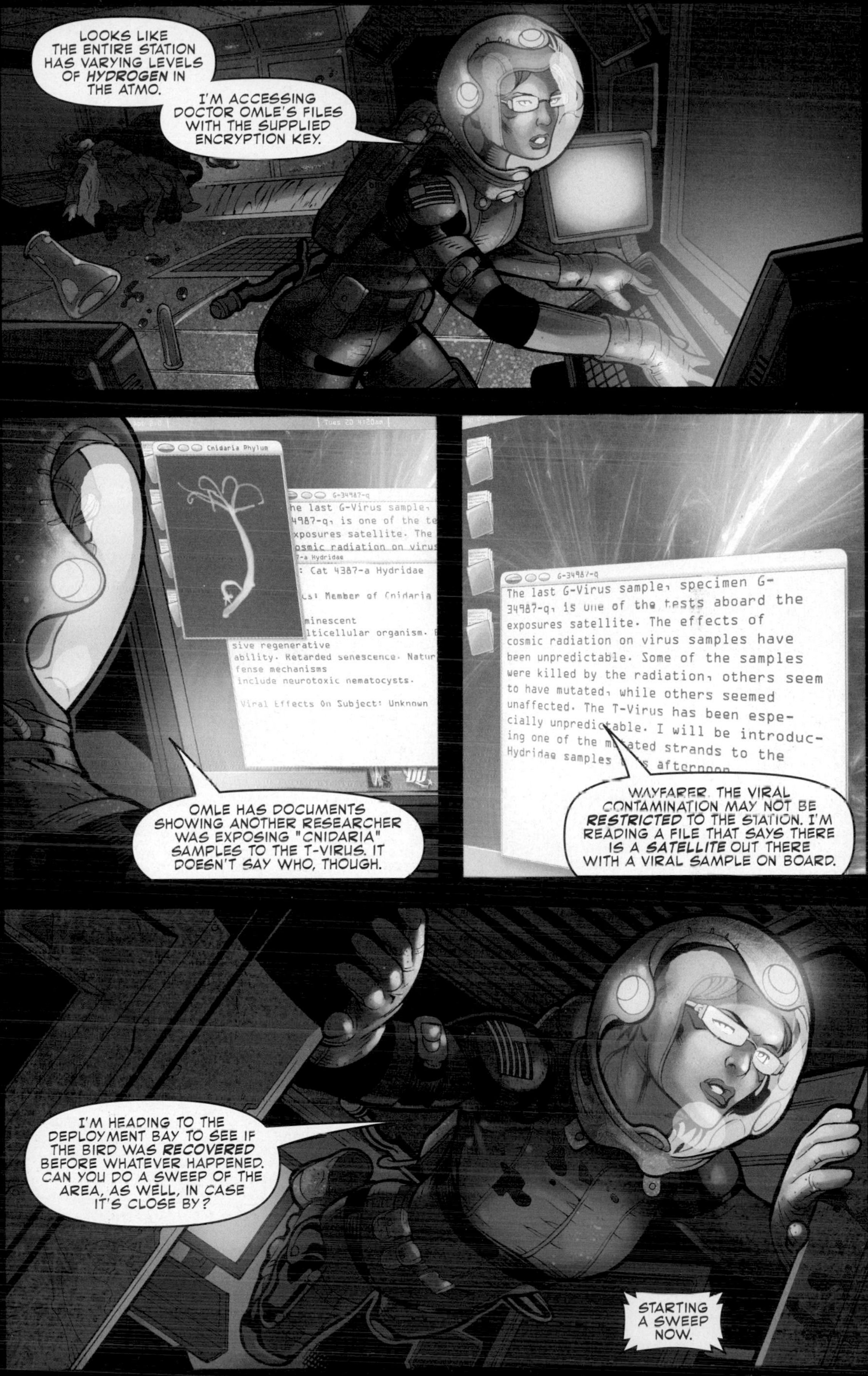
LOOKS LIKE THE ENTIRE STATION HAS VARYING LEVELS OF HYDROGEN IN THE ATMO.
I'M ACCESSING DOCTOR OMLE'S FILES WITH THE SUPPLIED ENCRYPTION KEY.
Cnidaria Phylum
Cat 4387-a Hydridae
ability. Retarded senescence.
fense mechanisms
include neurotoxic nematocysts.
Viral Effects On Subject: Unknown
OMLE HAS DOCUMENTS SHOWING ANOTHER RESEARCHER WAS EXPOSING "CNIDARIA" SAMPLES TO THE T-VIRUS. IT DOESN'T SAY WHO, THOUGH.
G-34987-q
The last G-Virus sample, specimen G-
34987-q, is one of the tests aboard the
exposures satellite. The effects of
cosmic radiation on virus samples have
been unpredictable. Some of the samples
were killed by the radiation, others seem
to have mutated, while others seemed
unaffected. The T-Virus has been especially unpredictable. I will be introduc-
WAYFARER. THE VIRAL CONTAMINATION MAY NOT BE RESTRICTED TO THE STATION. I'M READING A FILE THAT SAYS THERE IS A SATELLITE OUT THERE WITH A VIRAL SAMPLE ON BOARD.
I'M HEADING TO THE DEPLOYMENT BAY TO SEE IF THE BIRD WAS RECOVERED BEFORE WHATEVER HAPPENED. CAN YOU DO A SWEEP OF THE AREA, AS WELL, IN CASE IT'S CLOSE BY?
STARTING A SWEEP NOW.

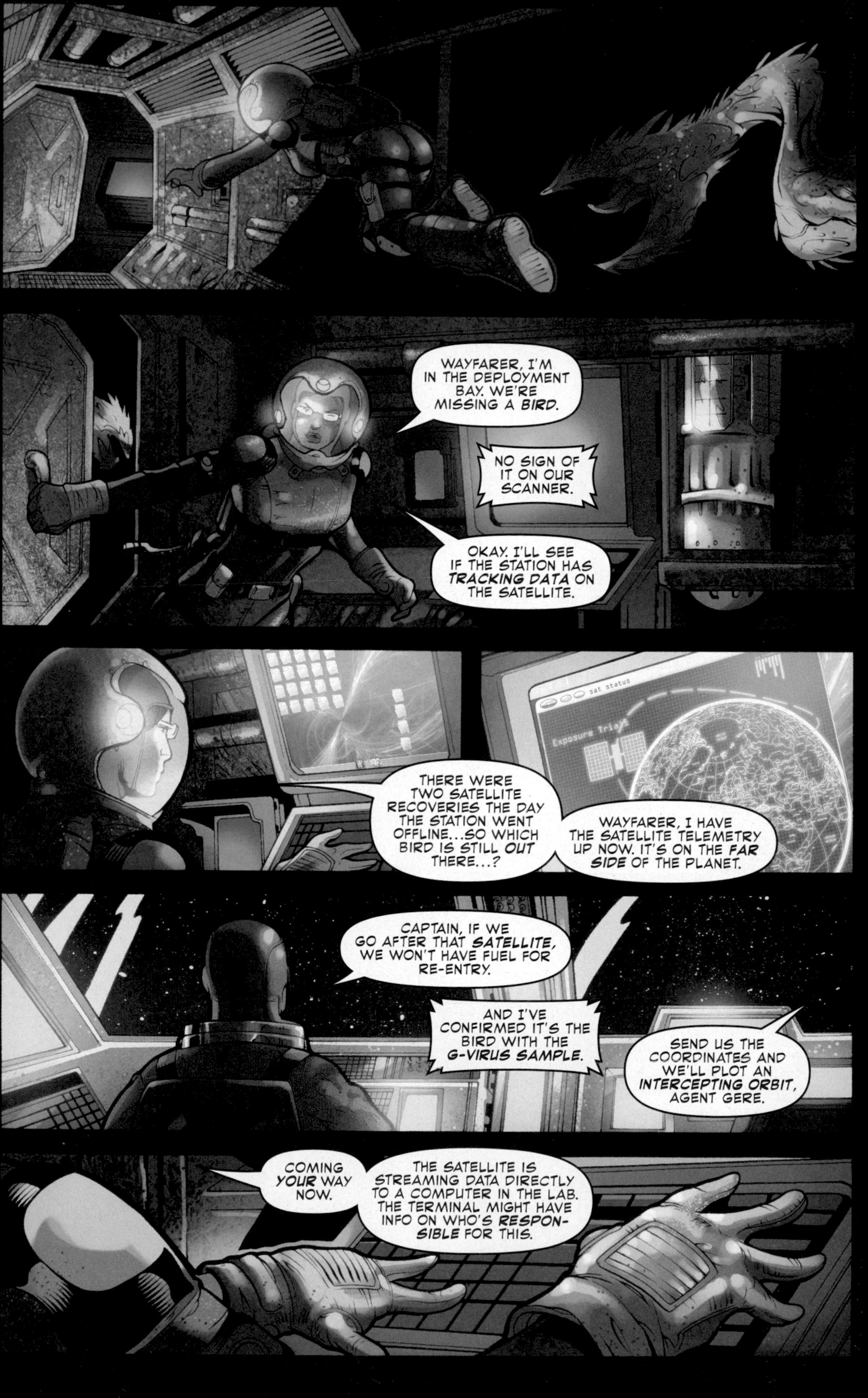
WAYFARER, I'M IN THE DEPLOYMENT BAY. WE'RE MISSING A BIRD.
NO SIGN OF IT ON OUR SCANNER.
OKAY. I'LL SEE IF THE STATION HAS TRACKING DATA ON THE SATELLITE.
sat status
Exposure Trial
THERE WERE TWO SATELLITE RECOVERIES THE DAY THE STATION WENT OFFLINE...SO WHICH BIRD IS STILL OUT THERE...?
WAYFARER, I HAVE THE SATELLITE TELEMETRY UP NOW. IT'S ON THE FAR SIDE OF THE PLANET.
CAPTAIN, IF WE GO AFTER THAT SATELLITE, WE WON'T HAVE FUEL FOR RE-ENTRY.
AND I'VE CONFIRMED IT'S THE BIRD WITH THE G-VIRUS SAMPLE.
SEND US THE COORDINATES AND WE'LL PLOT AN INTERCEPTING ORBIT, AGENT GERE.
COMING YOUR WAY NOW.
THE SATELLITE IS STREAMING DATA DIRECTLY TO A COMPUTER IN THE LAB. THE TERMINAL MIGHT HAVE INFO ON WHO'S RESPONSIBLE FOR THIS.

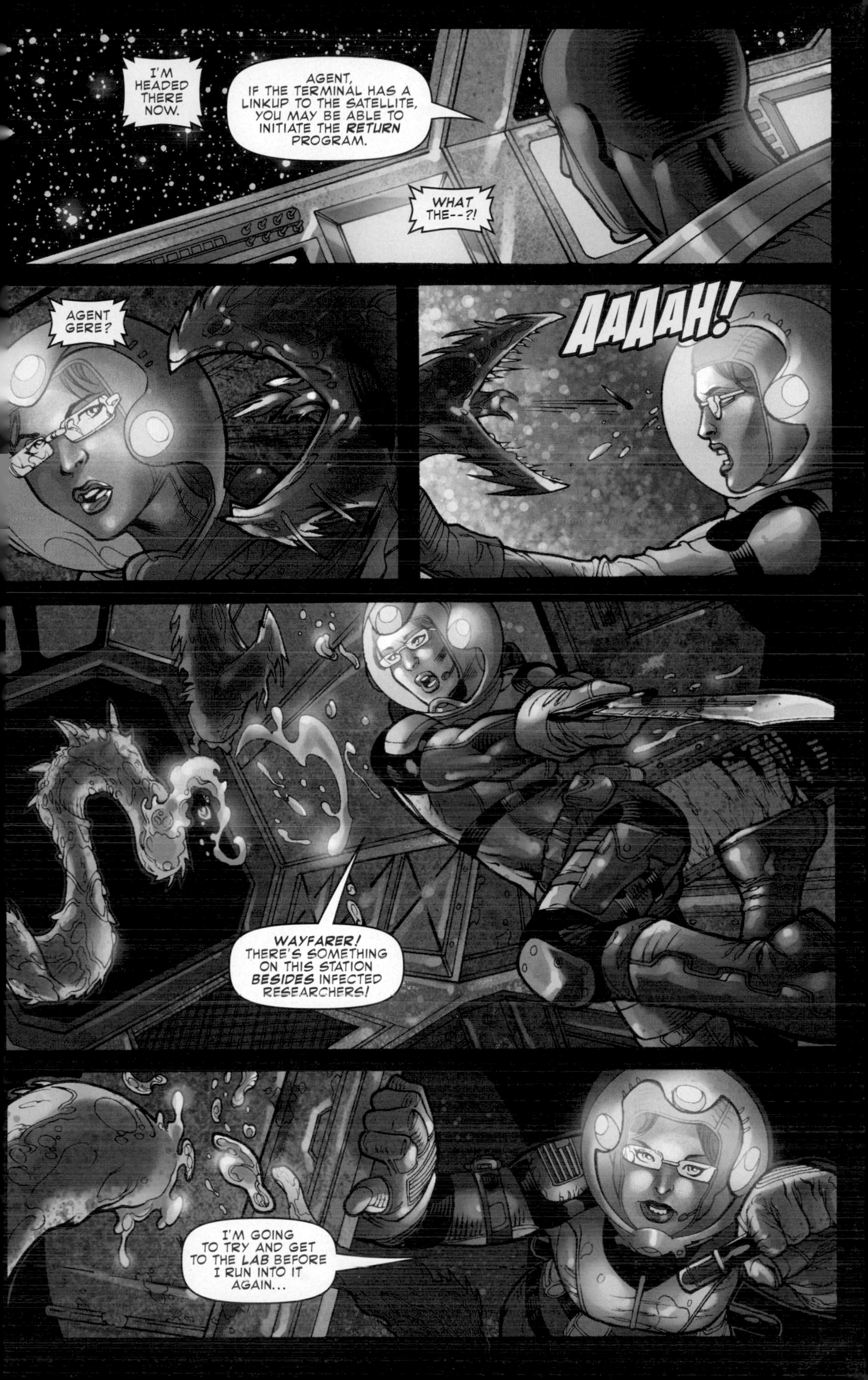
I'M HEADED THERE NOW.
AGENT, IF THE TERMINAL HAS A LINKUP TO THE SATELLITE, YOU MAY BE ABLE TO INITIATE THE *RETURN* PROGRAM.
WHAT THE--?!
AGENT GERE?
AAAAH!
WAYFARER! THERE'S SOMETHING ON THIS STATION *BESIDES* INFECTED RESEARCHERS!
I'M GOING TO TRY AND GET TO THE *LAB* BEFORE I RUN INTO IT AGAIN...

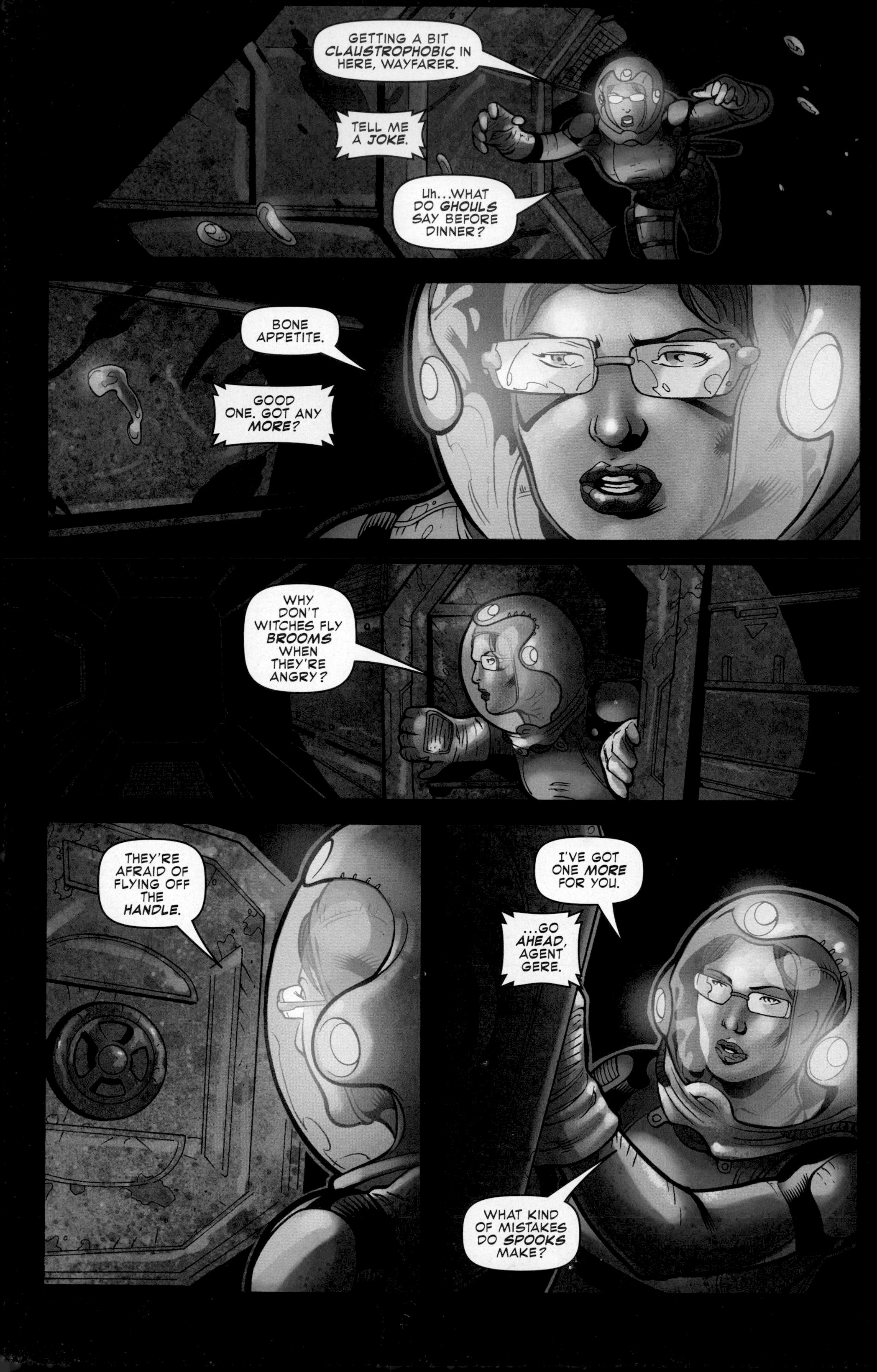
GETTING A BIT CLAUSTROPHOBIC IN HERE, WAYFARER.
TELL ME A JOKE.
Uh...WHAT DO GHOULS SAY BEFORE DINNER?
BONE APPETITE.
GOOD ONE. GOT ANY MORE?
WHY DON'T WITCHES FLY BROOMS WHEN THEY'RE ANGRY?
THEY'RE AFRAID OF FLYING OFF THE HANDLE.
I'VE GOT ONE MORE FOR YOU.
...GO AHEAD, AGENT GERE.
WHAT KIND OF MISTAKES DO SPOOKS MAKE?

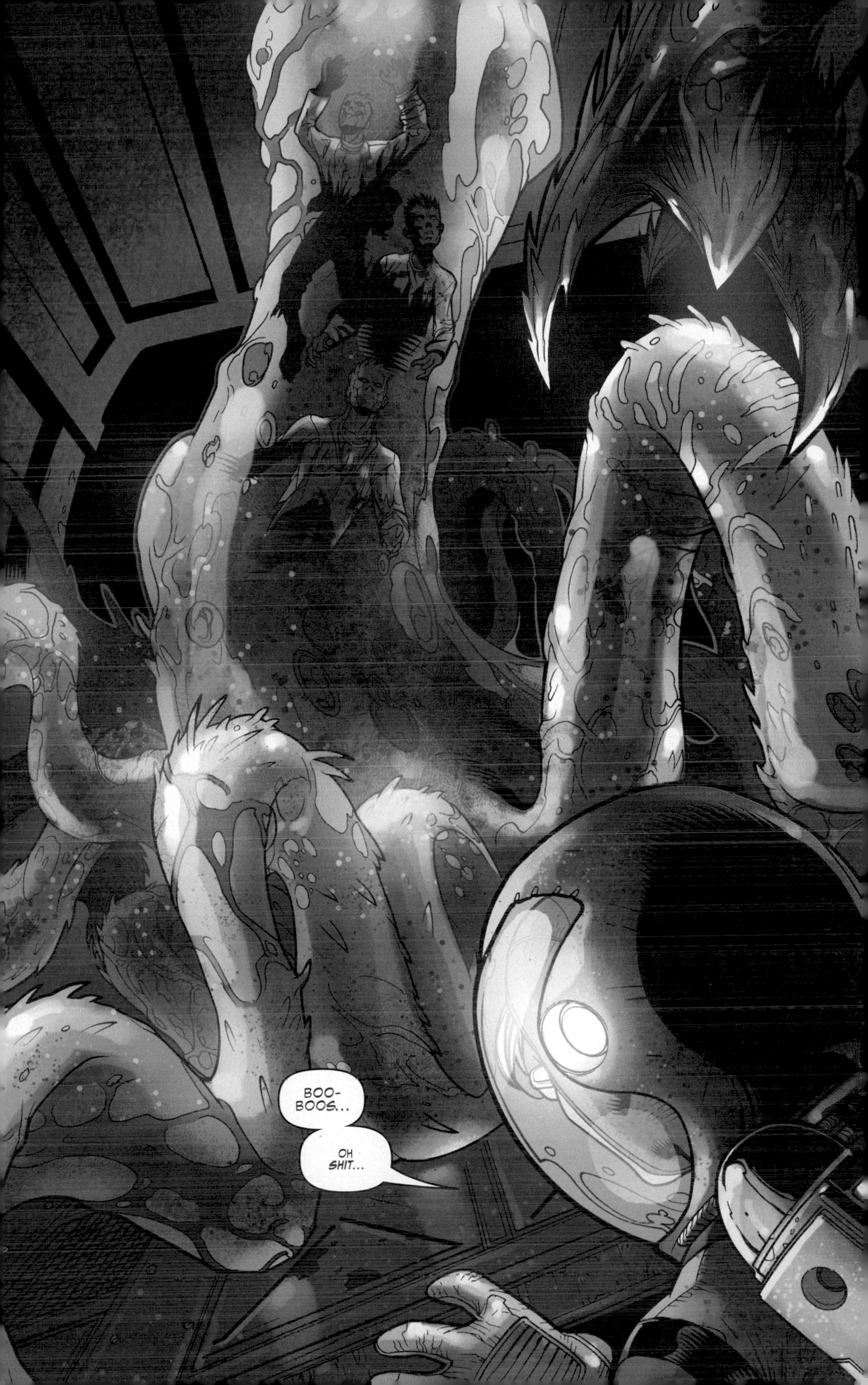
BOO-BOOS...
OH SHIT...

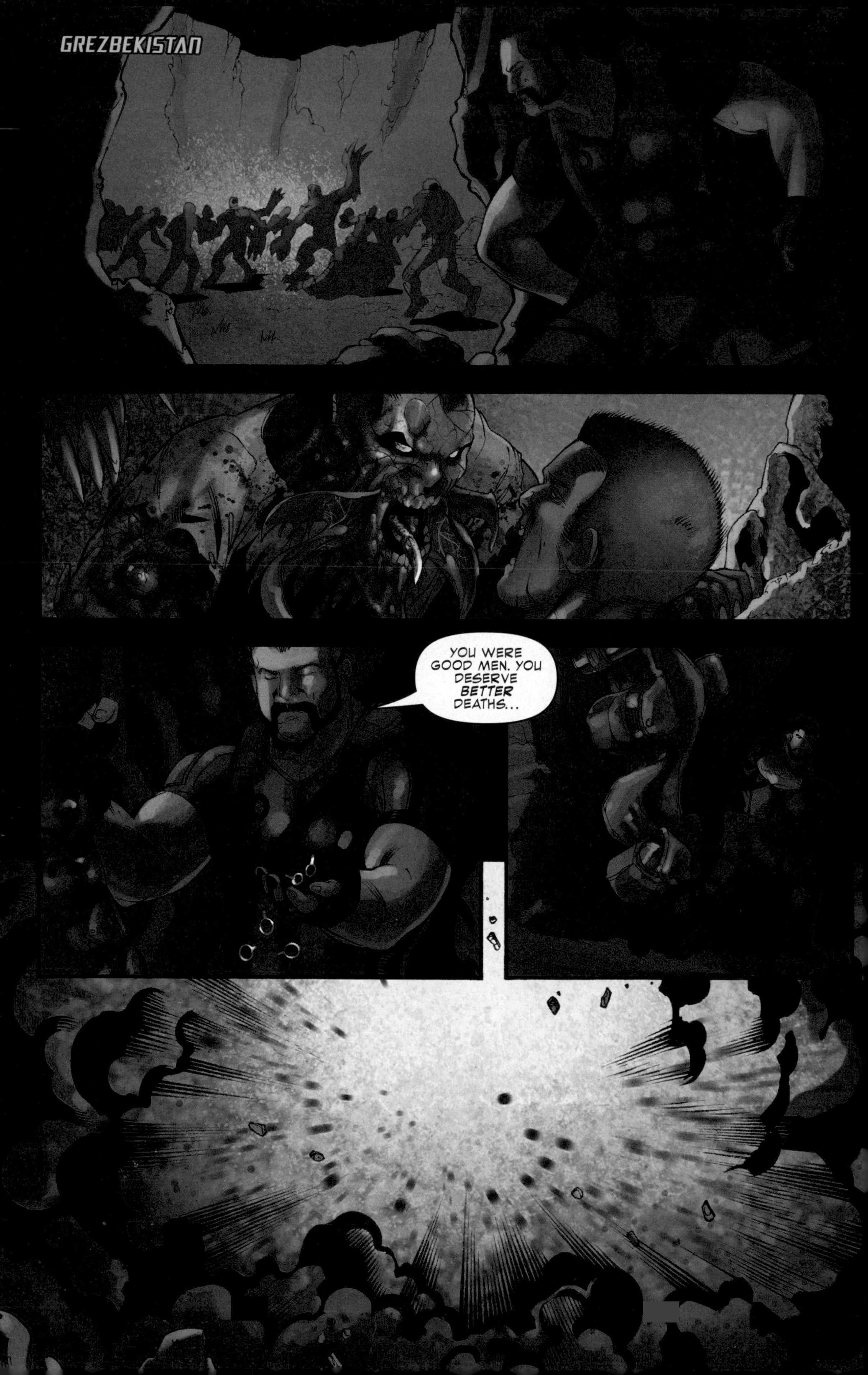
GREZBEKISTAN
YOU WERE GOOD MEN. YOU DESERVE BETTER DEATHS...

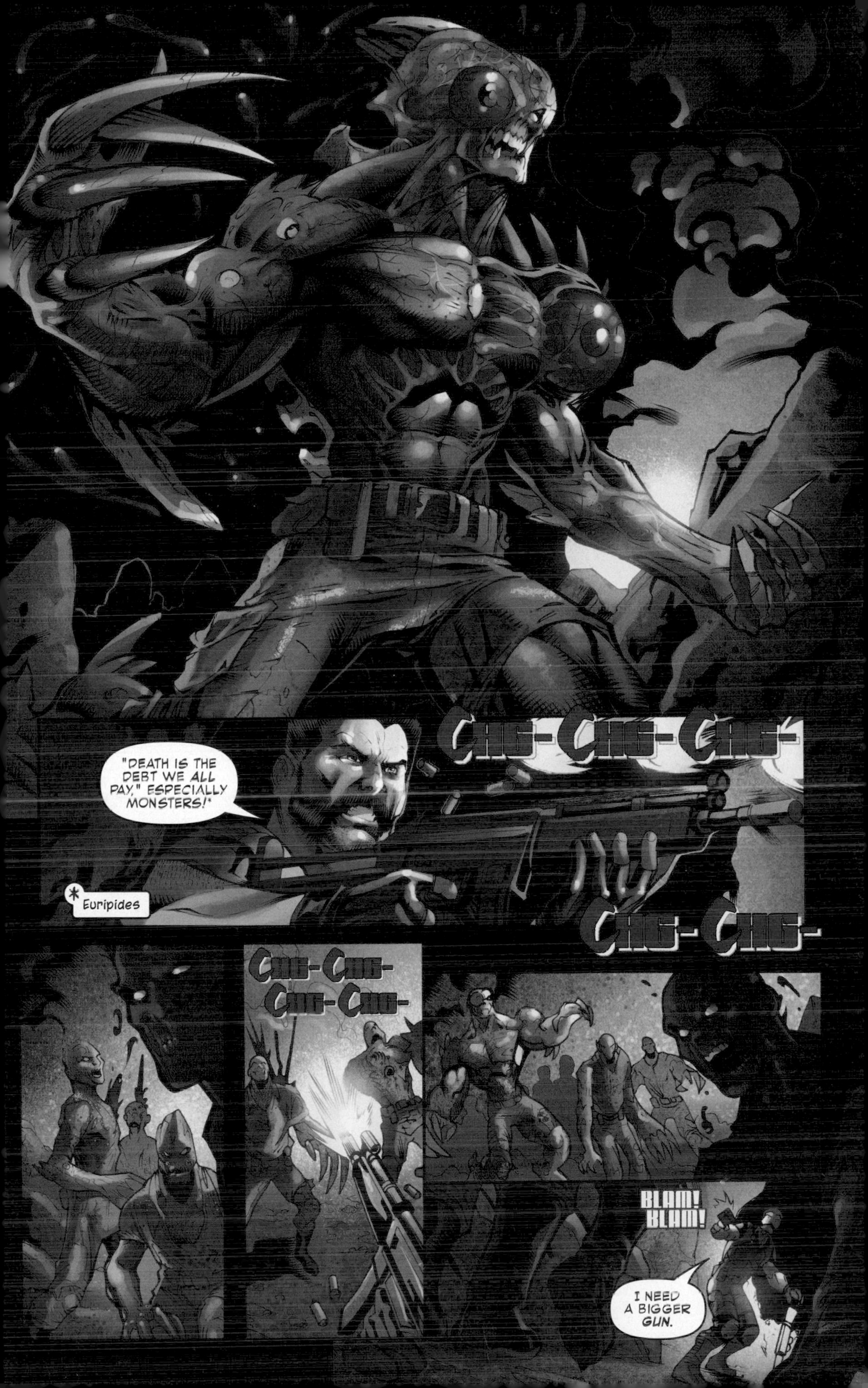
"DEATH IS THE DEBT WE ALL PAY," ESPECIALLY MONSTERS!*
CHG-CHG-CHG-
* Euripides
CHG-CHG-
CHG-CHG-
CHG-CHG-
BLAM! BLAM!
I NEED A BIGGER GUN.

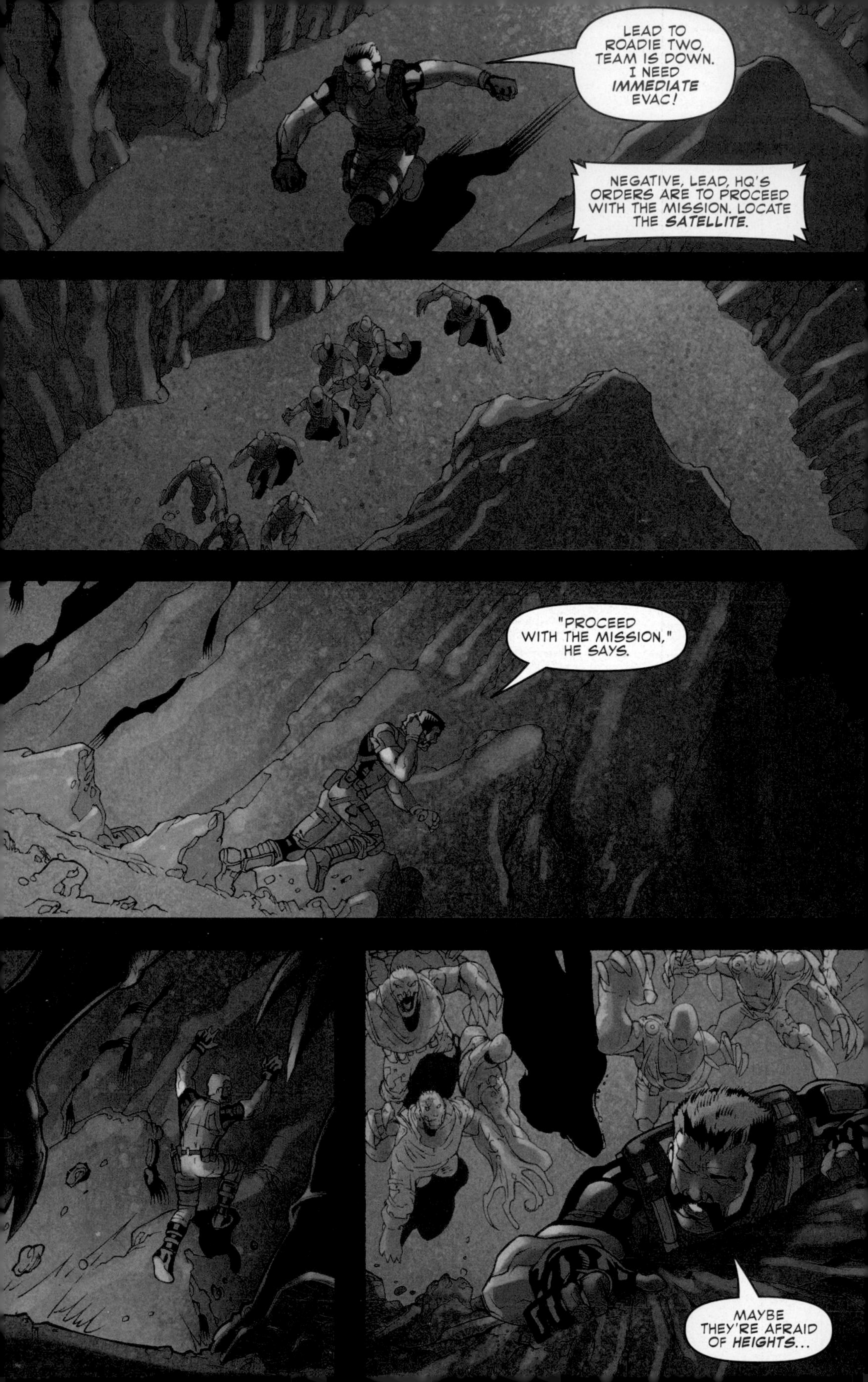
LEAD TO ROADIE TWO, TEAM IS DOWN. I NEED IMMEDIATE EVAC!
NEGATIVE, LEAD, HQ'S ORDERS ARE TO PROCEED WITH THE MISSION. LOCATE THE SATELLITE.
"PROCEED WITH THE MISSION," HE SAYS.
MAYBE THEY'RE AFRAID OF HEIGHTS...

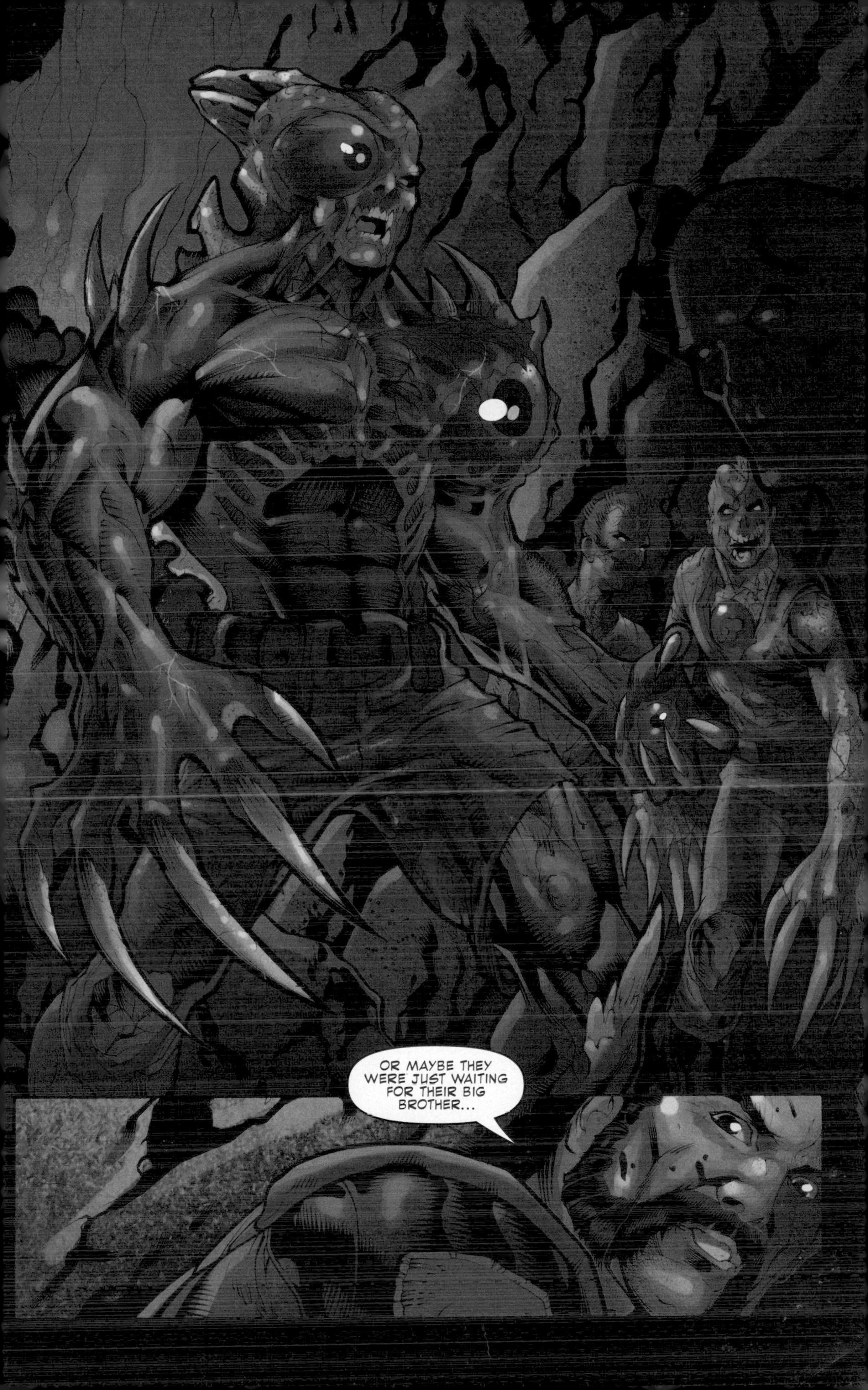
OR MAYBE THEY WERE JUST WAITING FOR THEIR BIG BROTHER...

RESIDENT EVIL 2
Cover by Kevin Sharpe

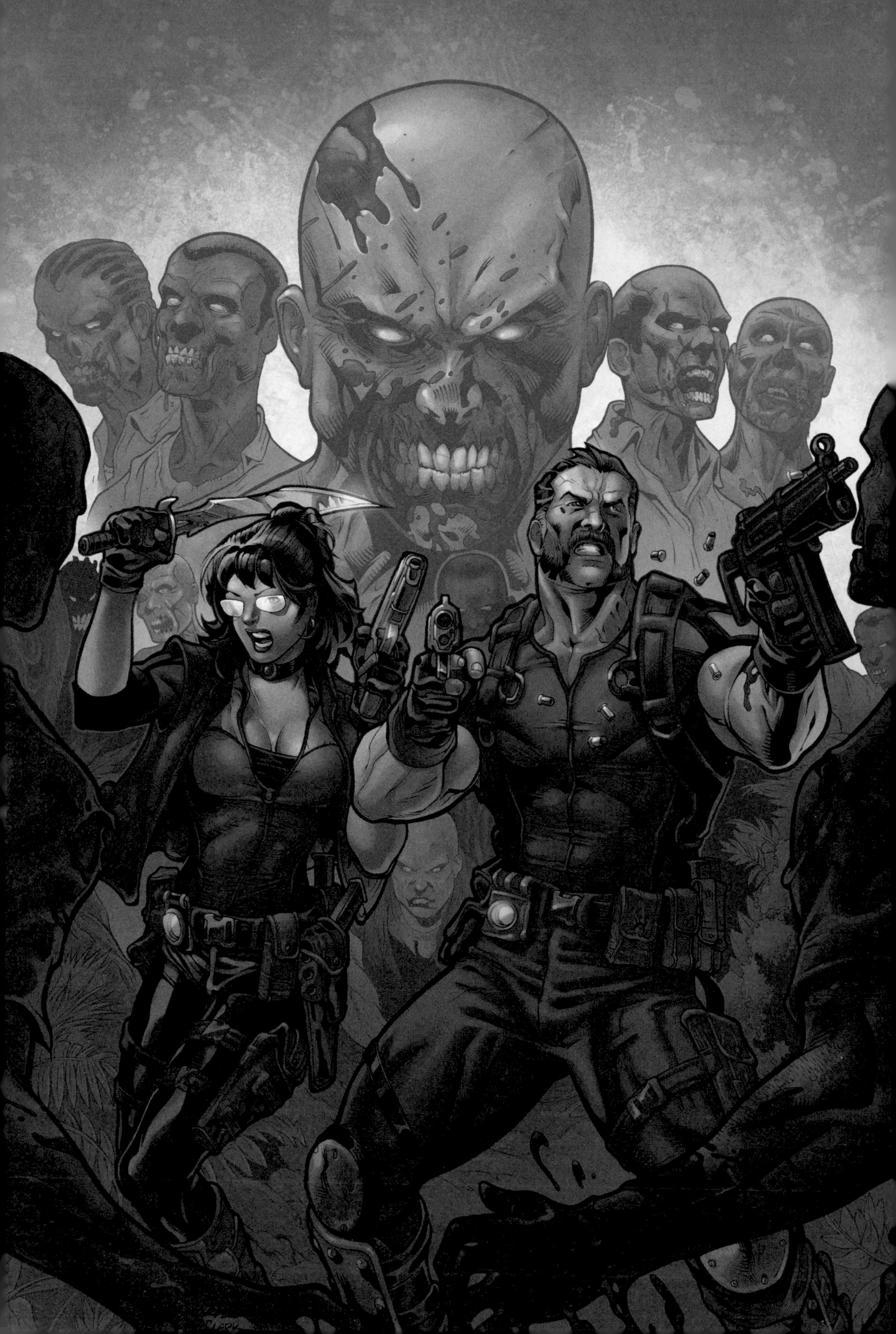

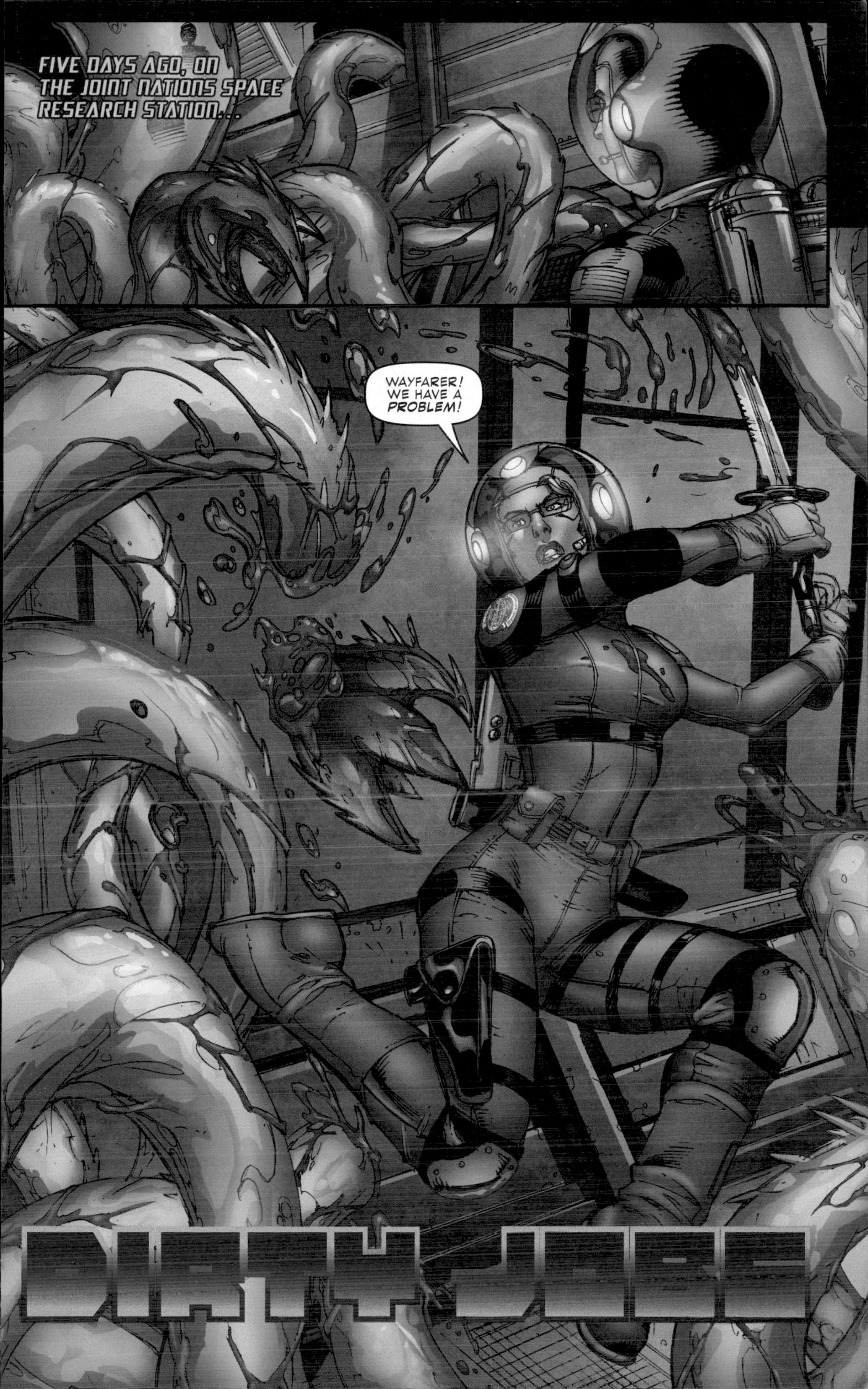
FIVE DAYS AGO, ON THE JOINT NATIONS SPACE RESEARCH STATION...
WAYFARER! WE HAVE A PROBLEM!
DIRTY JOBS

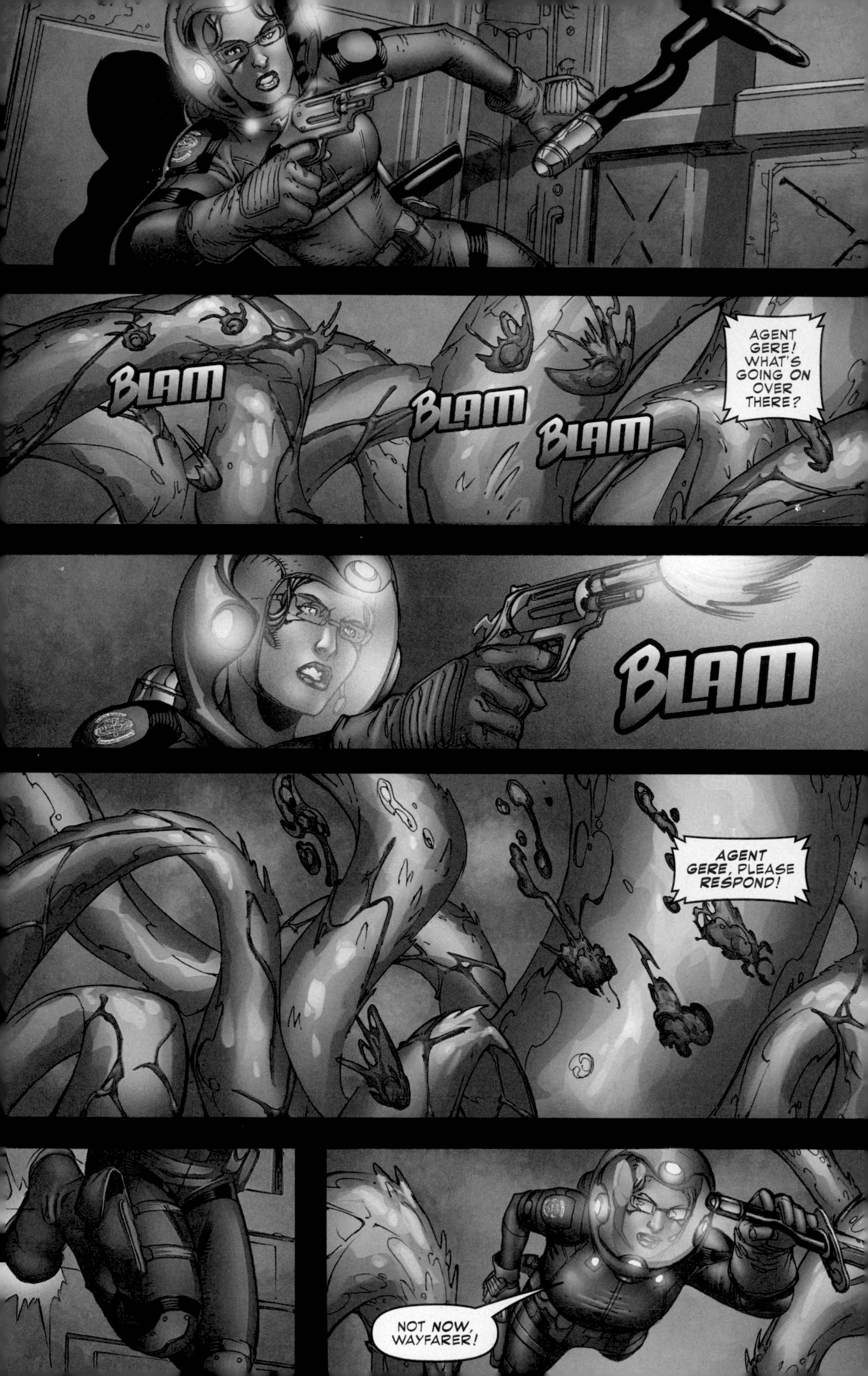
BLAM
BLAM
BLAM
AGENT GERE! WHAT'S GOING ON OVER THERE?
BLAM
AGENT GERE, PLEASE RESPOND!
NOT NOW, WAYFARER!

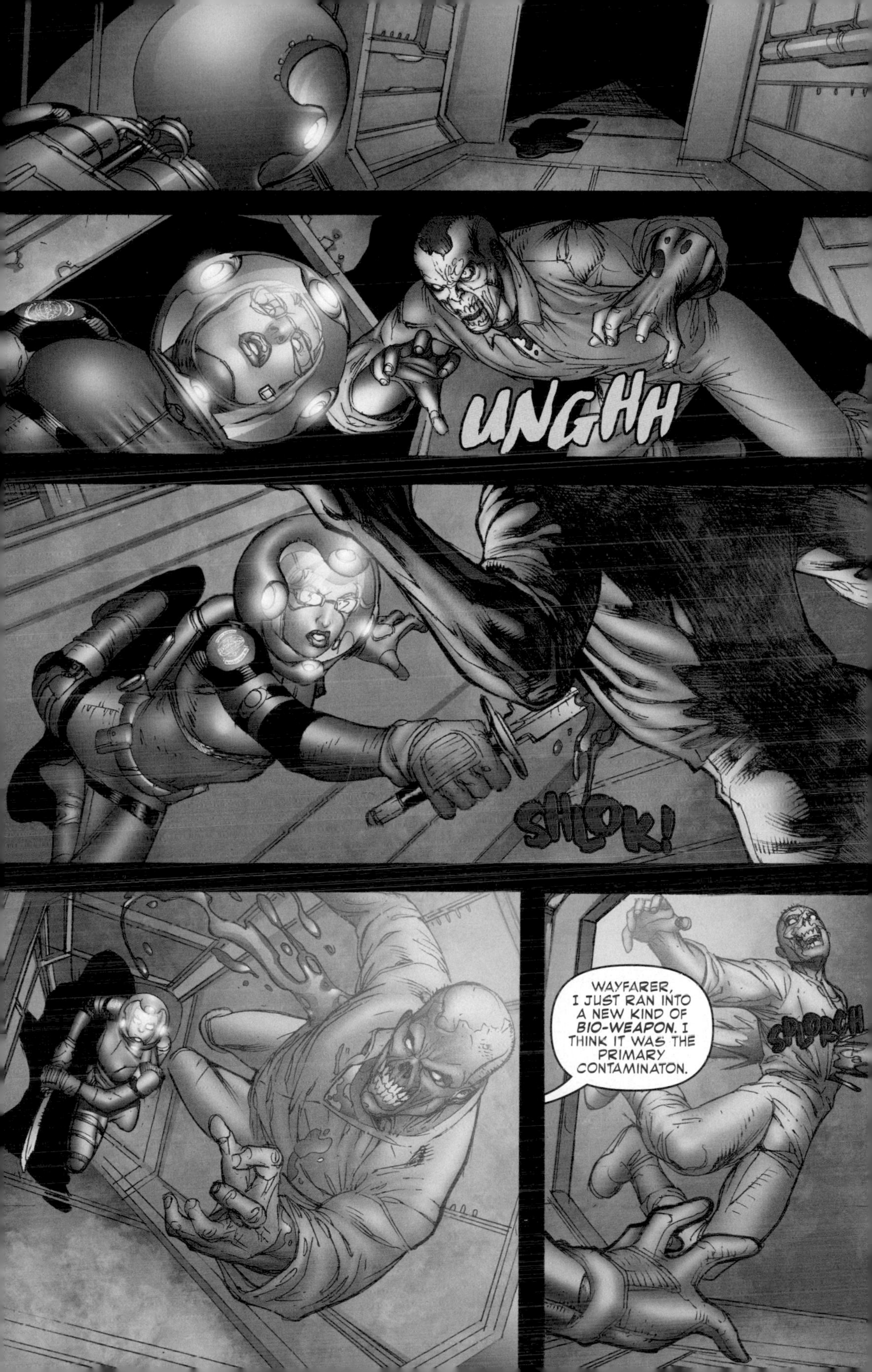
UNGHH
SHLOK!
WAYFARER, I JUST RAN INTO A NEW KIND OF BIO-WEAPON. I THINK IT WAS THE PRIMARY CONTAMINATON.
SPLORCH

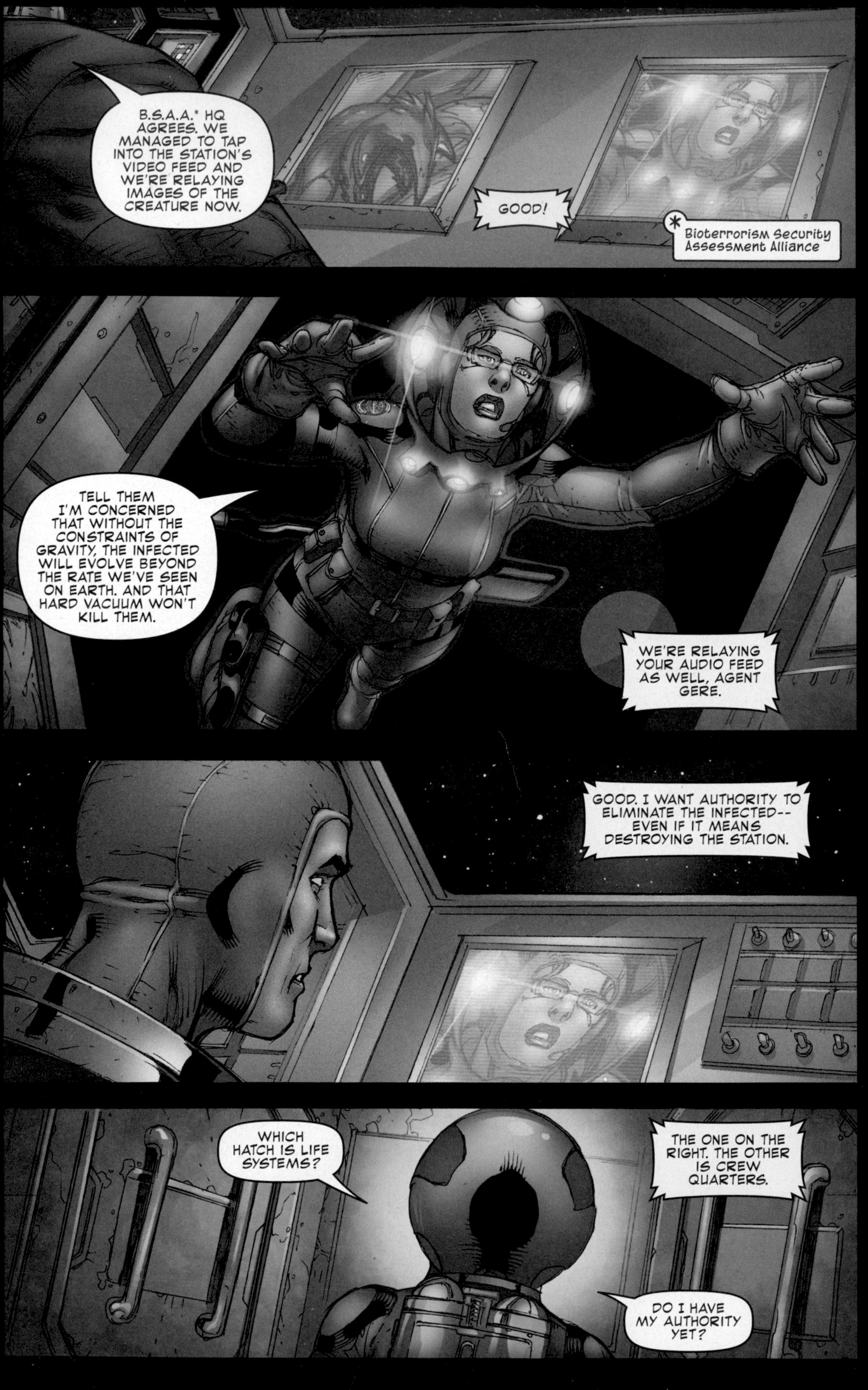
B.S.A.A.* HQ AGREES. WE MANAGED TO TAP INTO THE STATION'S VIDEO FEED AND WE'RE RELAYING IMAGES OF THE CREATURE NOW.
GOOD!
* Bioterrorism Security Assessment Alliance
TELL THEM I'M CONCERNED THAT WITHOUT THE CONSTRAINTS OF GRAVITY, THE INFECTED WILL EVOLVE BEYOND THE RATE WE'VE SEEN ON EARTH. AND THAT HARD VACUUM WON'T KILL THEM.
WE'RE RELAYING YOUR AUDIO FEED AS WELL, AGENT GERE.
GOOD. I WANT AUTHORITY TO ELIMINATE THE INFECTED-- EVEN IF IT MEANS DESTROYING THE STATION.
WHICH HATCH IS LIFE SYSTEMS?
THE ONE ON THE RIGHT. THE OTHER IS CREW QUARTERS.
DO I HAVE MY AUTHORITY YET?

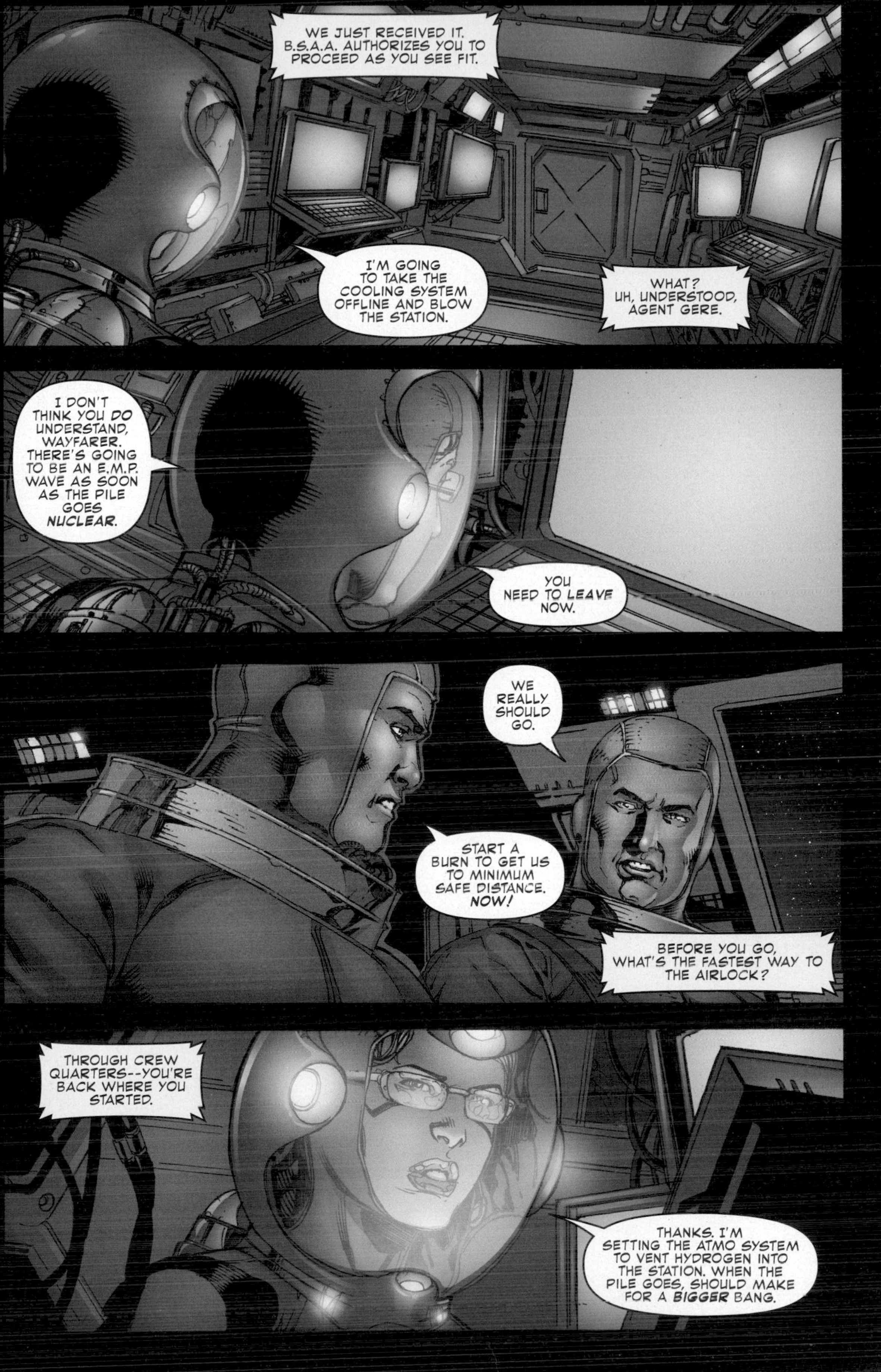
WE JUST RECEIVED IT. B.S.A.A. AUTHORIZES YOU TO PROCEED AS YOU SEE FIT.
I'M GOING TO TAKE THE COOLING SYSTEM OFFLINE AND BLOW THE STATION.
WHAT? UH, UNDERSTOOD, AGENT GERE.
I DON'T THINK YOU DO UNDERSTAND, WAYFARER. THERE'S GOING TO BE AN E.M.P. WAVE AS SOON AS THE PILE GOES NUCLEAR.
YOU NEED TO LEAVE NOW.
WE REALLY SHOULD GO.
START A BURN TO GET US TO MINIMUM SAFE DISTANCE. NOW!
BEFORE YOU GO, WHAT'S THE FASTEST WAY TO THE AIRLOCK?
THROUGH CREW QUARTERS--YOU'RE BACK WHERE YOU STARTED.
THANKS. I'M SETTING THE ATMO SYSTEM TO VENT HYDROGEN INTO THE STATION. WHEN THE PILE GOES, SHOULD MAKE FOR A BIGGER BANG.

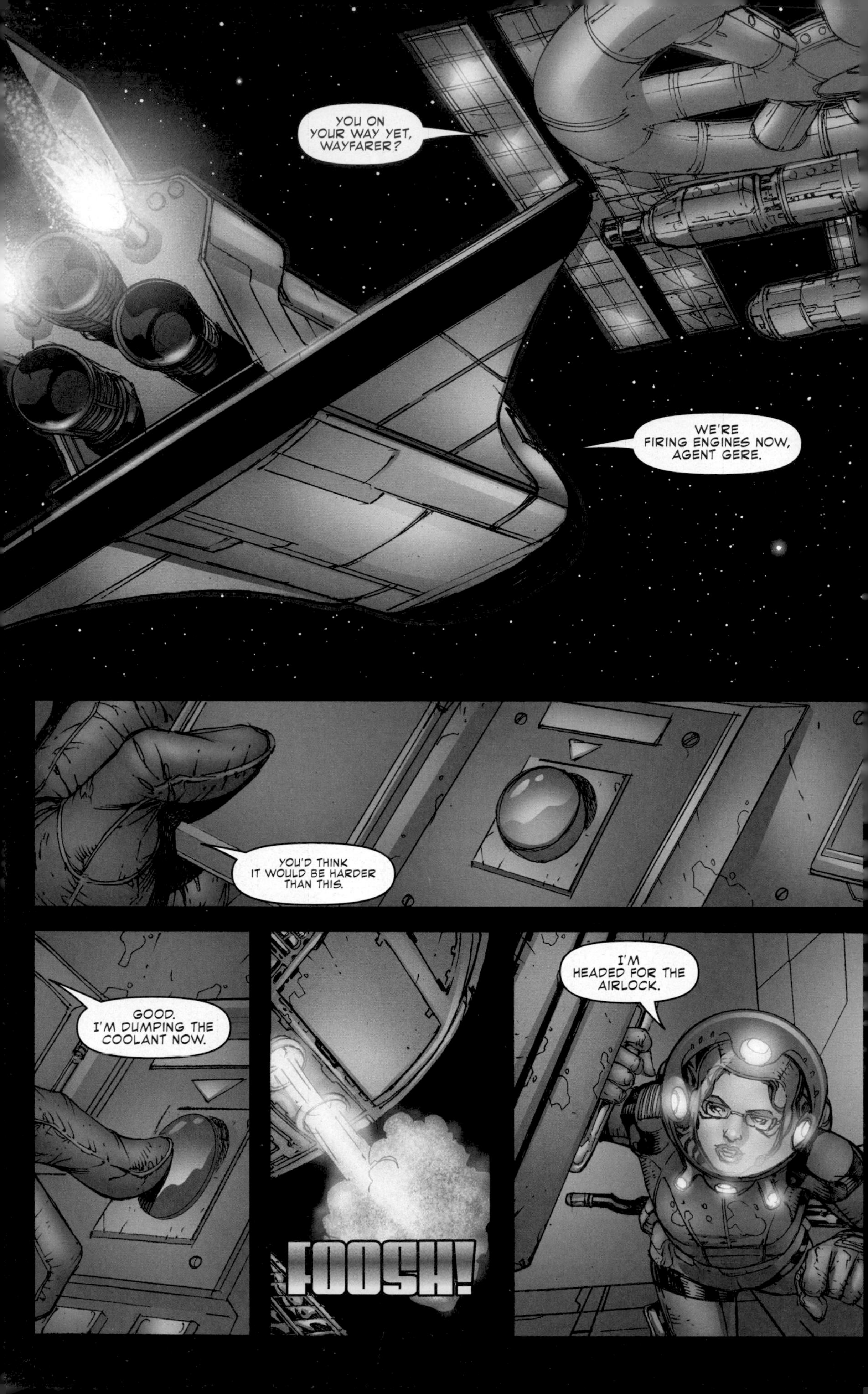
YOU ON YOUR WAY YET, WAYFARER?
WE'RE FIRING ENGINES NOW, AGENT GERE.
YOU'D THINK IT WOULD BE HARDER THAN THIS.
GOOD. I'M DUMPING THE COOLANT NOW.
FOOSH!
I'M HEADED FOR THE AIRLOCK.

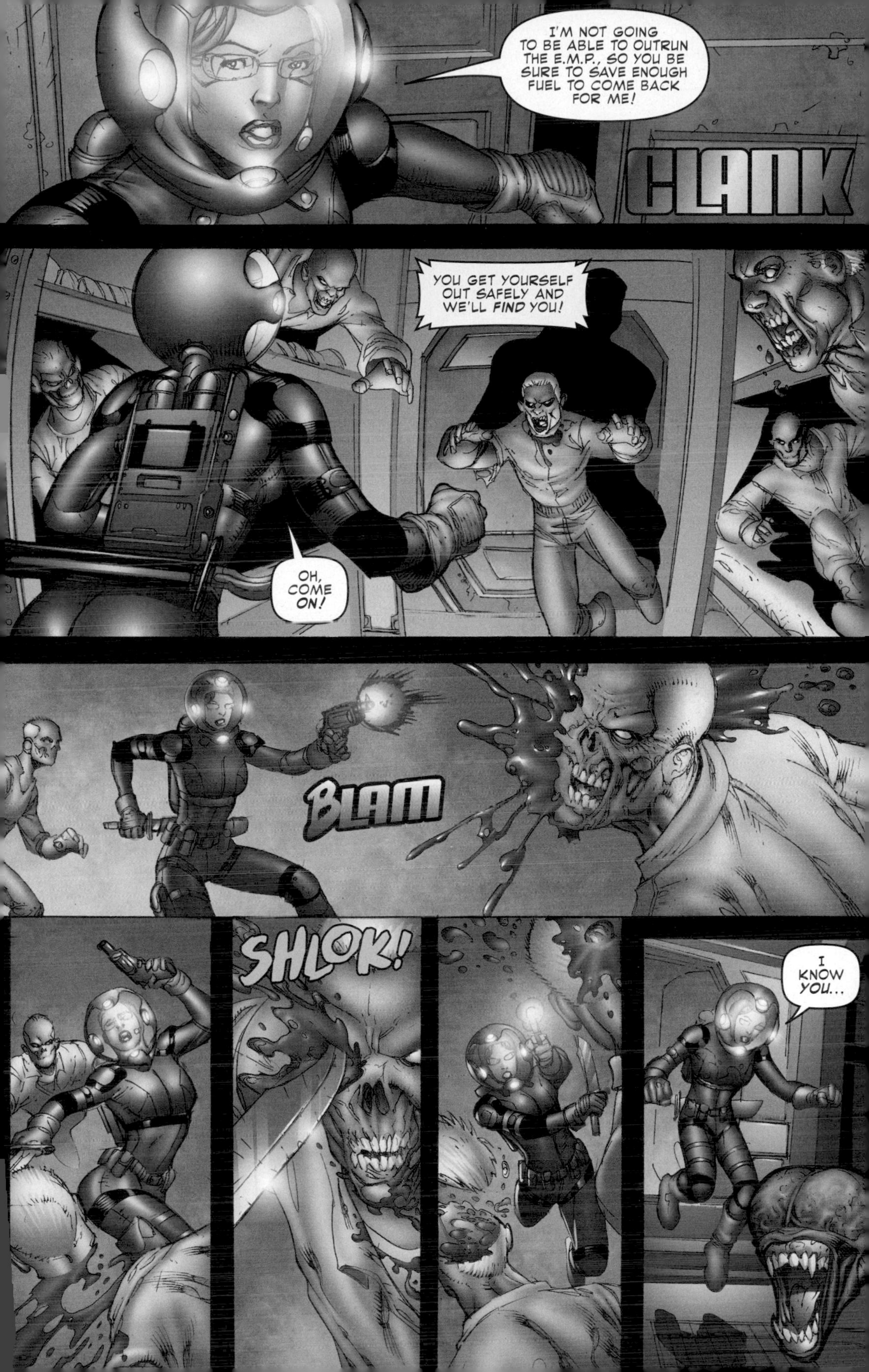
I'M NOT GOING TO BE ABLE TO OUTRUN THE E.M.P., SO YOU BE SURE TO SAVE ENOUGH FUEL TO COME BACK FOR ME!
CLANK
YOU GET YOURSELF OUT SAFELY AND WE'LL FIND YOU!
OH, COME ON!
BLAM
SHLOK!
I KNOW YOU...

WE'RE *CLEAR*, AGENT GERE, HAVE YOU MADE IT OUT YET?

ALMOST! RETRIEVING H.H.M.U.* NOW.

* Hand-Held Maneuvering Unit

FINGERS CROSSED...

FWOOSH

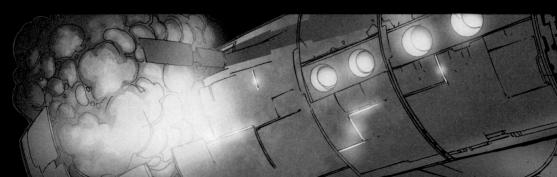

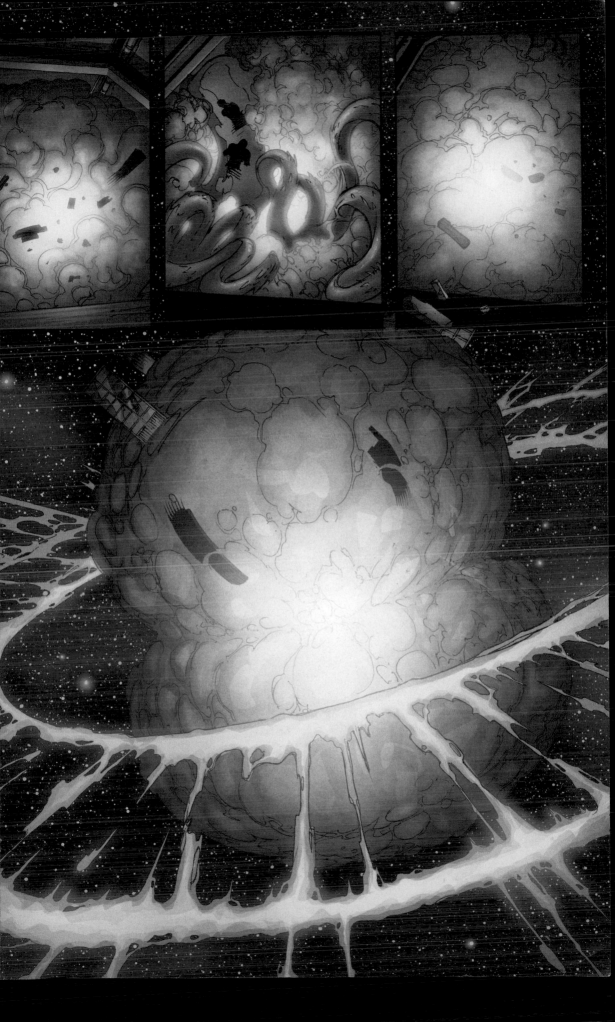

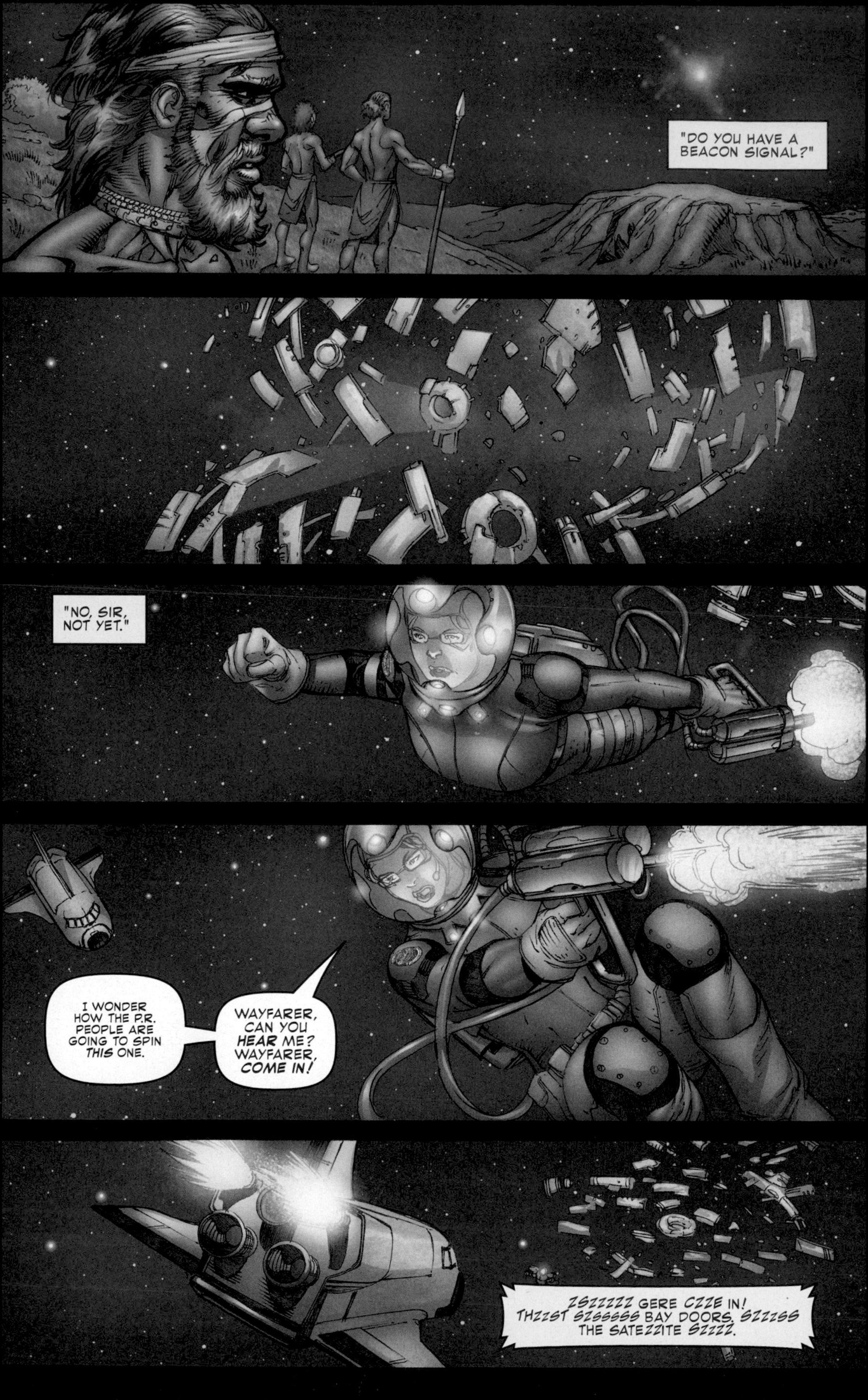
"DO YOU HAVE A BEACON SIGNAL?"
"NO, SIR, NOT YET."
I WONDER HOW THE P.R. PEOPLE ARE GOING TO SPIN THIS ONE.
WAYFARER, CAN YOU HEAR ME? WAYFARER, COME IN!
ZSZZZZZ GERE CZZE IN! THZZST SZSSSSS BAY DOORS, SZZZSS THE SATEZZITE SZZZZ.

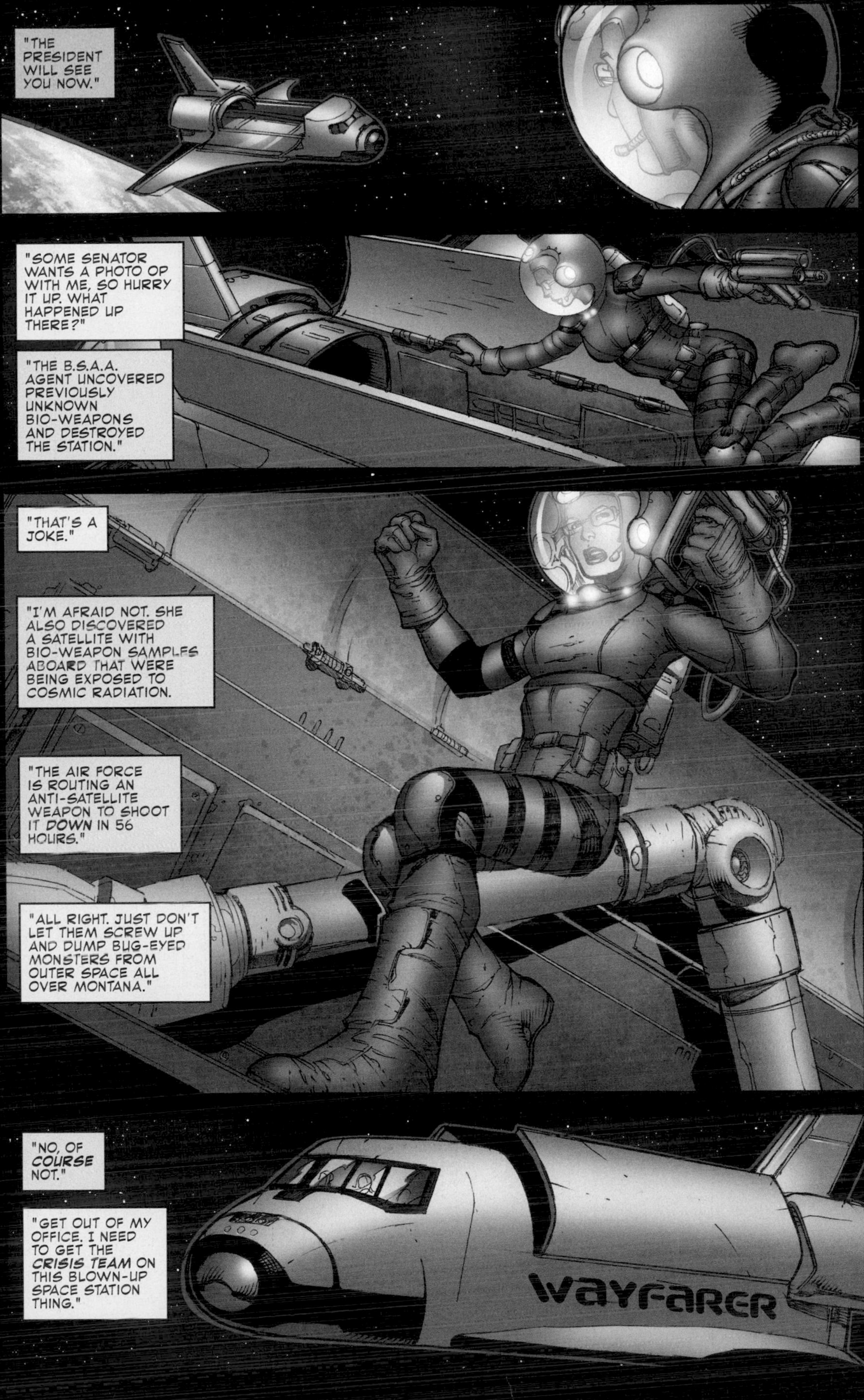
"THE PRESIDENT WILL SEE YOU NOW."
"SOME SENATOR WANTS A PHOTO OP WITH ME, SO HURRY IT UP. WHAT HAPPENED UP THERE?"
"THE B.S.A.A. AGENT UNCOVERED PREVIOUSLY UNKNOWN BIO-WEAPONS AND DESTROYED THE STATION."
"THAT'S A JOKE."
"I'M AFRAID NOT. SHE ALSO DISCOVERED A SATELLITE WITH BIO-WEAPON SAMPLES ABOARD THAT WERE BEING EXPOSED TO COSMIC RADIATION.
"THE AIR FORCE IS ROUTING AN ANTI-SATELLITE WEAPON TO SHOOT IT DOWN IN 56 HOURS."
"ALL RIGHT. JUST DON'T LET THEM SCREW UP AND DUMP BUG-EYED MONSTERS FROM OUTER SPACE ALL OVER MONTANA."
"NO, OF COURSE NOT."
"GET OUT OF MY OFFICE. I NEED TO GET THE CRISIS TEAM ON THIS BLOWN-UP SPACE STATION THING."
WAYFARER

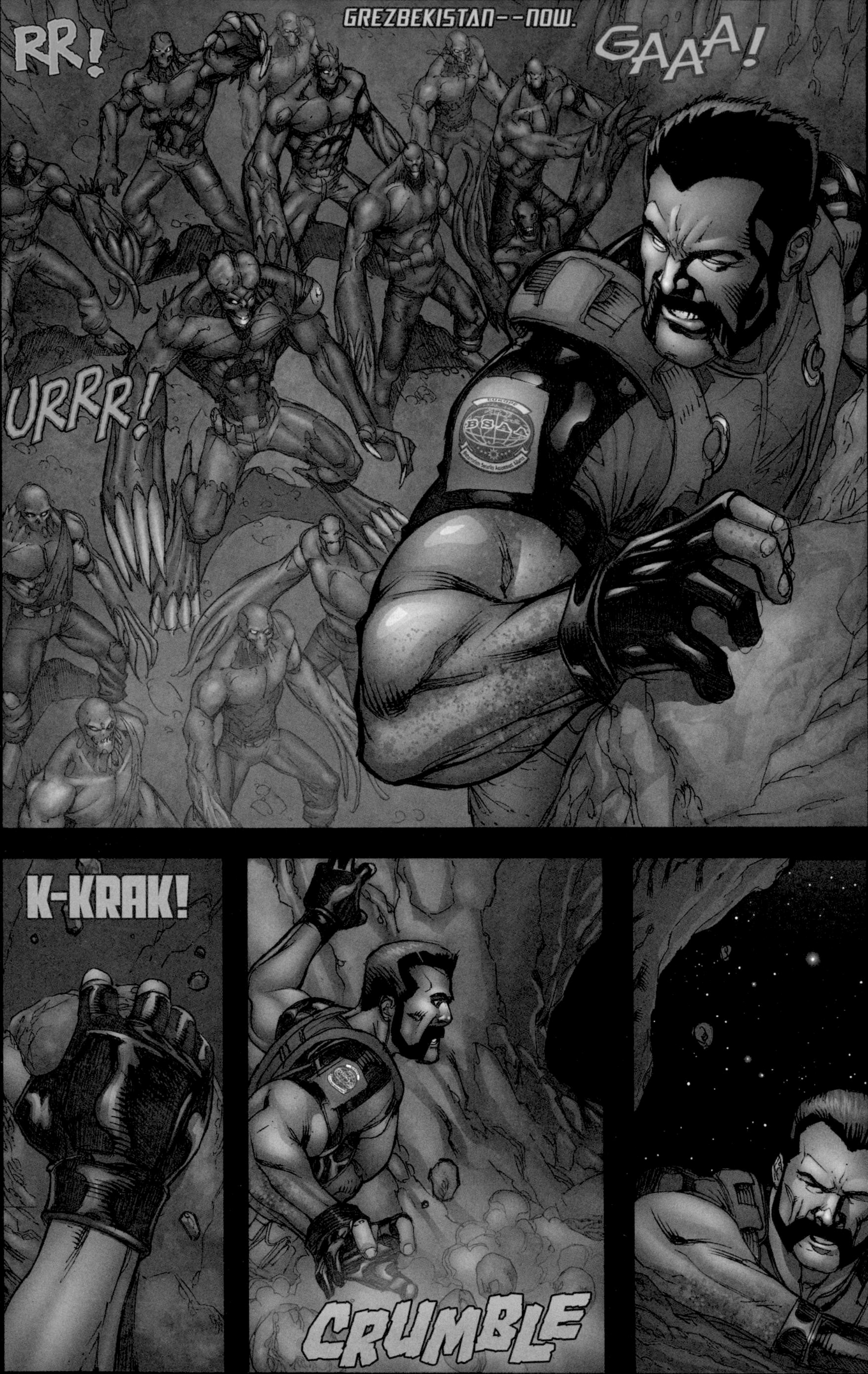
GREZBEKISTAN--NOW.
RR!
GAAA!
URRR!
K-KRAK!
CRUMBLE

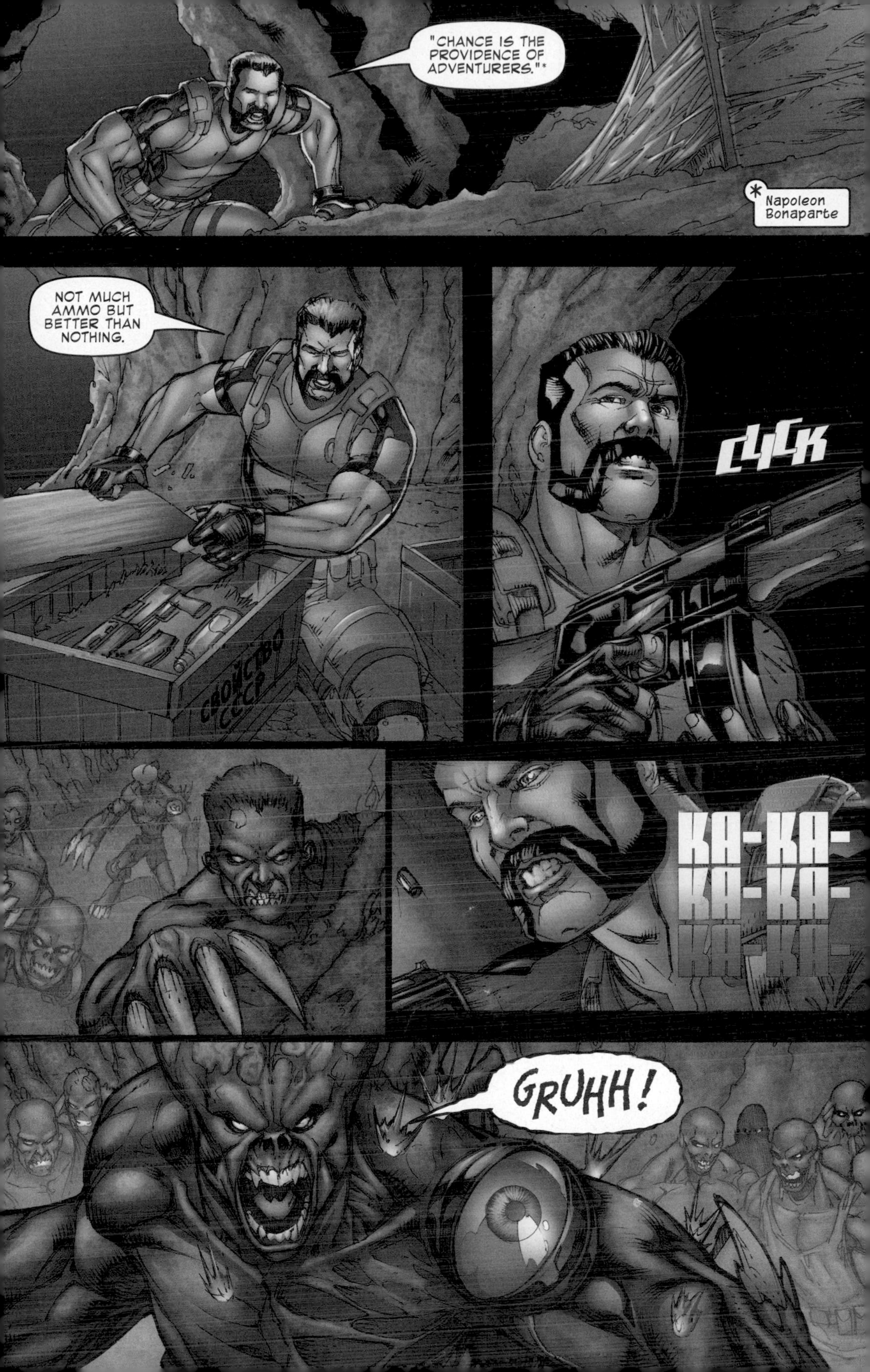
"CHANCE IS THE PROVIDENCE OF ADVENTURERS."*
* Napoleon Bonaparte
NOT MUCH AMMO BUT BETTER THAN NOTHING.
СВОЙСТВО СССР
CLICK
KA-KA-KA-KA-KA-KA-
GRUHH!

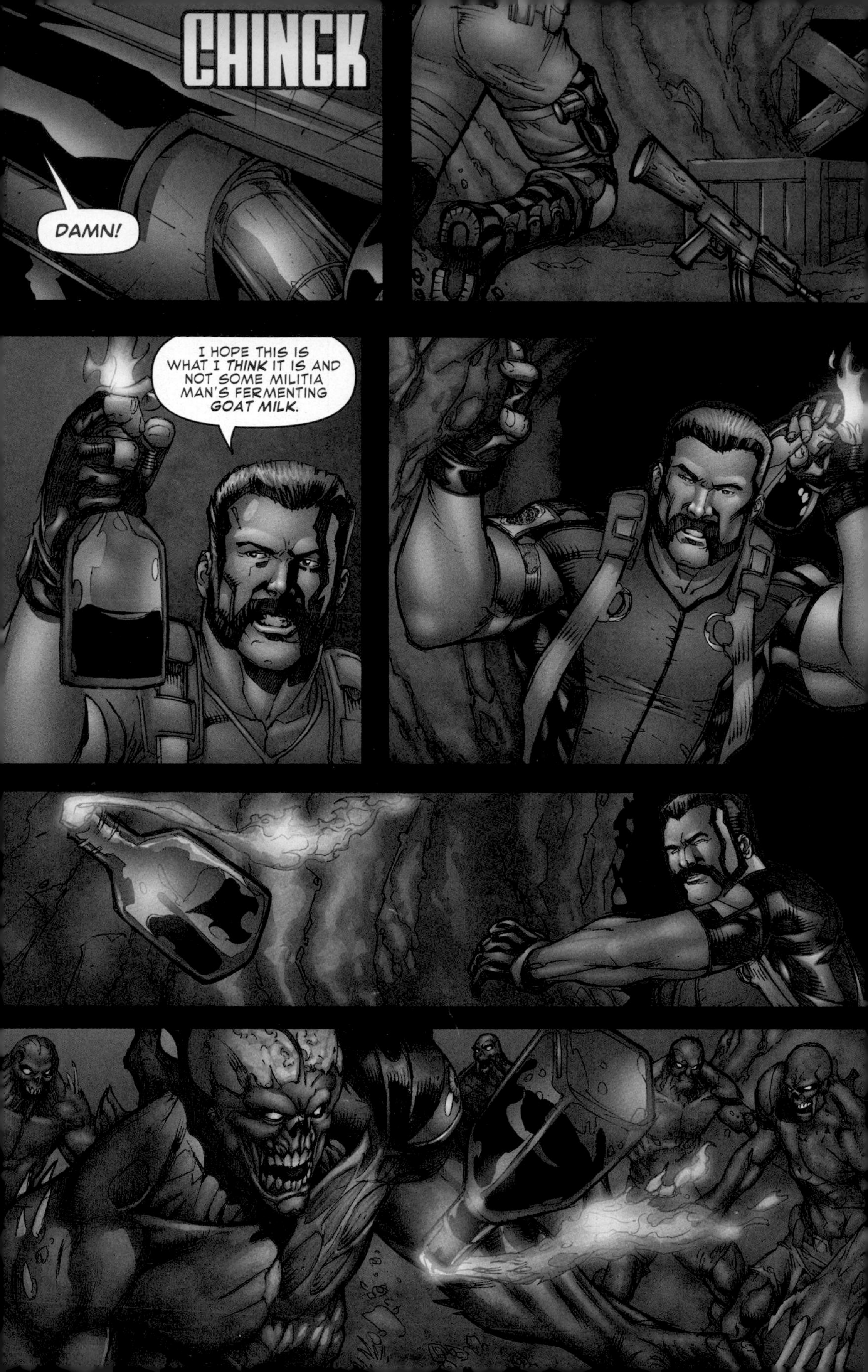
CHINGK
DAMN!
I HOPE THIS IS WHAT I THINK IT IS AND NOT SOME MILITIA MAN'S FERMENTING GOAT MILK.

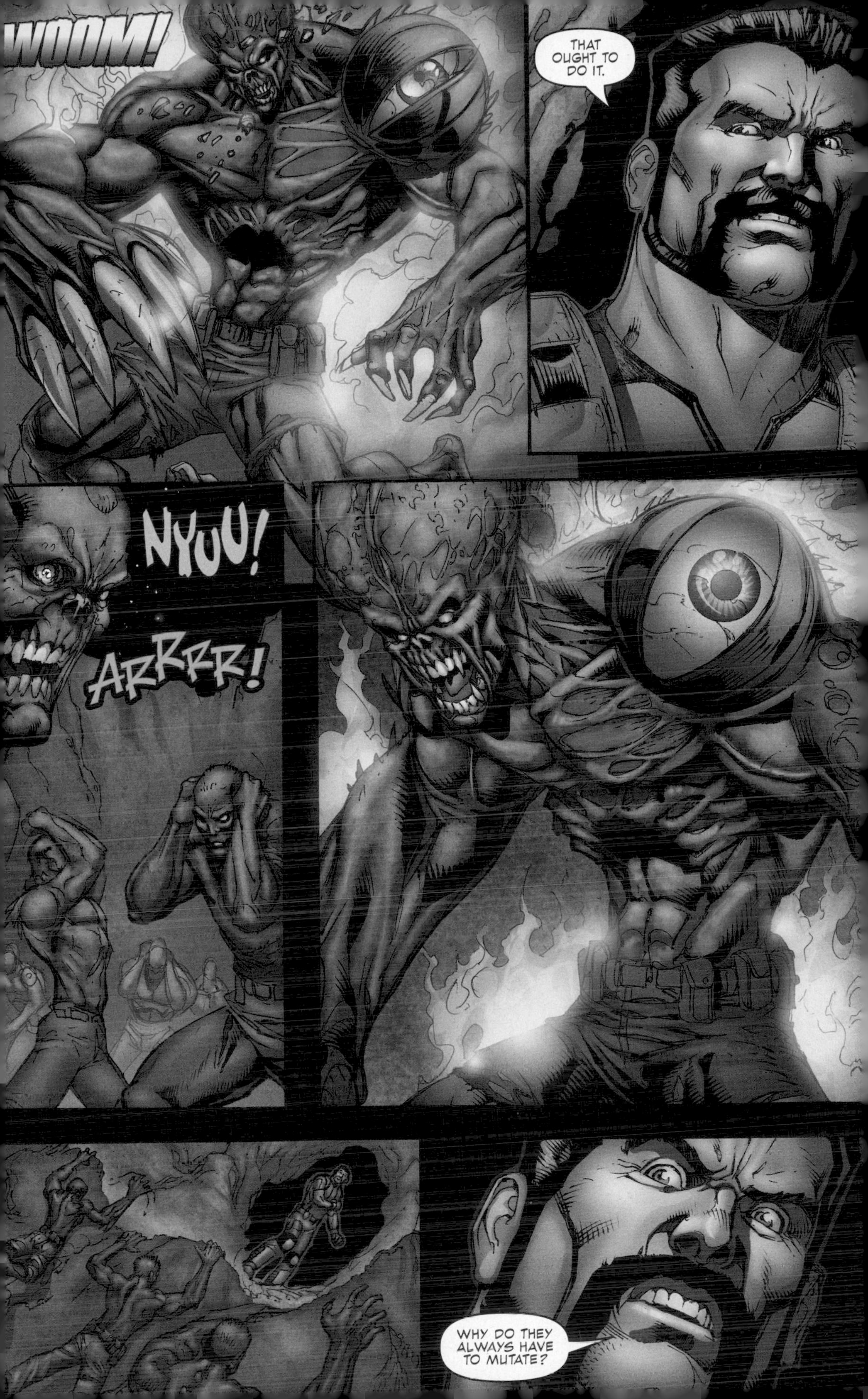
WOOM!
THAT OUGHT TO DO IT.
NYUU!
ARRRR!
WHY DO THEY ALWAYS HAVE TO MUTATE?

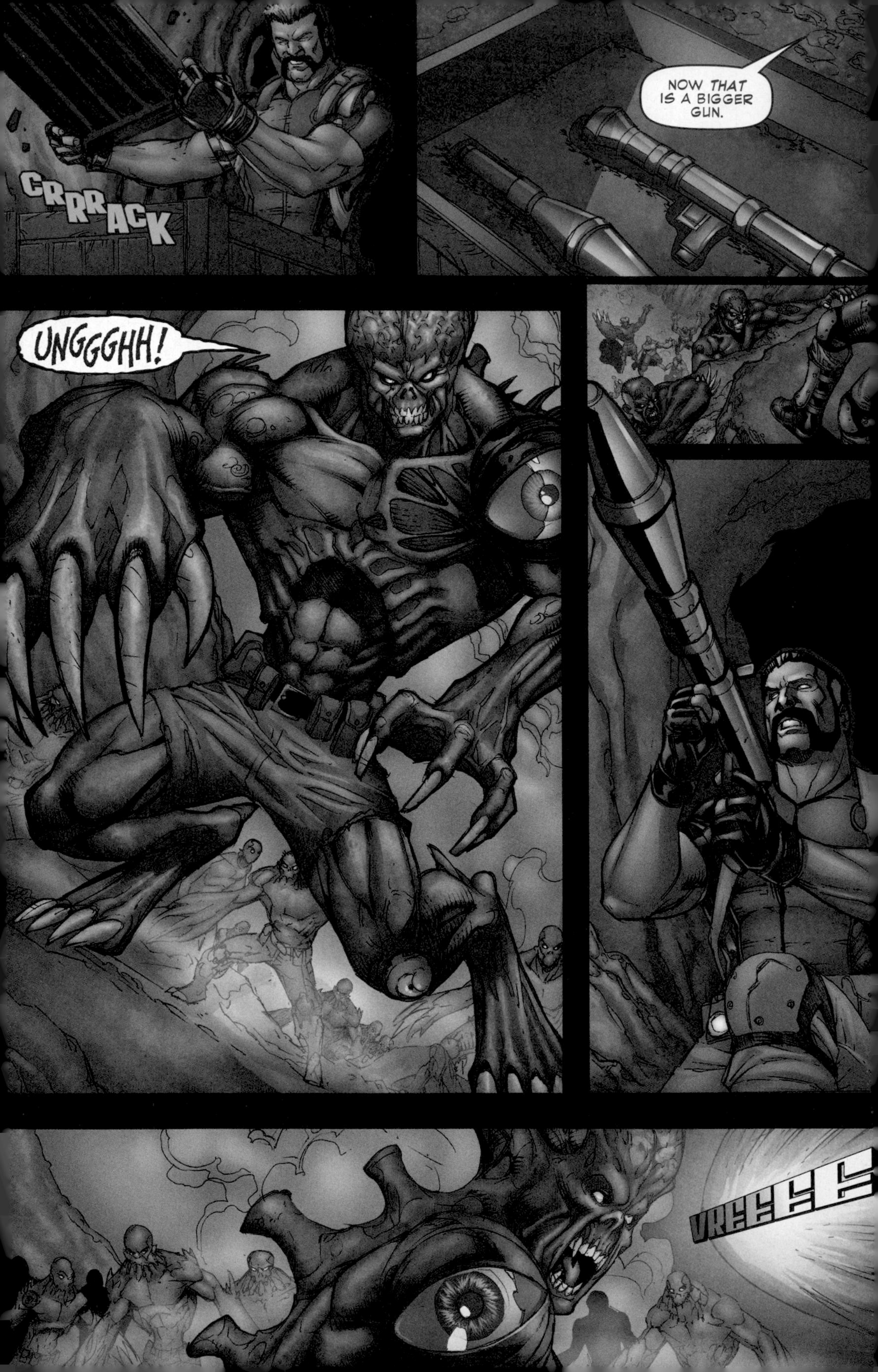
CRRRACK
NOW *THAT* IS A BIGGER GUN.
UNGGGHH!
VREEEE

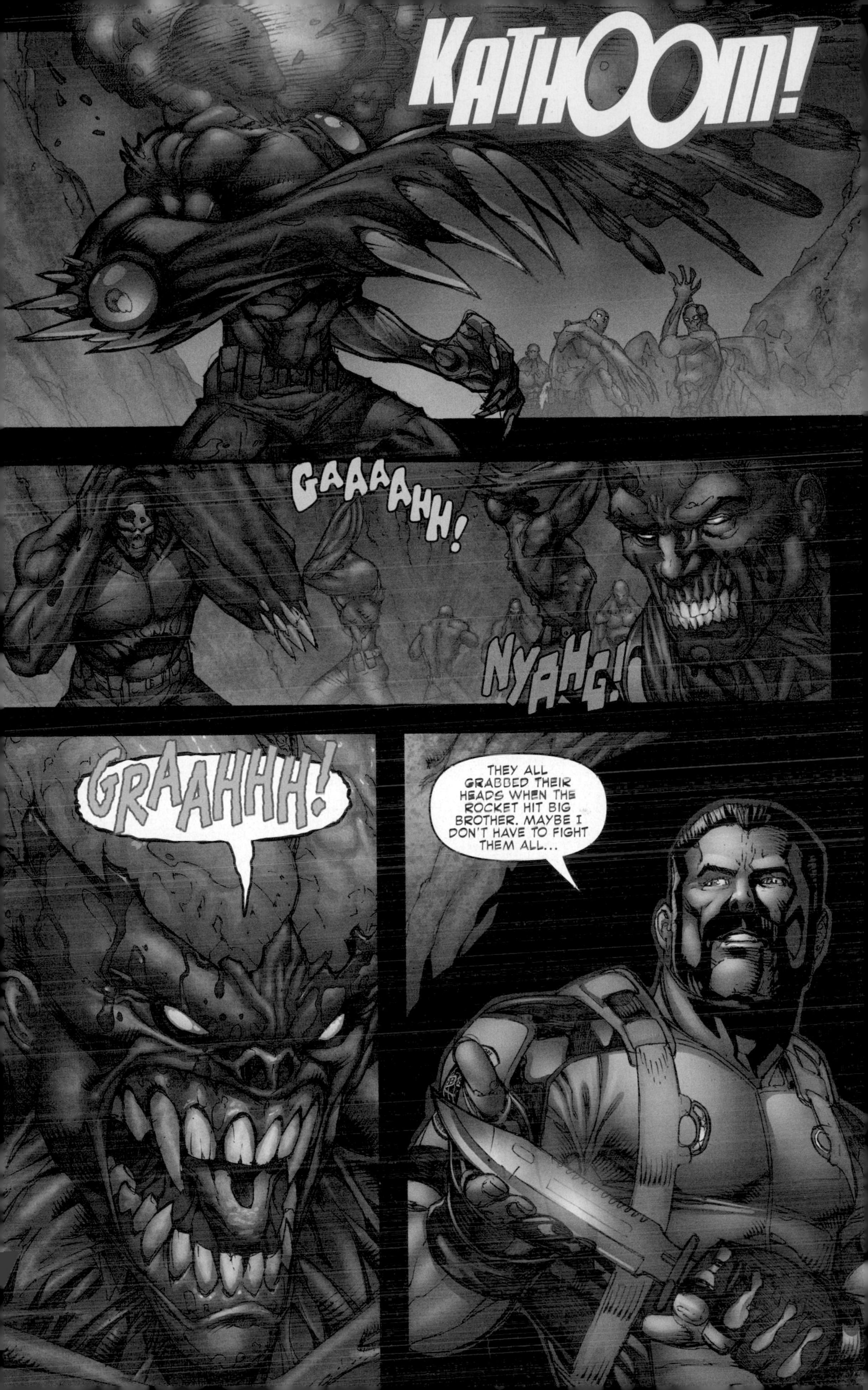
KATHOOOM!
GAAAAHH!
NYAHG!
GRAAHHH!
THEY ALL GRABBED THEIR HEADS WHEN THE ROCKET HIT BIG BROTHER. MAYBE I DON'T HAVE TO FIGHT THEM ALL...

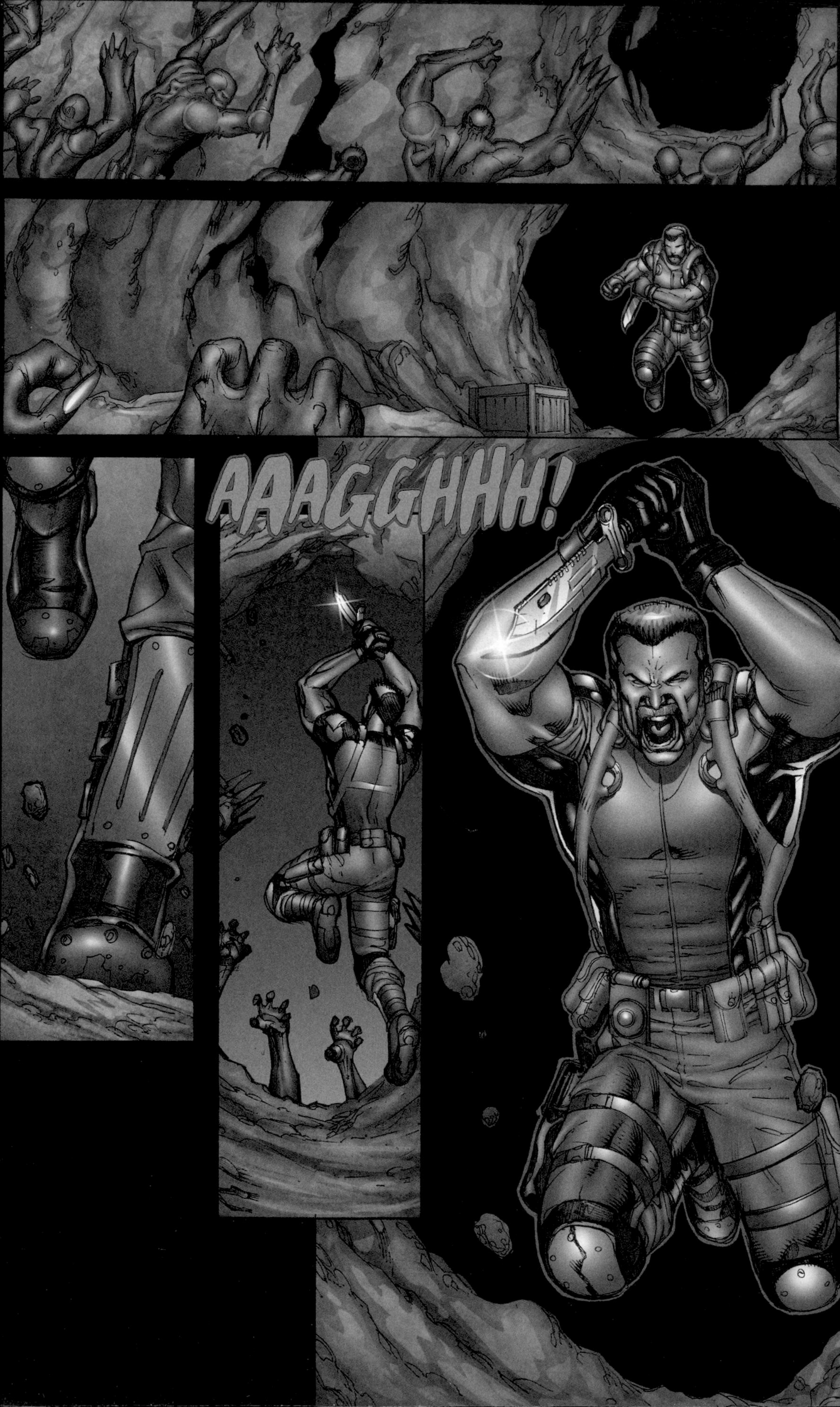
AAAGGHHH!

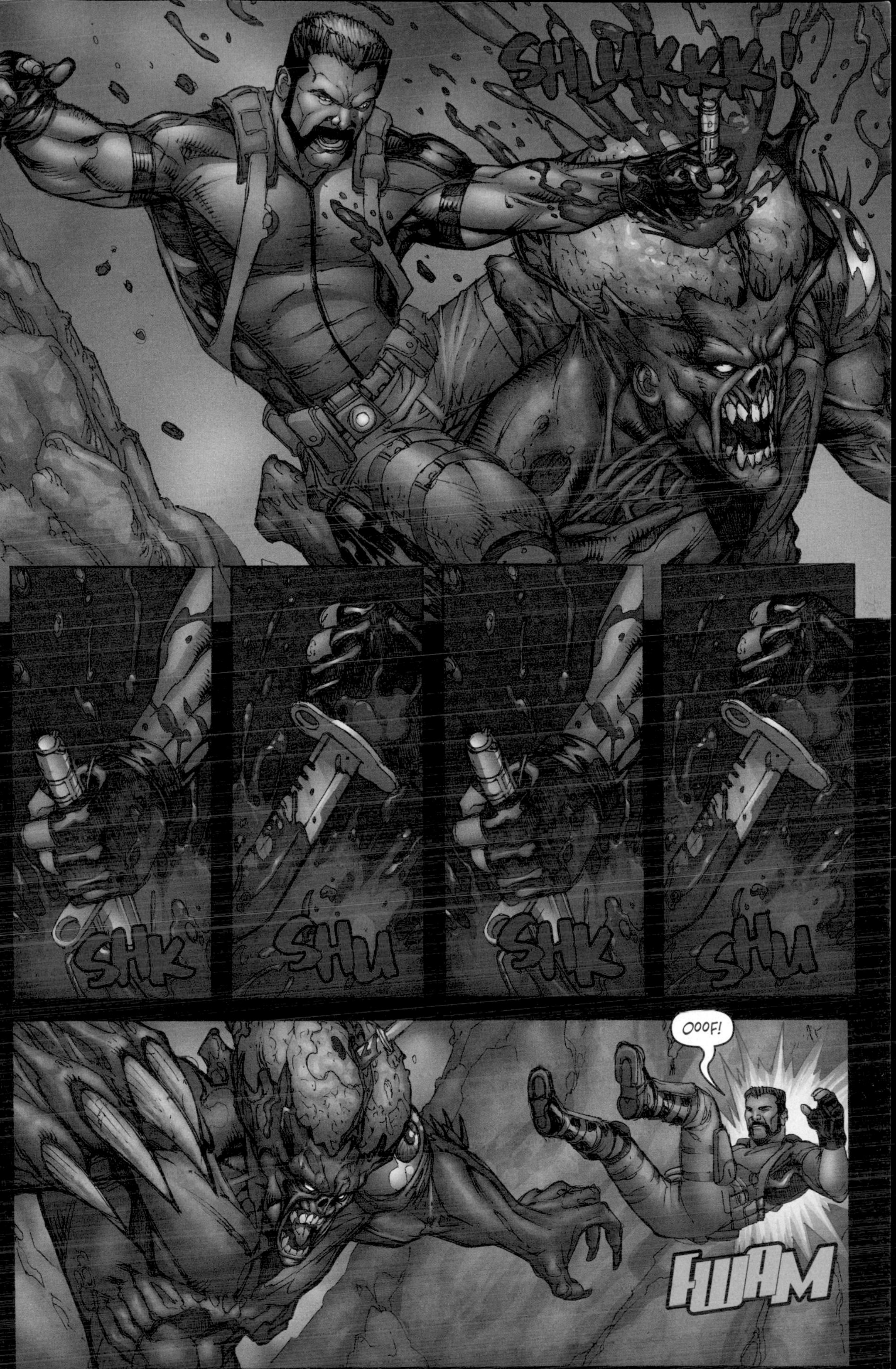
SHLUKKK!
SHK
SHU
SHK
SHU
OOOF!
FWAM

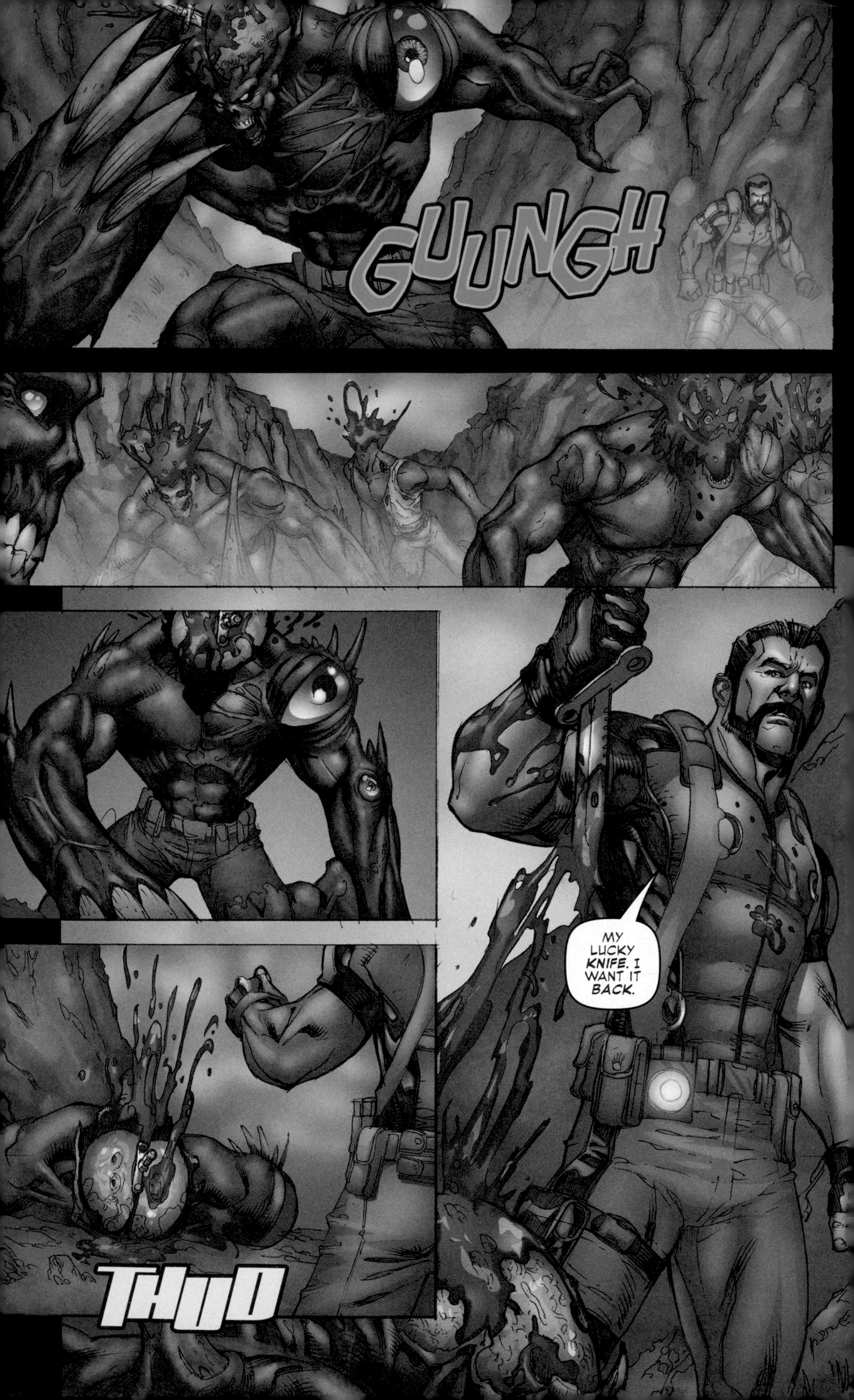
GUUNGH
MY LUCKY KNIFE. I WANT IT BACK.
THUD

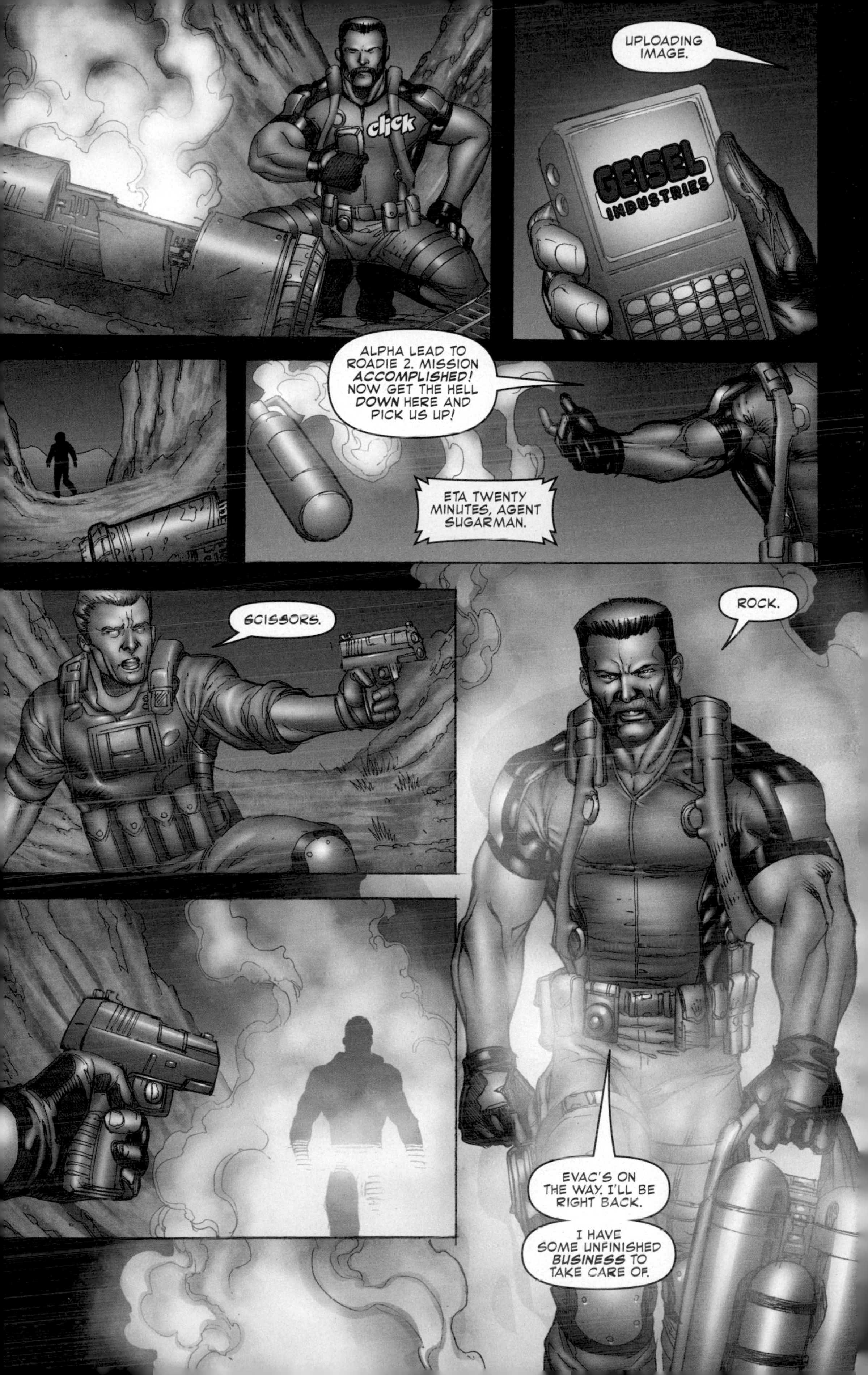
click
UPLOADING IMAGE.
GEISEL INDUSTRIES
ALPHA LEAD TO ROADIE 2. MISSION ACCOMPLISHED! NOW GET THE HELL DOWN HERE AND PICK US UP!
ETA TWENTY MINUTES, AGENT SUGARMAN.
SCISSORS.
ROCK.
EVAC'S ON THE WAY. I'LL BE RIGHT BACK.
I HAVE SOME UNFINISHED BUSINESS TO TAKE CARE OF.

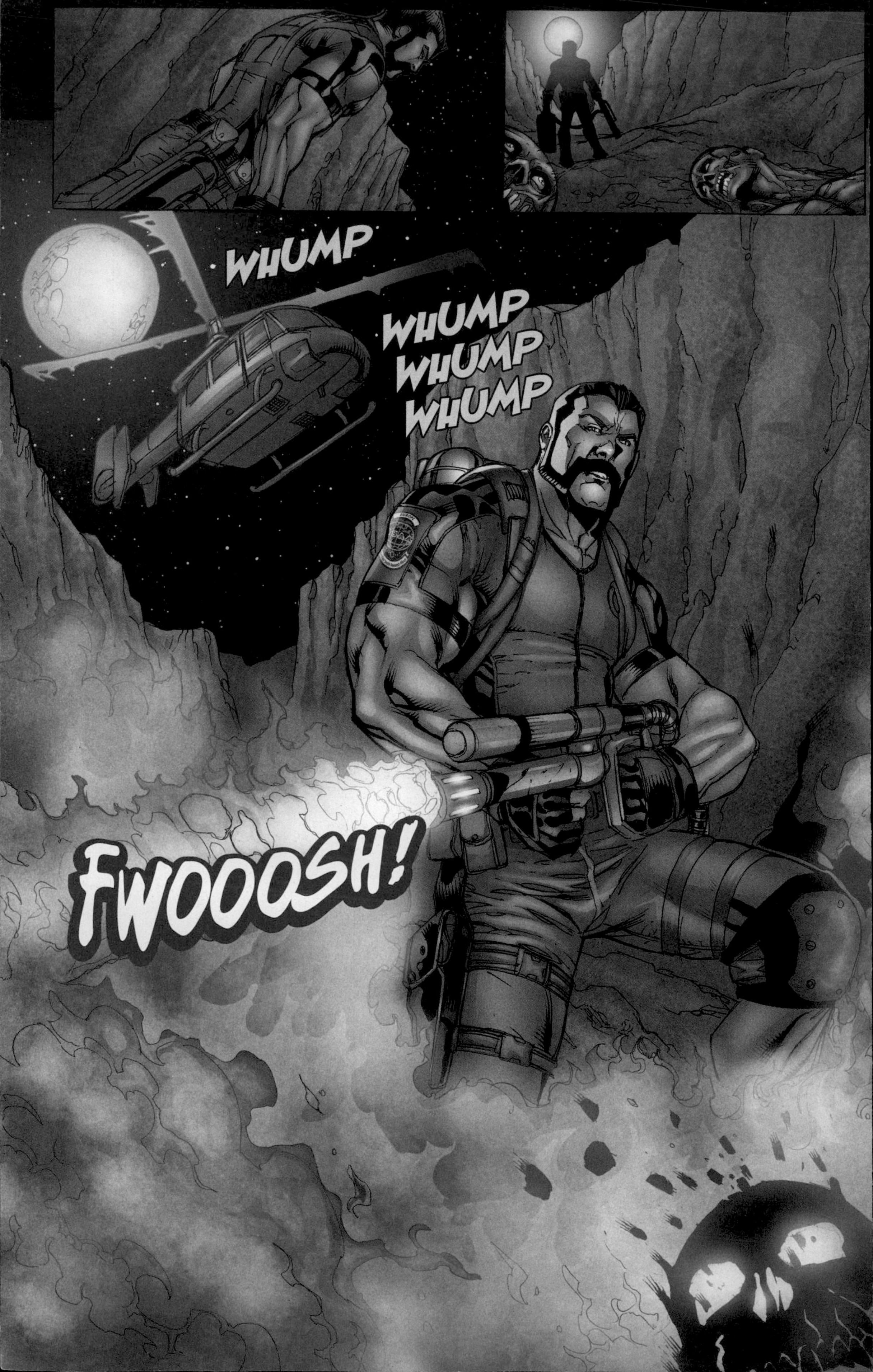
WHUMP
WHUMP
WHUMP
WHUMP
FWOOOSH!

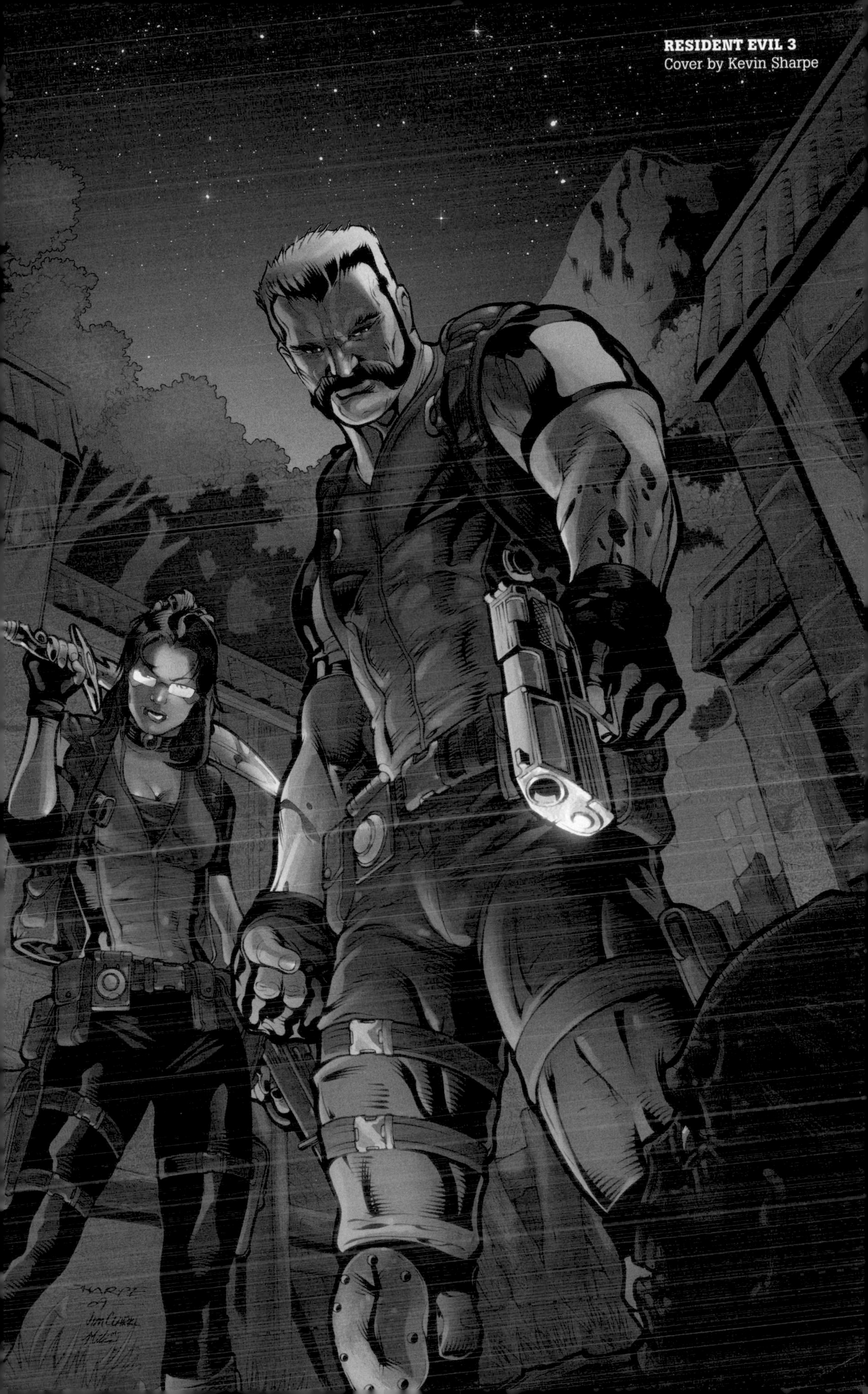

RESIDENT EVIL 3
Cover by Kevin Sharpe

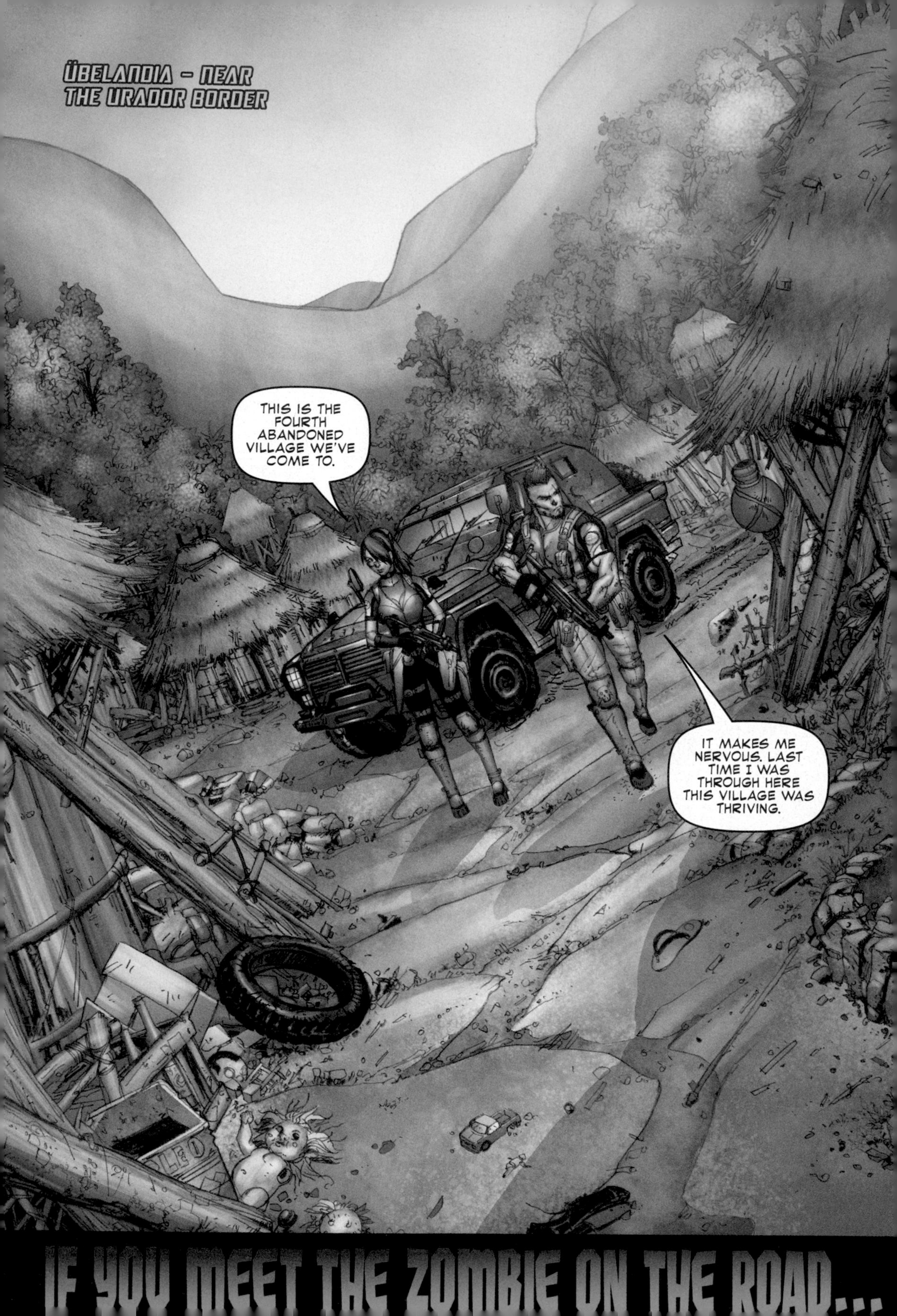
ÜBELANDIA - NEAR THE URADOR BORDER
THIS IS THE FOURTH ABANDONED VILLAGE WE'VE COME TO.
IT MAKES ME NERVOUS. LAST TIME I WAS THROUGH HERE THIS VILLAGE WAS THRIVING.
IF YOU MEET THE ZOMBIE ON THE ROAD...

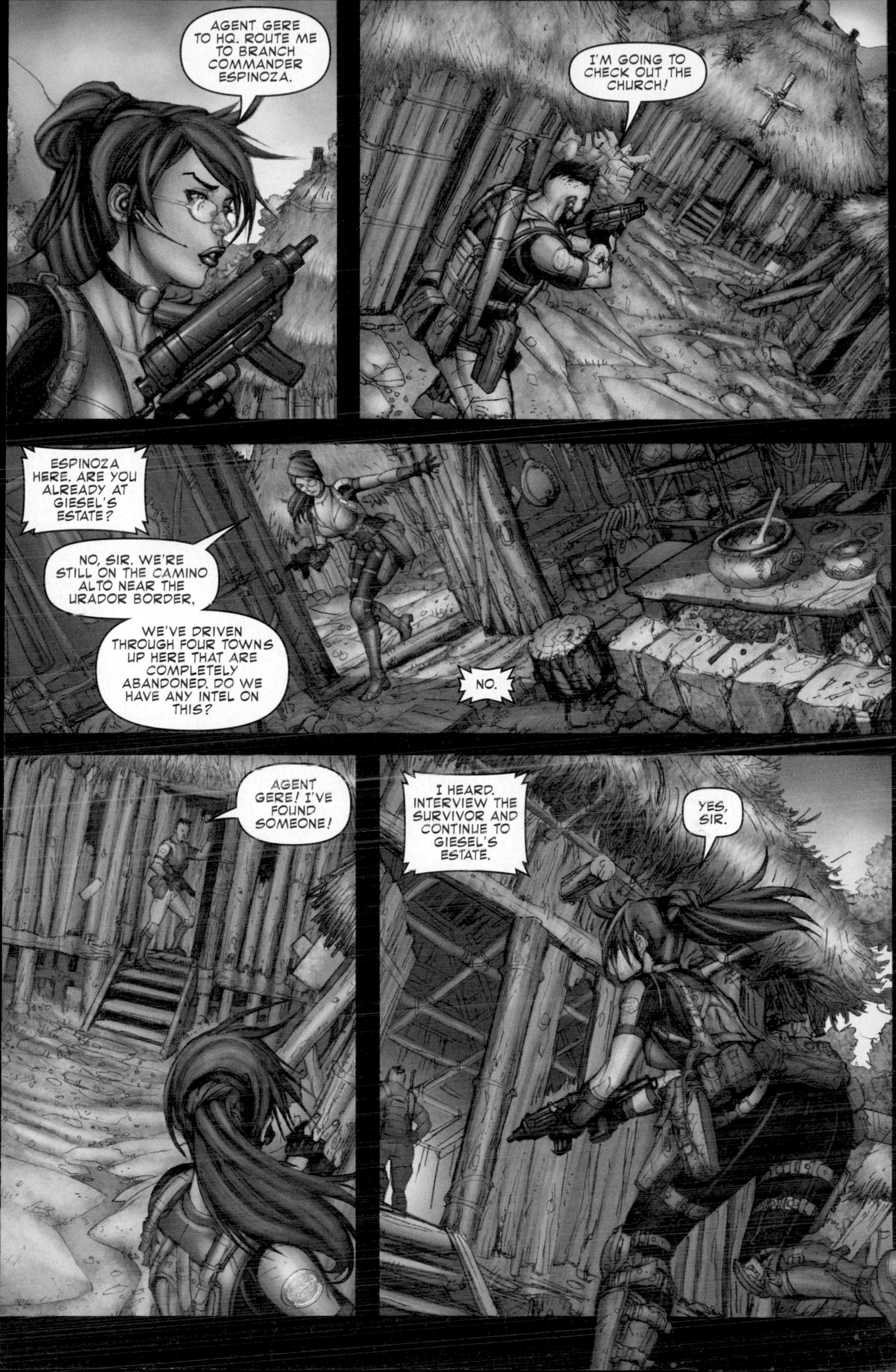
AGENT GERE TO HQ. ROUTE ME TO BRANCH COMMANDER ESPINOZA.
I'M GOING TO CHECK OUT THE CHURCH!
ESPINOZA HERE. ARE YOU ALREADY AT GIESEL'S ESTATE?
NO, SIR. WE'RE STILL ON THE CAMINO ALTO NEAR THE URADOR BORDER.
WE'VE DRIVEN THROUGH FOUR TOWNS UP HERE THAT ARE COMPLETELY ABANDONED. DO WE HAVE ANY INTEL ON THIS?
NO.
AGENT GERE! I'VE FOUND SOMEONE!
I HEARD. INTERVIEW THE SURVIVOR AND CONTINUE TO GIESEL'S ESTATE.
YES, SIR.

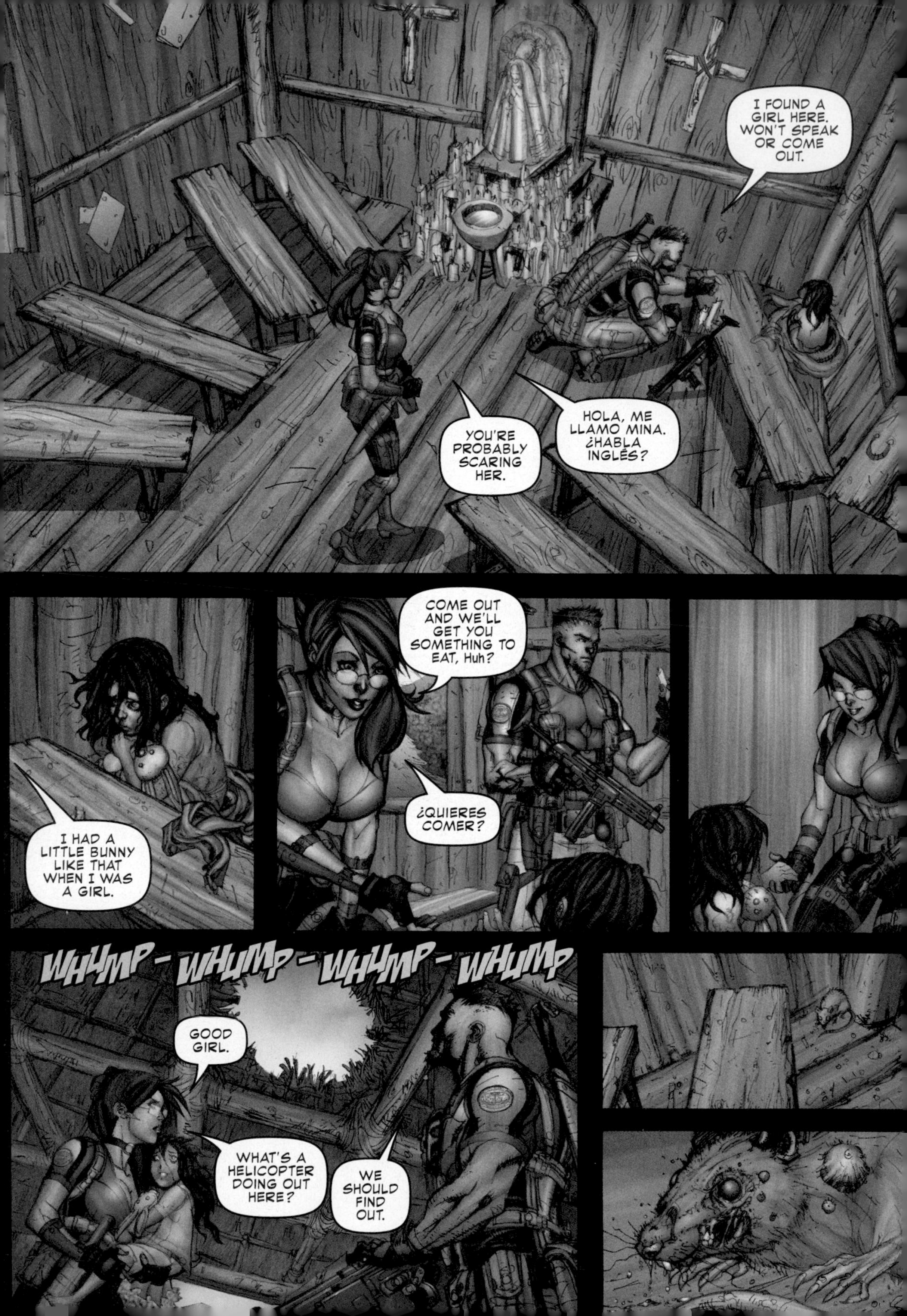
I FOUND A GIRL HERE. WON'T SPEAK OR COME OUT.
HOLA, ME LLAMO MINA. ¿HABLA INGLÉS?
YOU'RE PROBABLY SCARING HER.
I HAD A LITTLE BUNNY LIKE THAT WHEN I WAS A GIRL.
COME OUT AND WE'LL GET YOU SOMETHING TO EAT, Huh?
¿QUIERES COMER?
WHUMP - WHUMP - WHUMP - WHUMP
GOOD GIRL.
WHAT'S A HELICOPTER DOING OUT HERE?
WE SHOULD FIND OUT.

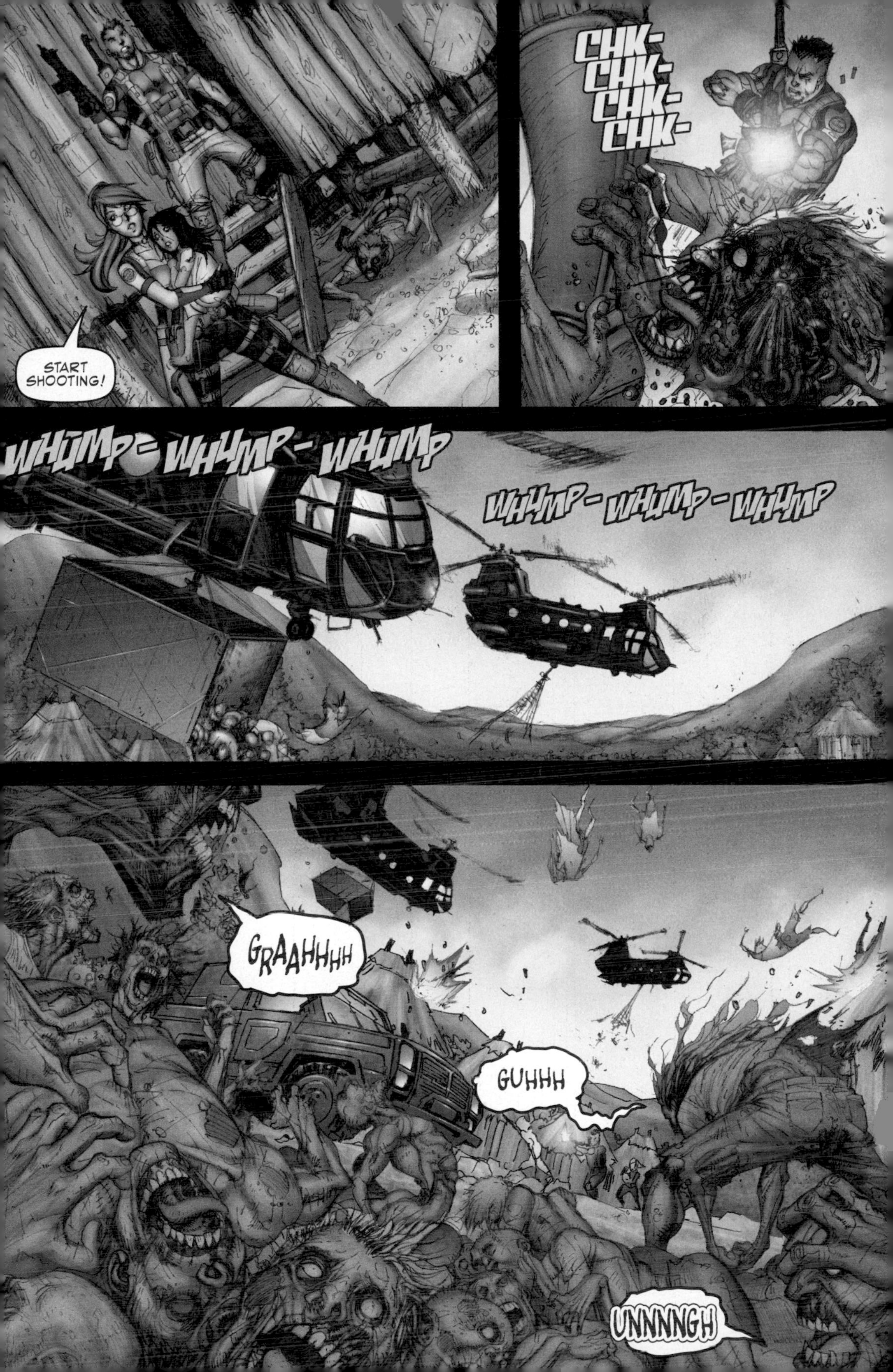
START SHOOTING!
CHK-CHK-CHK-CHK-
WHUMP-WHUMP-WHUMP
WHUMP-WHUMP-WHUMP
GRAAHHHH
GUHHH
UNNNNGH

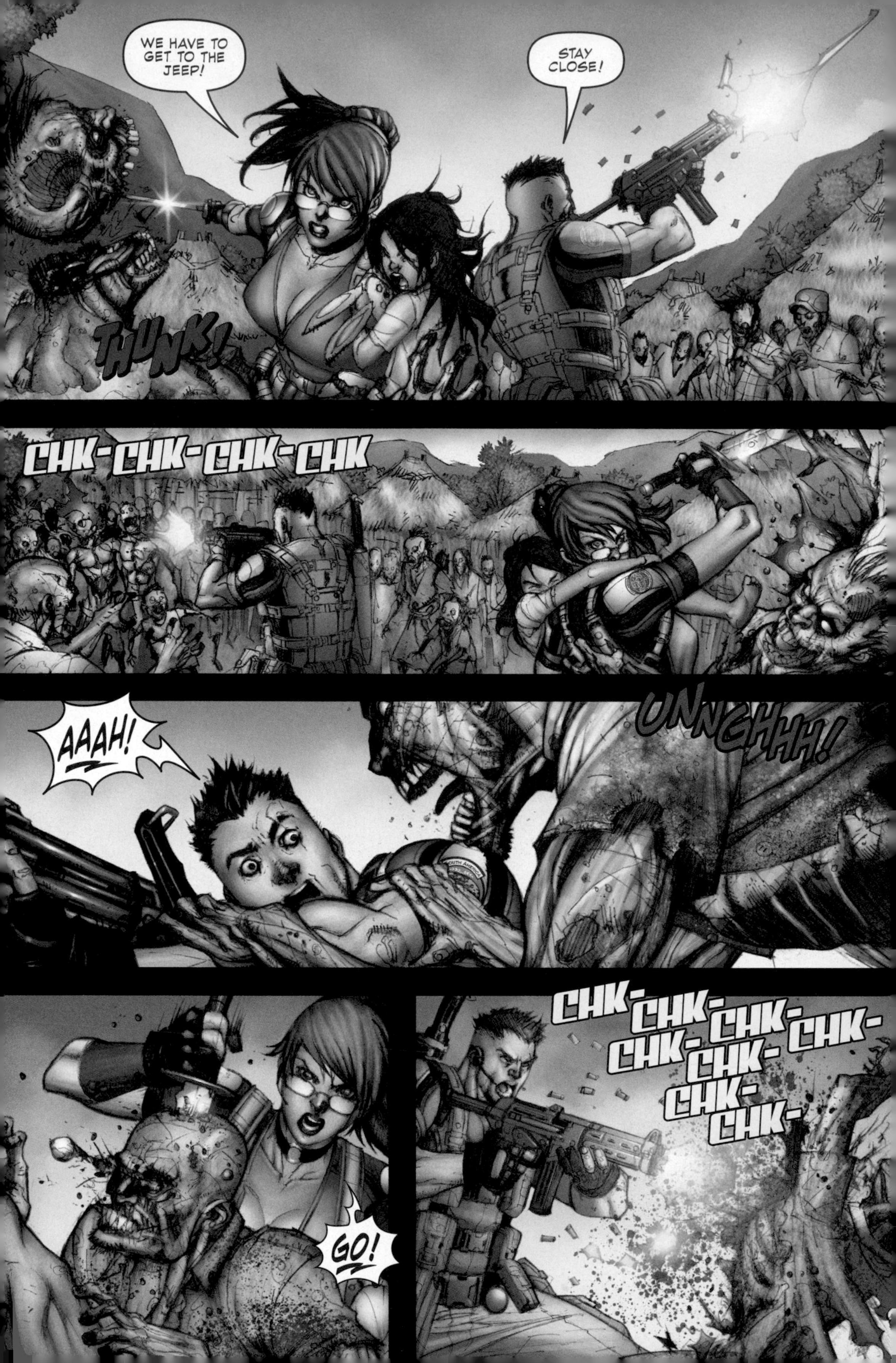
WE HAVE TO GET TO THE JEEP!
STAY CLOSE!
THUNK!
CHK-CHK-CHK-CHK
AAAH!
UNNGHHH!
GO!
CHK-CHK-CHK-CHK-CHK-CHK-CHK-CHK-

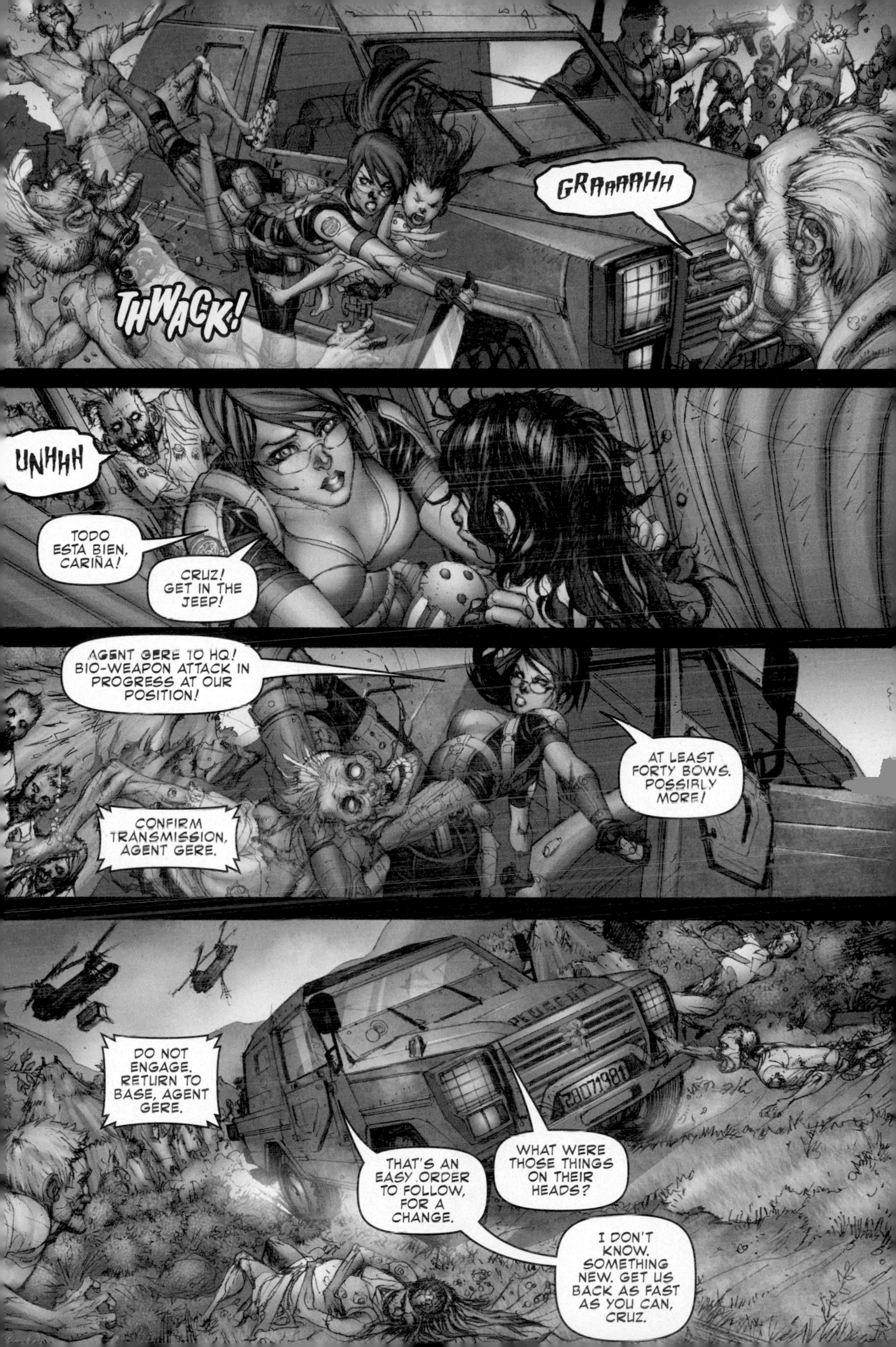
GRAAAAHH
THWACK!
UNHHH
TODO ESTA BIEN, CARIÑA!
CRUZ! GET IN THE JEEP!
AGENT GERE TO HQ! BIO-WEAPON ATTACK IN PROGRESS AT OUR POSITION!
AT LEAST FORTY BOWS. POSSIBLY MORE!
CONFIRM TRANSMISSION, AGENT GERE.
DO NOT ENGAGE. RETURN TO BASE, AGENT GERE.
WHAT WERE THOSE THINGS ON THEIR HEADS?
THAT'S AN EASY ORDER TO FOLLOW, FOR A CHANGE.
I DON'T KNOW. SOMETHING NEW. GET US BACK AS FAST AS YOU CAN, CRUZ.

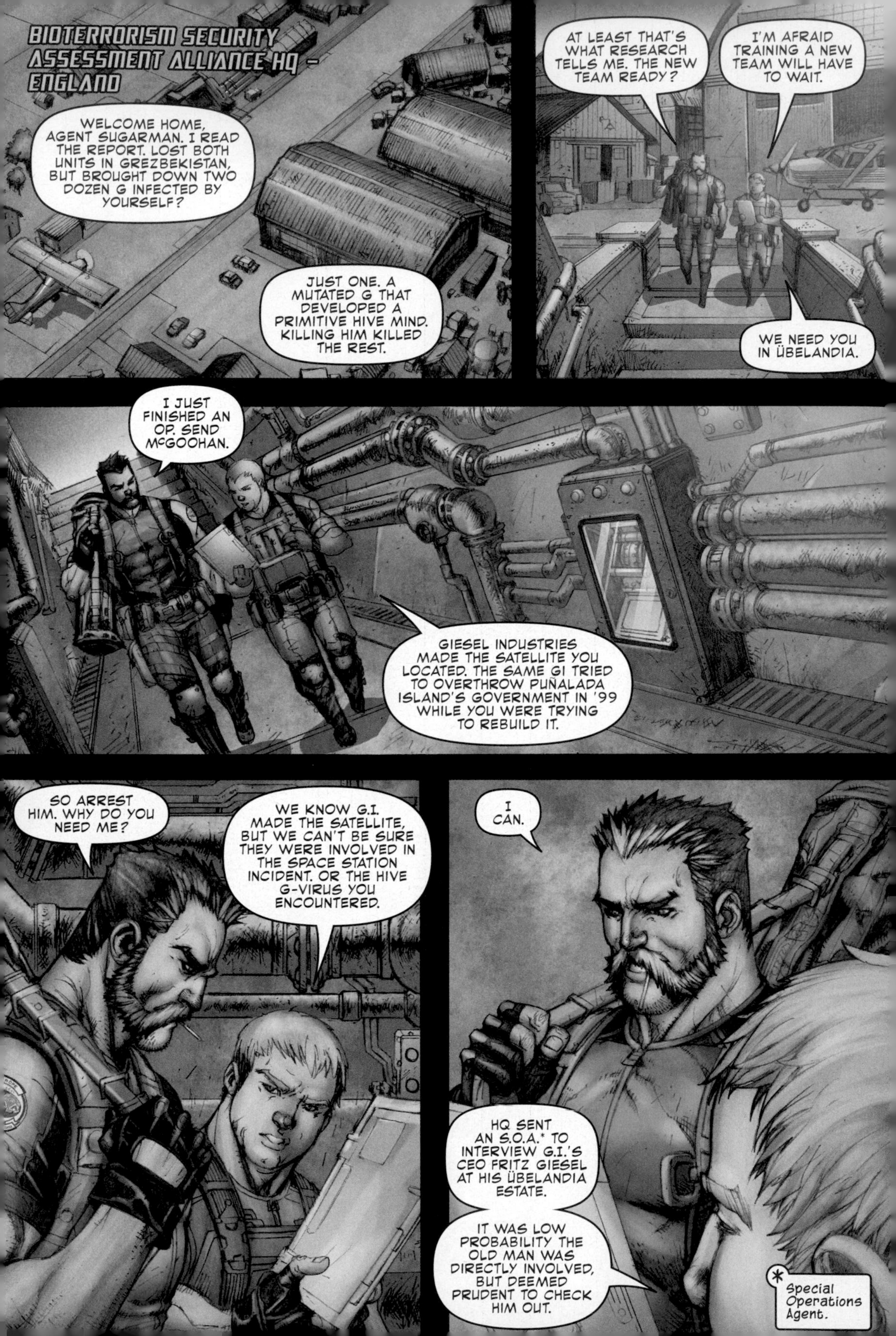

BIOTERRORISM SECURITY ASSESSMENT ALLIANCE HQ – ENGLAND
WELCOME HOME, AGENT SUGARMAN. I READ THE REPORT. LOST BOTH UNITS IN GREZBEKISTAN, BUT BROUGHT DOWN TWO DOZEN G INFECTED BY YOURSELF?
JUST ONE. A MUTATED G THAT DEVELOPED A PRIMITIVE HIVE MIND. KILLING HIM KILLED THE REST.
AT LEAST THAT'S WHAT RESEARCH TELLS ME. THE NEW TEAM READY?
I'M AFRAID TRAINING A NEW TEAM WILL HAVE TO WAIT.
WE NEED YOU IN ÜBELANDIA.
I JUST FINISHED AN OP. SEND McGOOHAN.
GIESEL INDUSTRIES MADE THE SATELLITE YOU LOCATED. THE SAME GI TRIED TO OVERTHROW PUÑALADA ISLAND'S GOVERNMENT IN '99 WHILE YOU WERE TRYING TO REBUILD IT.
SO ARREST HIM. WHY DO YOU NEED ME?
WE KNOW G.I. MADE THE SATELLITE, BUT WE CAN'T BE SURE THEY WERE INVOLVED IN THE SPACE STATION INCIDENT. OR THE HIVE G-VIRUS YOU ENCOUNTERED.
I CAN.
HQ SENT AN S.O.A.* TO INTERVIEW G.I.'S CEO FRITZ GIESEL AT HIS ÜBELANDIA ESTATE.
IT WAS LOW PROBABILITY THE OLD MAN WAS DIRECTLY INVOLVED, BUT DEEMED PRUDENT TO CHECK HIM OUT.
*Special Operations Agent.

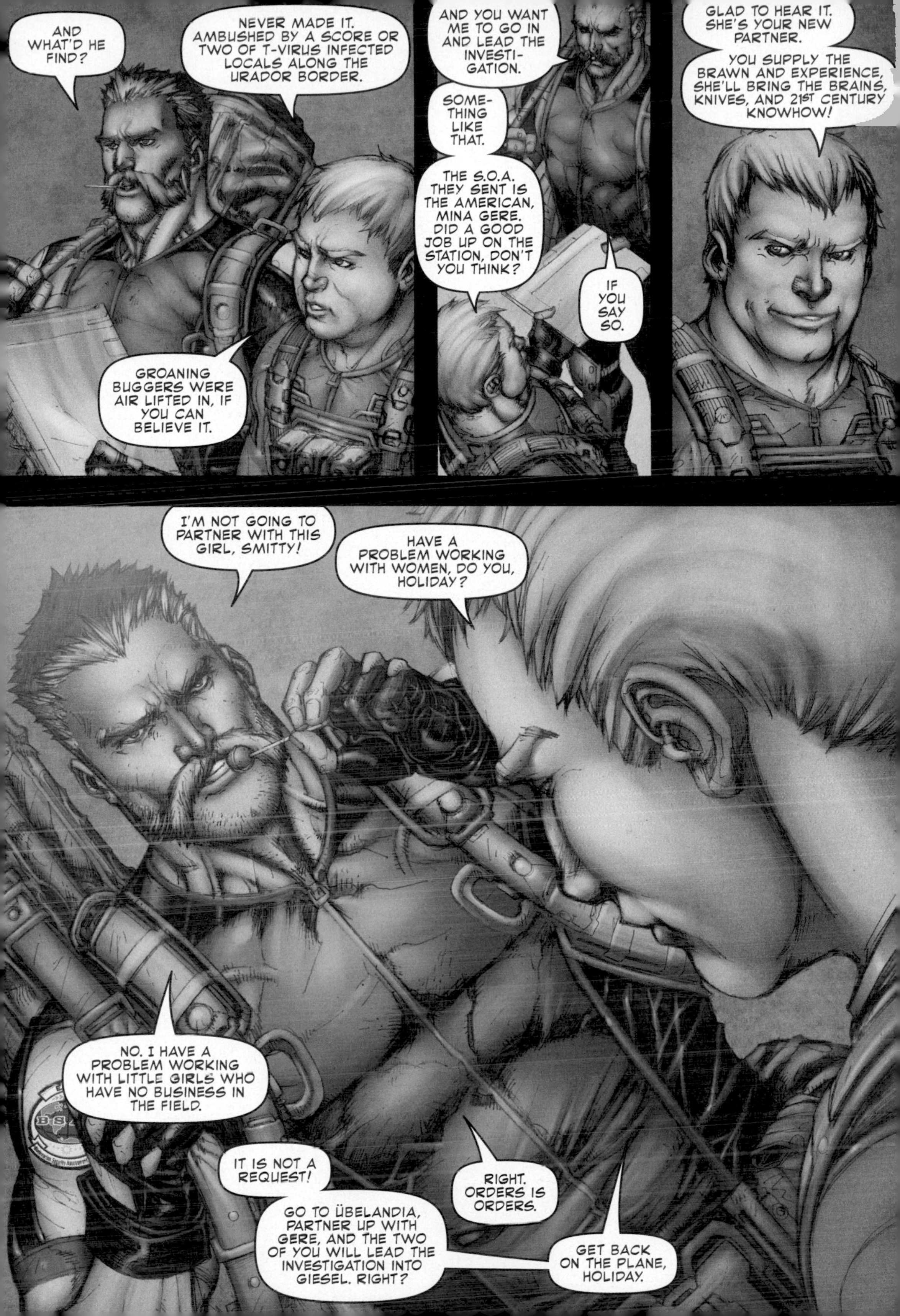
AND WHAT'D HE FIND?
NEVER MADE IT. AMBUSHED BY A SCORE OR TWO OF T-VIRUS INFECTED LOCALS ALONG THE URADOR BORDER.
GROANING BUGGERS WERE AIR LIFTED IN, IF YOU CAN BELIEVE IT.
AND YOU WANT ME TO GO IN AND LEAD THE INVESTI- GATION.
SOME- THING LIKE THAT.
THE S.O.A. THEY SENT IS THE AMERICAN, MINA GERE. DID A GOOD JOB UP ON THE STATION, DON'T YOU THINK?
IF YOU SAY SO.
GLAD TO HEAR IT. SHE'S YOUR NEW PARTNER.
YOU SUPPLY THE BRAWN AND EXPERIENCE, SHE'LL BRING THE BRAINS, KNIVES, AND 21ST CENTURY KNOWHOW!
I'M NOT GOING TO PARTNER WITH THIS GIRL, SMITTY!
HAVE A PROBLEM WORKING WITH WOMEN, DO YOU, HOLIDAY?
NO. I HAVE A PROBLEM WORKING WITH LITTLE GIRLS WHO HAVE NO BUSINESS IN THE FIELD.
IT IS NOT A REQUEST!
GO TO ÜBELANDIA, PARTNER UP WITH GERE, AND THE TWO OF YOU WILL LEAD THE INVESTIGATION INTO GIESEL. RIGHT?
RIGHT. ORDERS IS ORDERS.
GET BACK ON THE PLANE, HOLIDAY.

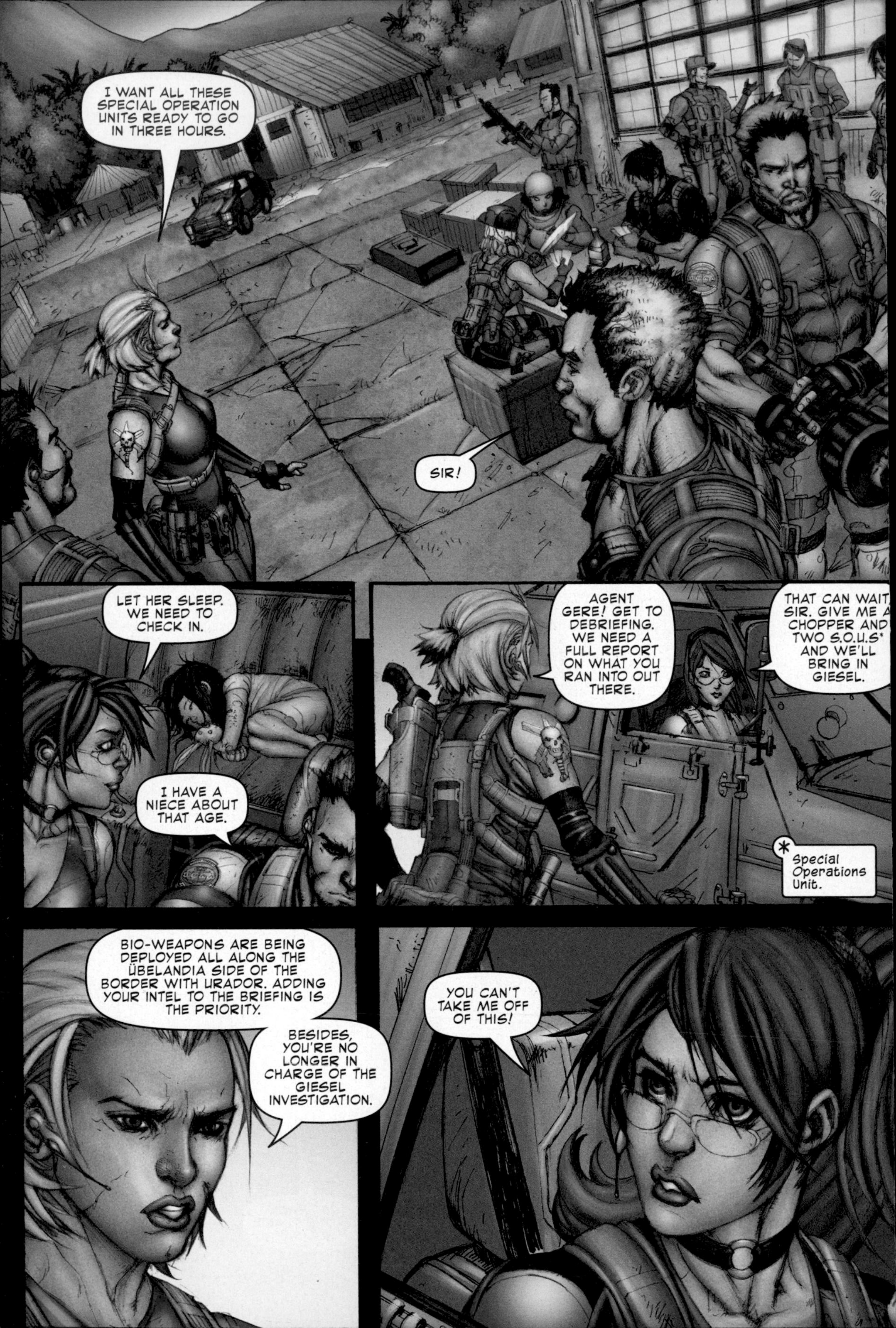
I WANT ALL THESE SPECIAL OPERATION UNITS READY TO GO IN THREE HOURS.
SIR!
LET HER SLEEP. WE NEED TO CHECK IN.
I HAVE A NIECE ABOUT THAT AGE.
AGENT GERE! GET TO DEBRIEFING. WE NEED A FULL REPORT ON WHAT YOU RAN INTO OUT THERE.
THAT CAN WAIT, SIR. GIVE ME A CHOPPER AND TWO S.O.U.S* AND WE'LL BRING IN GIESEL.
* Special Operations Unit.
BIO-WEAPONS ARE BEING DEPLOYED ALL ALONG THE ÜBELANDIA SIDE OF THE BORDER WITH URADOR. ADDING YOUR INTEL TO THE BRIEFING IS THE PRIORITY.
BESIDES, YOU'RE NO LONGER IN CHARGE OF THE GIESEL INVESTIGATION.
YOU CAN'T TAKE ME OFF OF THIS!

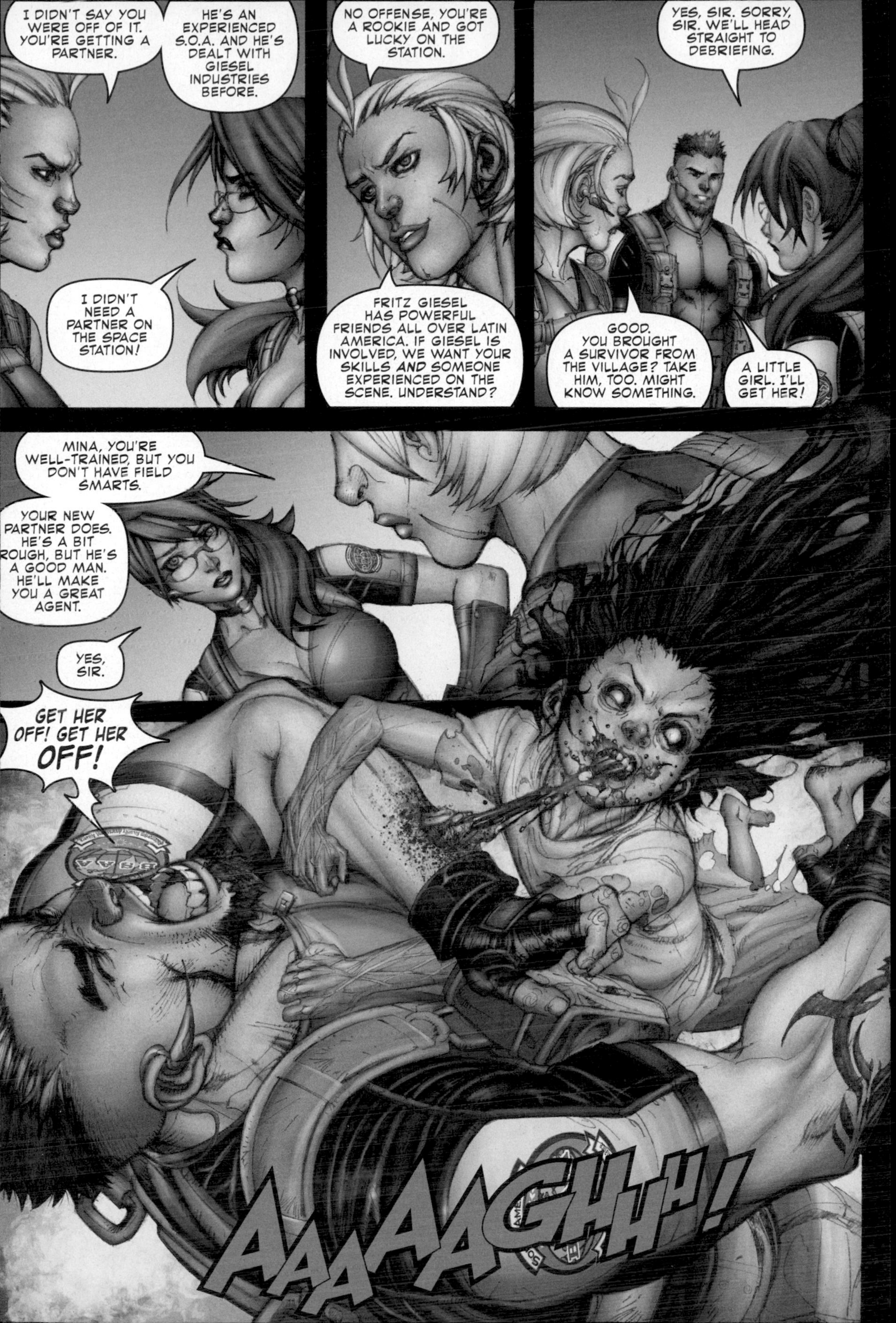
I DIDN'T SAY YOU WERE OFF OF IT. YOU'RE GETTING A PARTNER.
HE'S AN EXPERIENCED S.O.A. AND HE'S DEALT WITH GIESEL INDUSTRIES BEFORE.
I DIDN'T NEED A PARTNER ON THE SPACE STATION!
NO OFFENSE, YOU'RE A ROOKIE AND GOT LUCKY ON THE STATION.
FRITZ GIESEL HAS POWERFUL FRIENDS ALL OVER LATIN AMERICA. IF GIESEL IS INVOLVED, WE WANT YOUR SKILLS AND SOMEONE EXPERIENCED ON THE SCENE. UNDERSTAND?
YES, SIR. SORRY, SIR. WE'LL HEAD STRAIGHT TO DEBRIEFING.
GOOD. YOU BROUGHT A SURVIVOR FROM THE VILLAGE? TAKE HIM, TOO. MIGHT KNOW SOMETHING.
A LITTLE GIRL. I'LL GET HER!
MINA, YOU'RE WELL-TRAINED, BUT YOU DON'T HAVE FIELD SMARTS.
YOUR NEW PARTNER DOES. HE'S A BIT ROUGH, BUT HE'S A GOOD MAN. HE'LL MAKE YOU A GREAT AGENT.
YES, SIR.
GET HER OFF! GET HER OFF!
AAAAAGHHH!

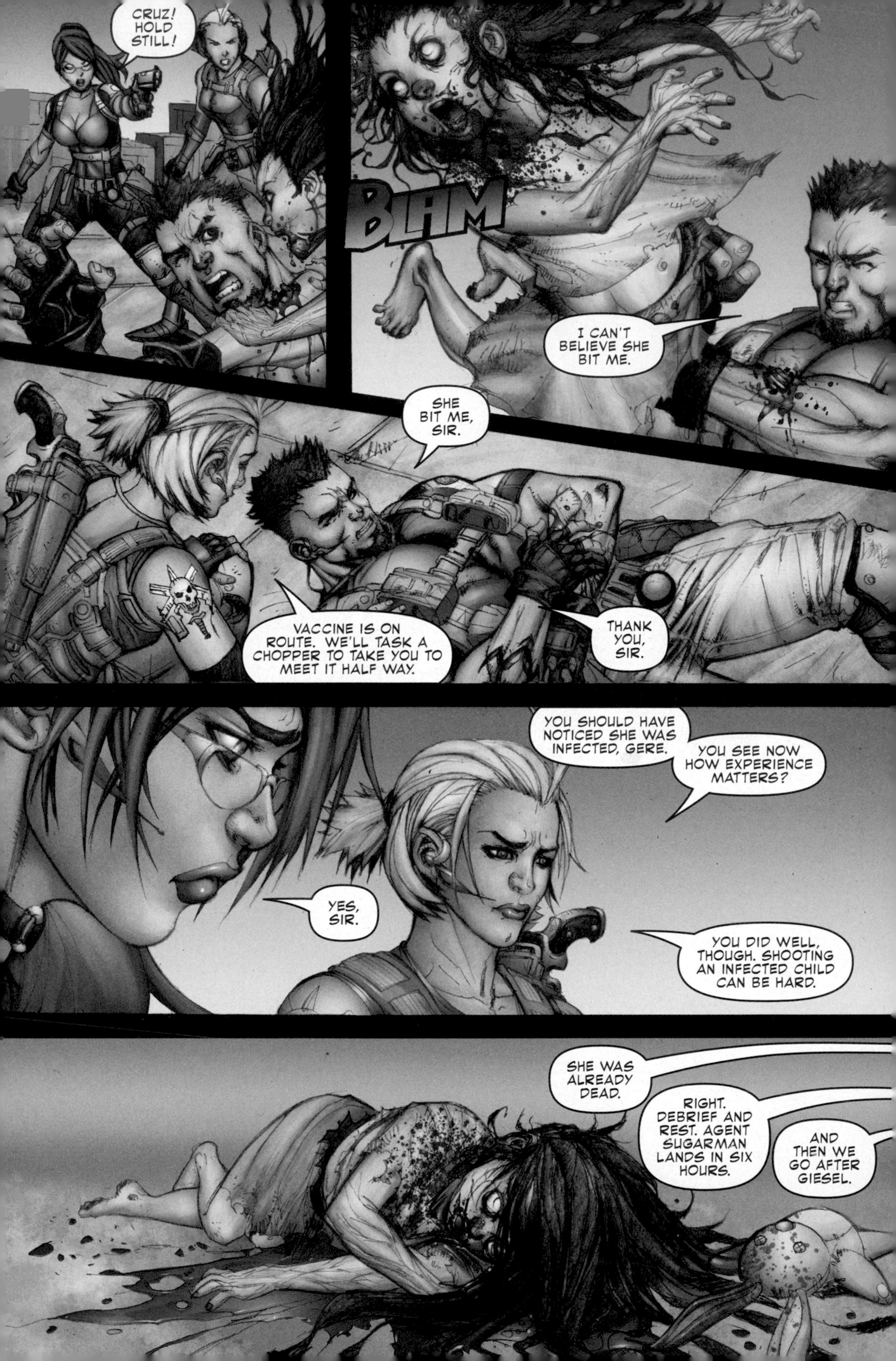
CRUZ! HOLD STILL!
BLAM
I CAN'T BELIEVE SHE BIT ME.
SHE BIT ME, SIR.
VACCINE IS ON ROUTE. WE'LL TASK A CHOPPER TO TAKE YOU TO MEET IT HALF WAY.
THANK YOU, SIR.
YOU SHOULD HAVE NOTICED SHE WAS INFECTED, GERE.
YOU SEE NOW HOW EXPERIENCE MATTERS?
YES, SIR.
YOU DID WELL, THOUGH. SHOOTING AN INFECTED CHILD CAN BE HARD.
SHE WAS ALREADY DEAD.
RIGHT. DEBRIEF AND REST. AGENT SUGARMAN LANDS IN SIX HOURS.
AND THEN WE GO AFTER GIESEL.

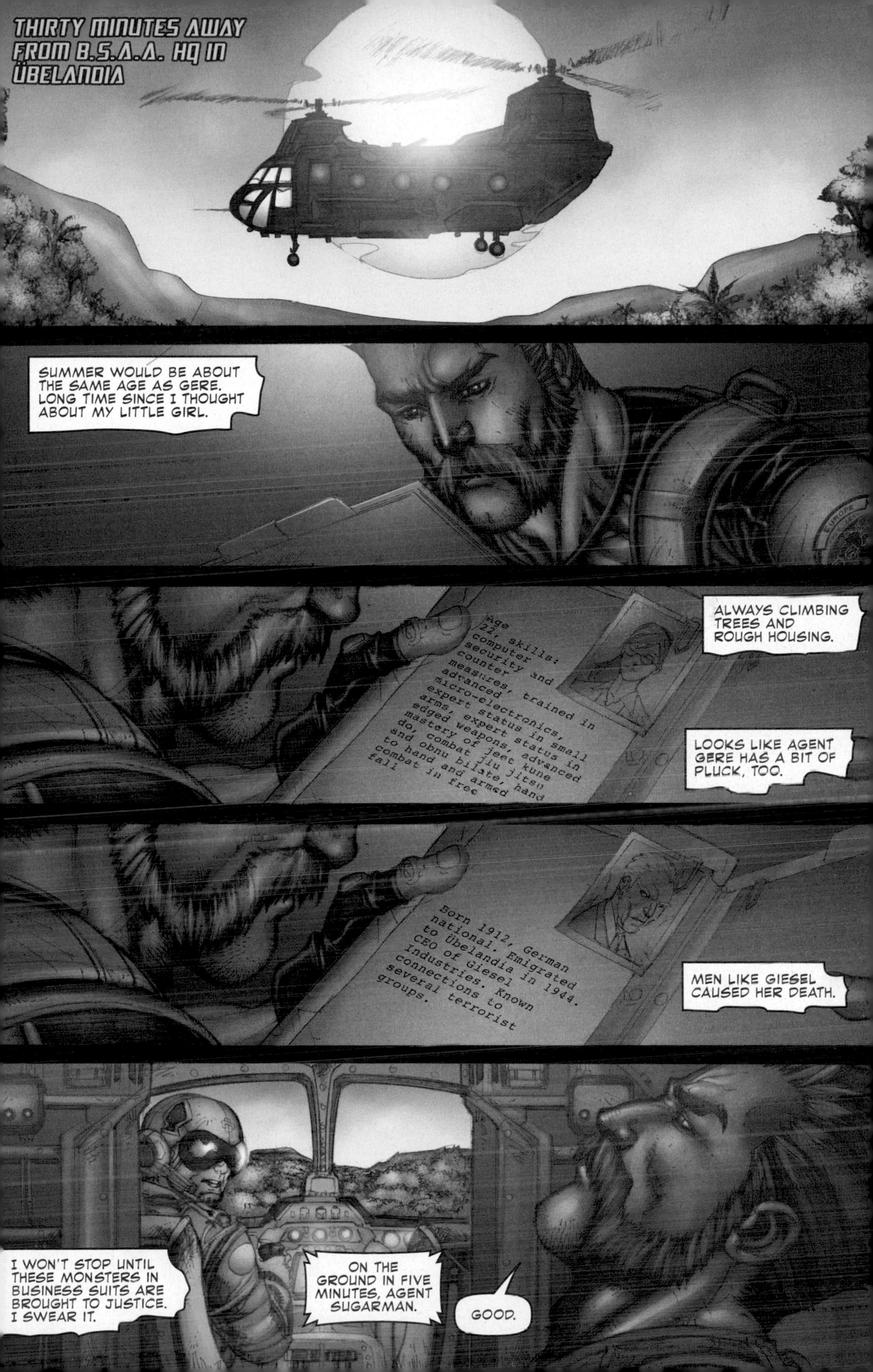
THIRTY MINUTES AWAY FROM B.S.A.A. HQ IN ÜBELANDIA
SUMMER WOULD BE ABOUT THE SAME AGE AS GERE. LONG TIME SINCE I THOUGHT ABOUT MY LITTLE GIRL.
Age 22, skills: computer security and counter measures, trained in advanced micro-electronics, expert status in small arms, expert status in edged weapons, advanced mastery of jeet kune do, combat jiu jitsu and obnu bilate, hand to hand and armed combat fall in free
ALWAYS CLIMBING TREES AND ROUGH HOUSING.
LOOKS LIKE AGENT GERE HAS A BIT OF PLUCK, TOO.
Born 1912, German national. Emigrated to Übelandia in 1944. CEO of Giesel Industries. Known connections to several terrorist groups.
MEN LIKE GIESEL CAUSED HER DEATH.
I WON'T STOP UNTIL THESE MONSTERS IN BUSINESS SUITS ARE BROUGHT TO JUSTICE. I SWEAR IT.
ON THE GROUND IN FIVE MINUTES, AGENT SUGARMAN.
GOOD.

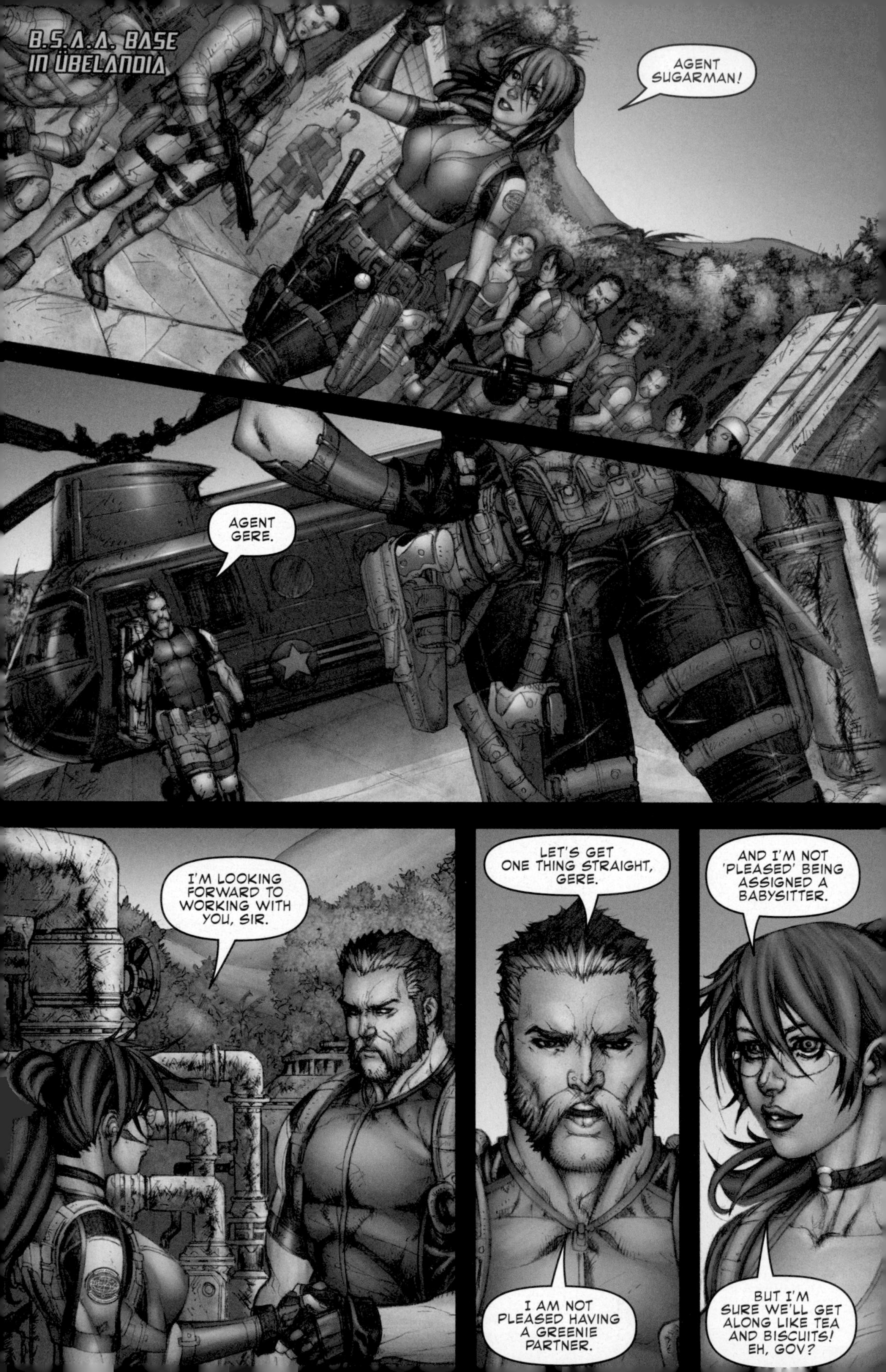

B.S.A.A. BASE IN ÜBELANDIA
AGENT SUGARMAN!
AGENT GERE.
I'M LOOKING FORWARD TO WORKING WITH YOU, SIR.
LET'S GET ONE THING STRAIGHT, GERE.
I AM NOT PLEASED HAVING A GREENIE PARTNER.
AND I'M NOT 'PLEASED' BEING ASSIGNED A BABYSITTER.
BUT I'M SURE WE'LL GET ALONG LIKE TEA AND BISCUITS! EH, GOV?

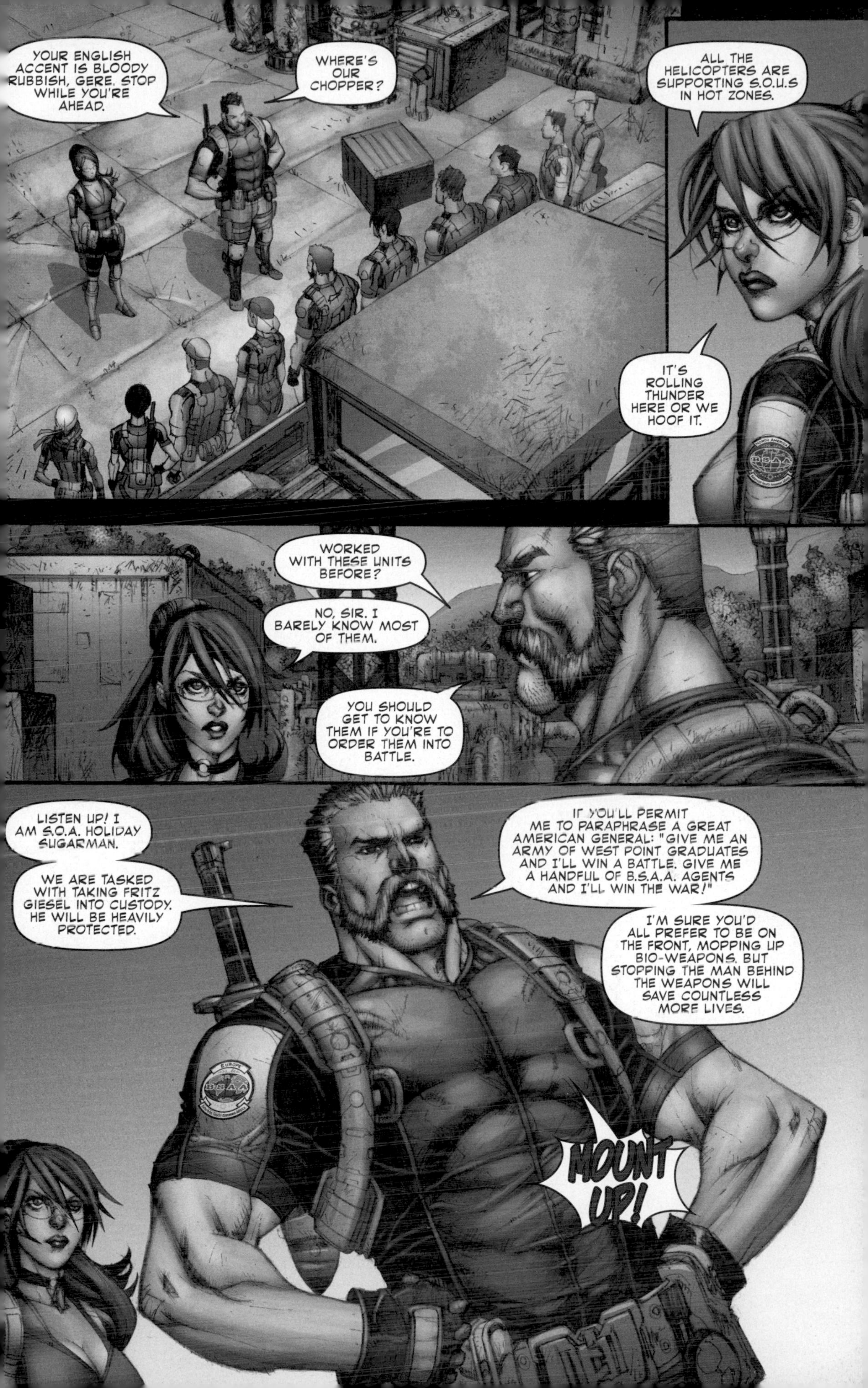

YOUR ENGLISH ACCENT IS BLOODY RUBBISH, GERE. STOP WHILE YOU'RE AHEAD.
WHERE'S OUR CHOPPER?
ALL THE HELICOPTERS ARE SUPPORTING S.O.U.S IN HOT ZONES.
IT'S ROLLING THUNDER HERE OR WE HOOF IT.
WORKED WITH THESE UNITS BEFORE?
NO, SIR. I BARELY KNOW MOST OF THEM.
YOU SHOULD GET TO KNOW THEM IF YOU'RE TO ORDER THEM INTO BATTLE.
LISTEN UP! I AM S.O.A. HOLIDAY SUGARMAN.
WE ARE TASKED WITH TAKING FRITZ GIESEL INTO CUSTODY. HE WILL BE HEAVILY PROTECTED.
IF YOU'LL PERMIT ME TO PARAPHRASE A GREAT AMERICAN GENERAL: "GIVE ME AN ARMY OF WEST POINT GRADUATES AND I'LL WIN A BATTLE. GIVE ME A HANDFUL OF B.S.A.A. AGENTS AND I'LL WIN THE WAR!"
I'M SURE YOU'D ALL PREFER TO BE ON THE FRONT, MOPPING UP BIO-WEAPONS, BUT STOPPING THE MAN BEHIND THE WEAPONS WILL SAVE COUNTLESS MORE LIVES.
MOUNT UP!

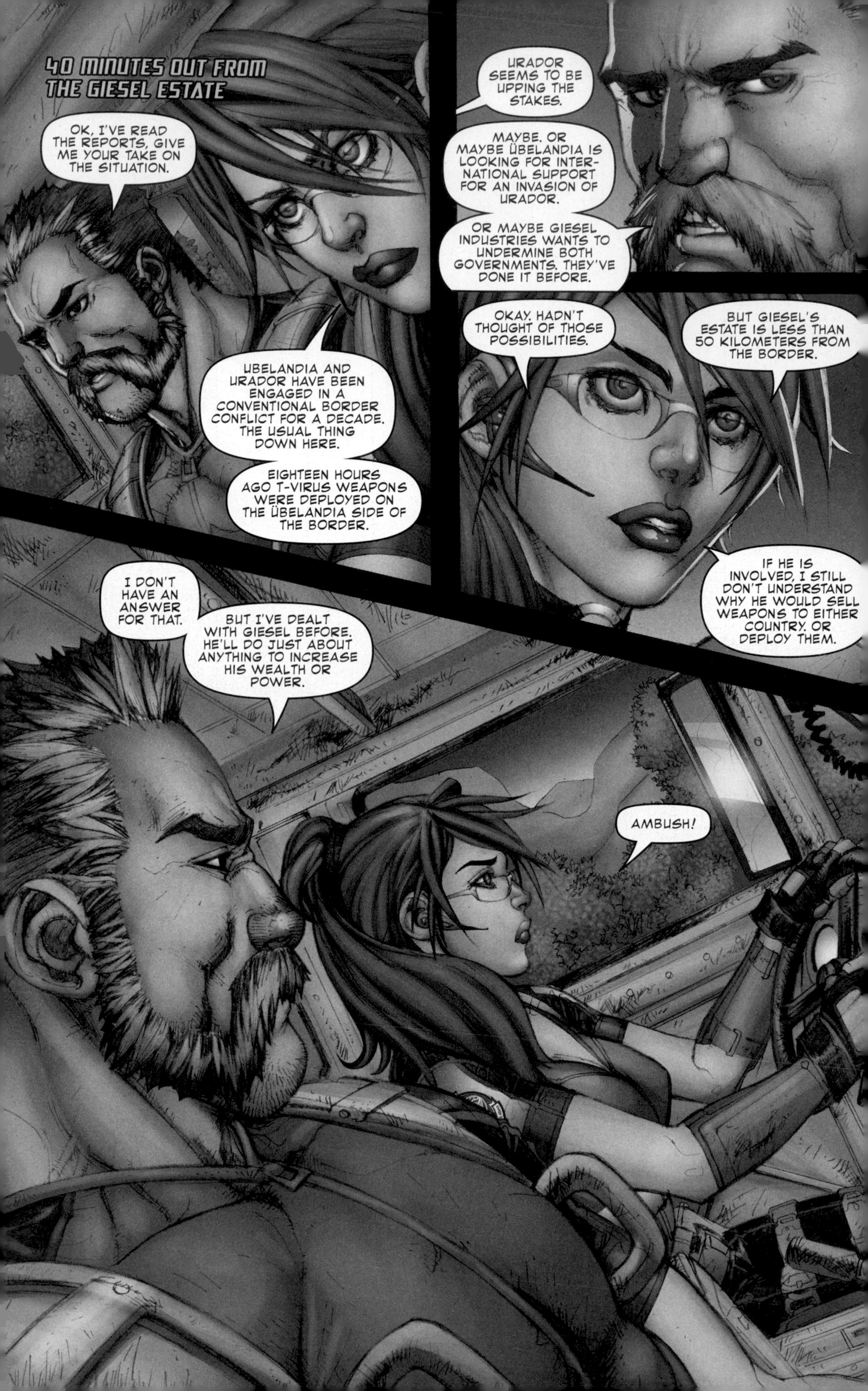
40 MINUTES OUT FROM THE GIESEL ESTATE
OK, I'VE READ THE REPORTS, GIVE ME YOUR TAKE ON THE SITUATION.
UBELANDIA AND URADOR HAVE BEEN ENGAGED IN A CONVENTIONAL BORDER CONFLICT FOR A DECADE. THE USUAL THING DOWN HERE.
EIGHTEEN HOURS AGO T-VIRUS WEAPONS WERE DEPLOYED ON THE ÜBELANDIA SIDE OF THE BORDER.
URADOR SEEMS TO BE UPPING THE STAKES.
MAYBE. OR MAYBE ÜBELANDIA IS LOOKING FOR INTERNATIONAL SUPPORT FOR AN INVASION OF URADOR.
OR MAYBE GIESEL INDUSTRIES WANTS TO UNDERMINE BOTH GOVERNMENTS. THEY'VE DONE IT BEFORE.
OKAY. HADN'T THOUGHT OF THOSE POSSIBILITIES.
BUT GIESEL'S ESTATE IS LESS THAN 50 KILOMETERS FROM THE BORDER.
IF HE IS INVOLVED, I STILL DON'T UNDERSTAND WHY HE WOULD SELL WEAPONS TO EITHER COUNTRY. OR DEPLOY THEM.
I DON'T HAVE AN ANSWER FOR THAT.
BUT I'VE DEALT WITH GIESEL BEFORE. HE'LL DO JUST ABOUT ANYTHING TO INCREASE HIS WEALTH OR POWER.
AMBUSH!

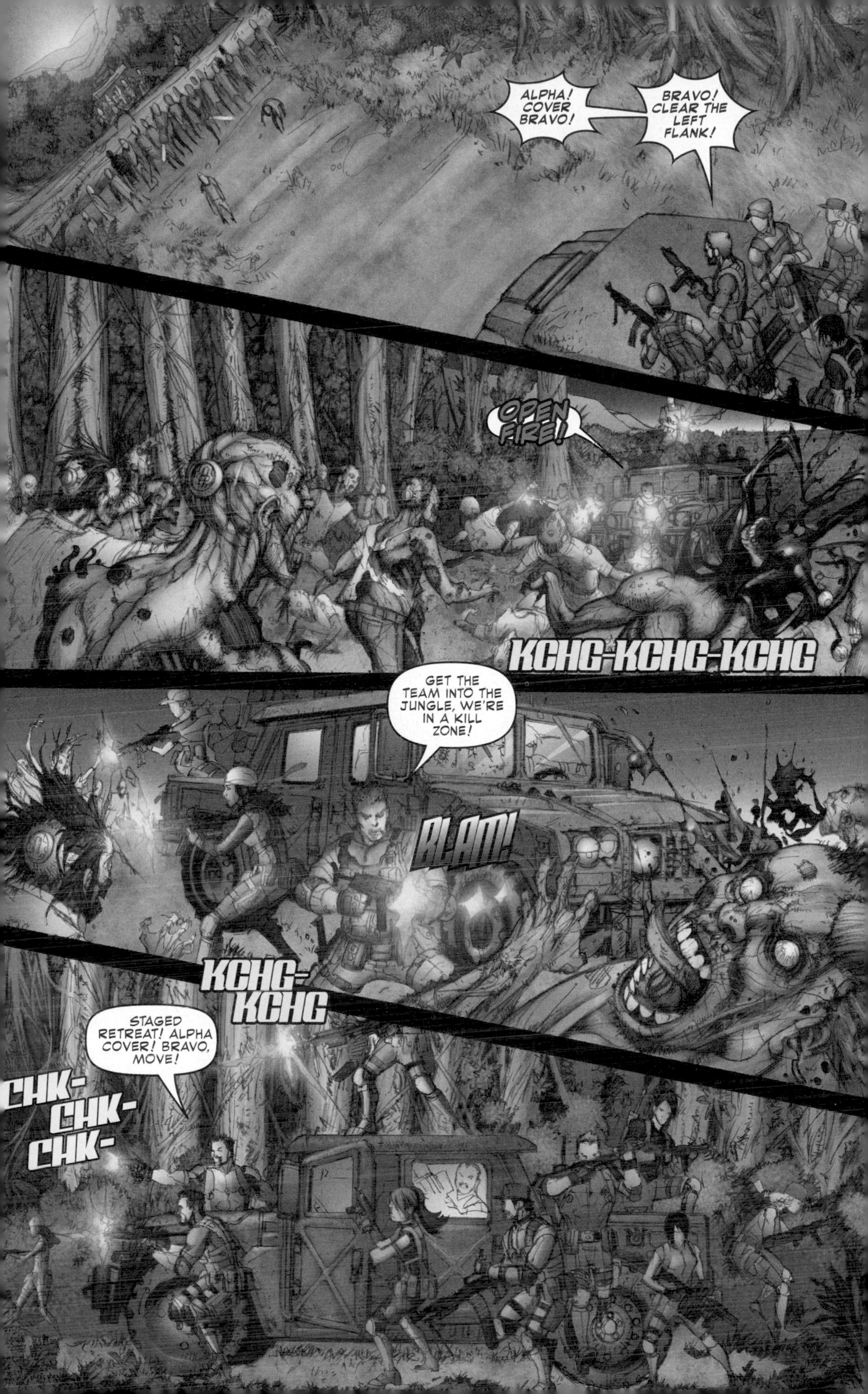
ALPHA! COVER BRAVO!
BRAVO! CLEAR THE LEFT FLANK!
OPEN FIRE!
KCHG-KCHG-KCHG
GET THE TEAM INTO THE JUNGLE, WE'RE IN A KILL ZONE!
BLAM!
KCHG-KCHG
STAGED RETREAT! ALPHA COVER! BRAVO, MOVE!
CHK-CHK-CHK-

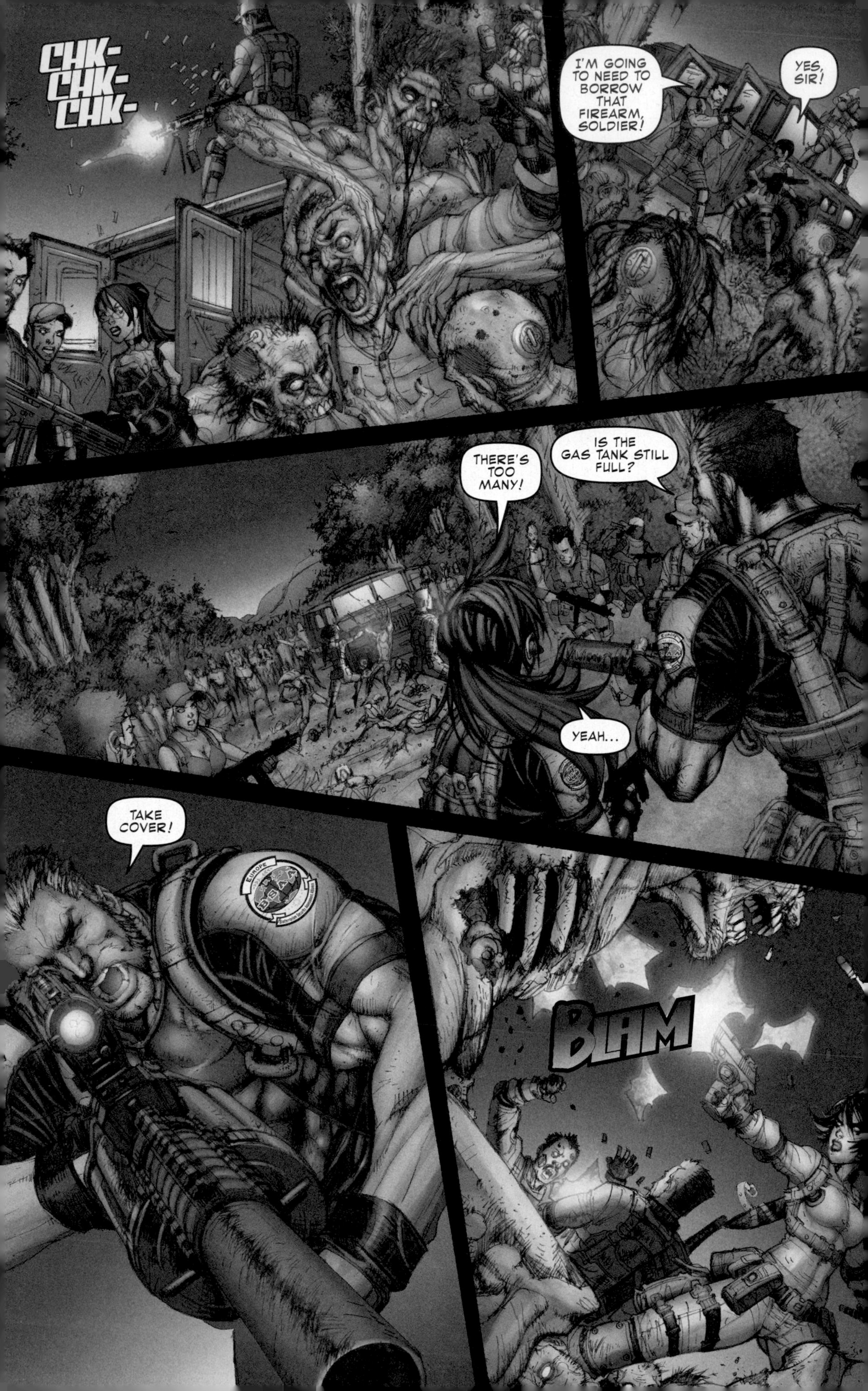
CHK-CHK-CHK-
I'M GOING TO NEED TO BORROW THAT FIREARM, SOLDIER!
YES, SIR!
THERE'S TOO MANY!
IS THE GAS TANK STILL FULL?
YEAH...
TAKE COVER!
BLAM

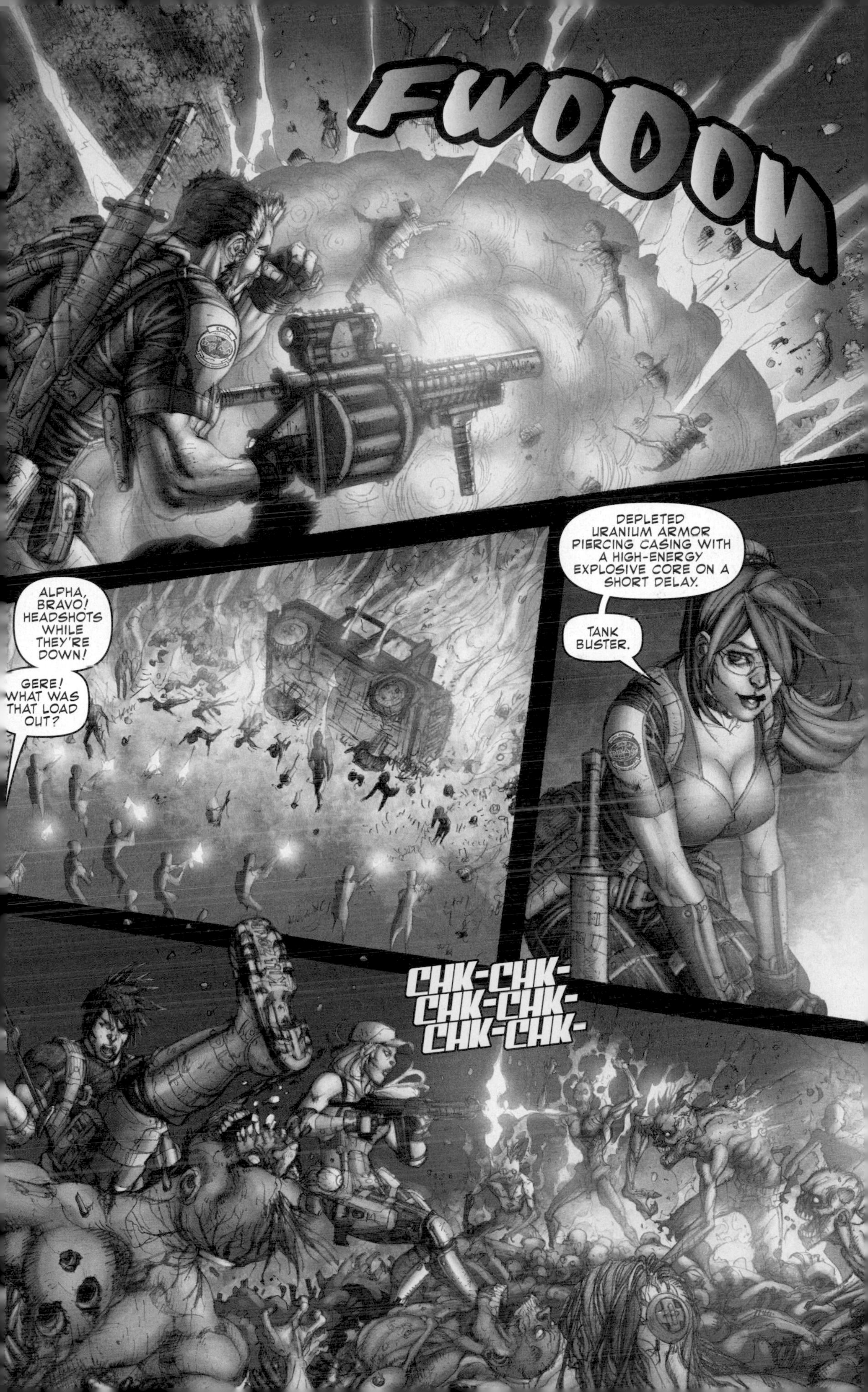
FWOOOM
ALPHA, BRAVO! HEADSHOTS WHILE THEY'RE DOWN!
GERE! WHAT WAS THAT LOAD OUT?
DEPLETED URANIUM ARMOR PIERCING CASING WITH A HIGH-ENERGY EXPLOSIVE CORE ON A SHORT DELAY.
TANK BUSTER.
CHK-CHK-CHK-CHK-CHK-CHK-

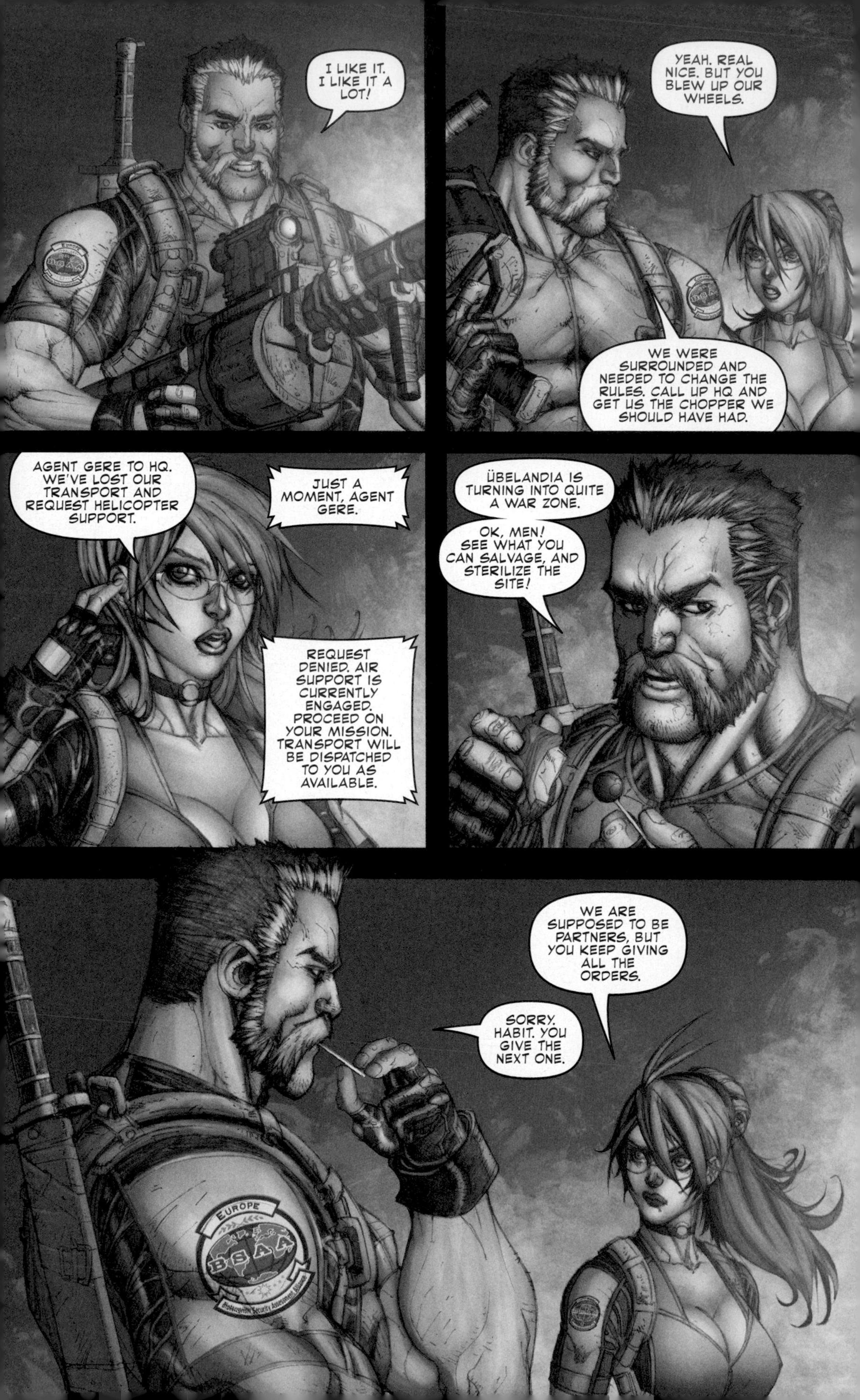
I LIKE IT. I LIKE IT A LOT!
YEAH. REAL NICE. BUT YOU BLEW UP OUR WHEELS.
WE WERE SURROUNDED AND NEEDED TO CHANGE THE RULES. CALL UP HQ AND GET US THE CHOPPER WE SHOULD HAVE HAD.
AGENT GERE TO HQ. WE'VE LOST OUR TRANSPORT AND REQUEST HELICOPTER SUPPORT.
JUST A MOMENT, AGENT GERE.
REQUEST DENIED. AIR SUPPORT IS CURRENTLY ENGAGED. PROCEED ON YOUR MISSION. TRANSPORT WILL BE DISPATCHED TO YOU AS AVAILABLE.
ÜBELANDIA IS TURNING INTO QUITE A WAR ZONE.
OK, MEN! SEE WHAT YOU CAN SALVAGE, AND STERILIZE THE SITE!
WE ARE SUPPOSED TO BE PARTNERS, BUT YOU KEEP GIVING ALL THE ORDERS.
SORRY. HABIT. YOU GIVE THE NEXT ONE.
EUROPE
BSAA

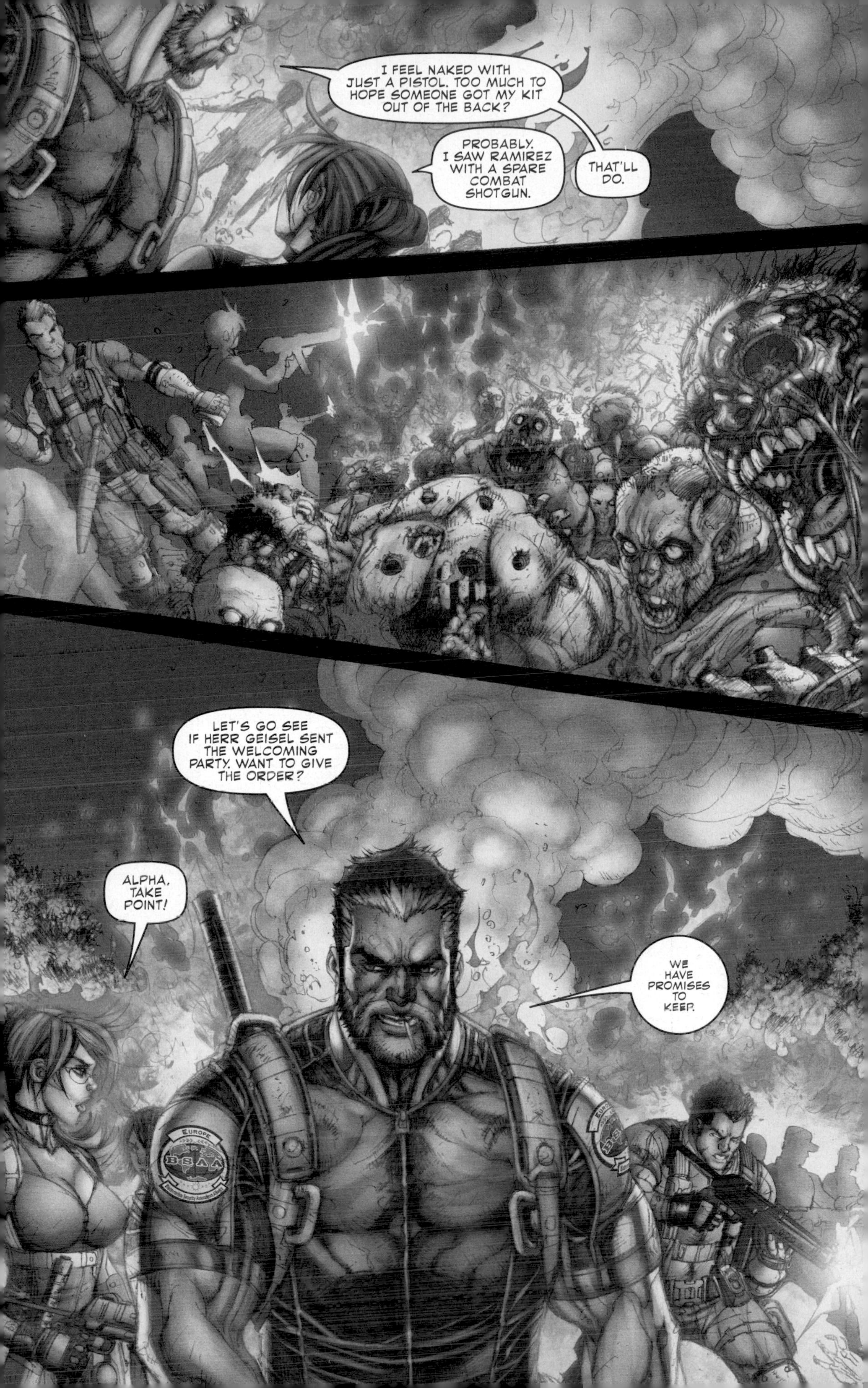
I FEEL NAKED WITH JUST A PISTOL. TOO MUCH TO HOPE SOMEONE GOT MY KIT OUT OF THE BACK?
PROBABLY. I SAW RAMIREZ WITH A SPARE COMBAT SHOTGUN.
THAT'LL DO.
LET'S GO SEE IF HERR GEISEL SENT THE WELCOMING PARTY. WANT TO GIVE THE ORDER?
ALPHA, TAKE POINT!
WE HAVE PROMISES TO KEEP.
EUROPE
BSAA

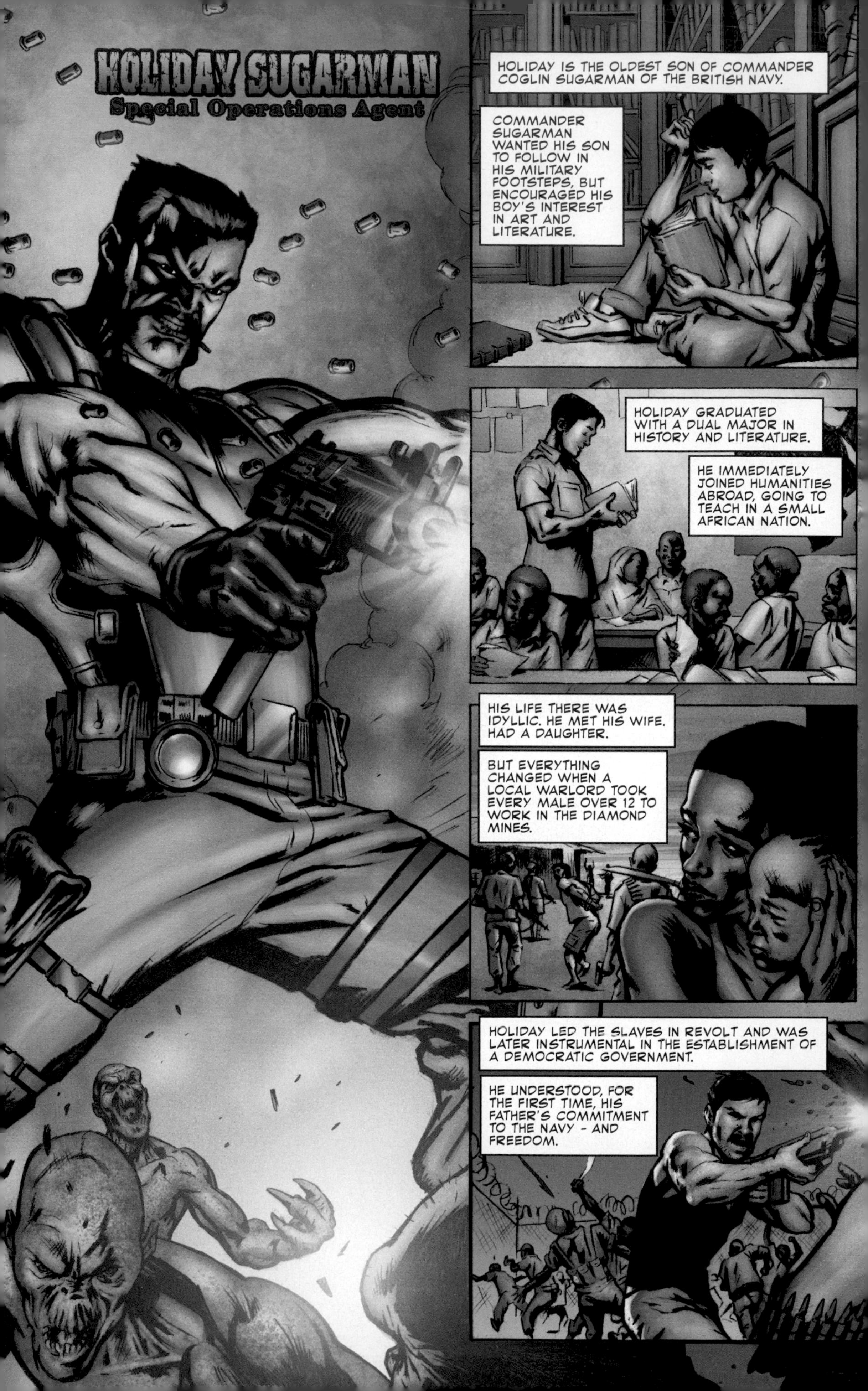
HOLIDAY SUGARMAN
Special Operations Agent
HOLIDAY IS THE OLDEST SON OF COMMANDER COGLIN SUGARMAN OF THE BRITISH NAVY.
COMMANDER SUGARMAN WANTED HIS SON TO FOLLOW IN HIS MILITARY FOOTSTEPS, BUT ENCOURAGED HIS BOY'S INTEREST IN ART AND LITERATURE.
HOLIDAY GRADUATED WITH A DUAL MAJOR IN HISTORY AND LITERATURE.
HE IMMEDIATELY JOINED HUMANITIES ABROAD, GOING TO TEACH IN A SMALL AFRICAN NATION.
HIS LIFE THERE WAS IDYLLIC. HE MET HIS WIFE. HAD A DAUGHTER.
BUT EVERYTHING CHANGED WHEN A LOCAL WARLORD TOOK EVERY MALE OVER 12 TO WORK IN THE DIAMOND MINES.
HOLIDAY LED THE SLAVES IN REVOLT AND WAS LATER INSTRUMENTAL IN THE ESTABLISHMENT OF A DEMOCRATIC GOVERNMENT.
HE UNDERSTOOD, FOR THE FIRST TIME, HIS FATHER'S COMMITMENT TO THE NAVY - AND FREEDOM.

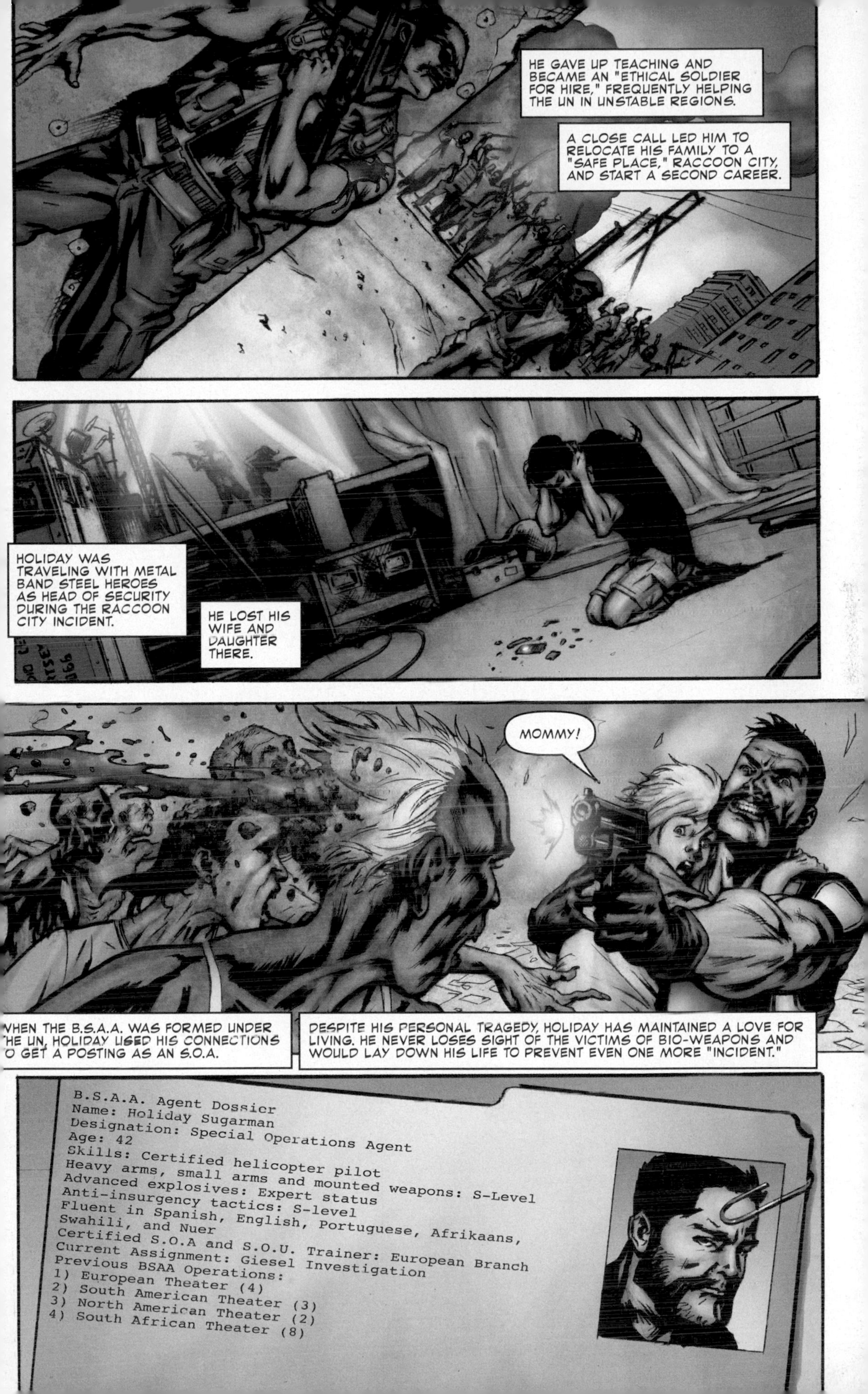

HE GAVE UP TEACHING AND BECAME AN "ETHICAL SOLDIER FOR HIRE," FREQUENTLY HELPING THE UN IN UNSTABLE REGIONS.
A CLOSE CALL LED HIM TO RELOCATE HIS FAMILY TO A "SAFE PLACE," RACCOON CITY, AND START A SECOND CAREER.
HOLIDAY WAS TRAVELING WITH METAL BAND STEEL HEROES AS HEAD OF SECURITY DURING THE RACCOON CITY INCIDENT.
HE LOST HIS WIFE AND DAUGHTER THERE.
MOMMY!
WHEN THE B.S.A.A. WAS FORMED UNDER
HE UN, HOLIDAY USED HIS CONNECTIONS
O GET A POSTING AS AN S.O.A.
DESPITE HIS PERSONAL TRAGEDY, HOLIDAY HAS MAINTAINED A LOVE FOR LIVING. HE NEVER LOSES SIGHT OF THE VICTIMS OF BIO-WEAPONS AND WOULD LAY DOWN HIS LIFE TO PREVENT EVEN ONE MORE "INCIDENT."
B.S.A.A. Agent Dossier
Name: Holiday Sugarman
Designation: Special Operations Agent
Age: 42
Skills: Certified helicopter pilot
Heavy arms, small arms and mounted weapons: S-Level
Advanced explosives: Expert status
Anti-insurgency tactics: S-level
Fluent in Spanish, English, Portuguese, Afrikaans, Swahili, and Nuer
Certified S.O.A and S.O.U. Trainer: European Branch
Current Assignment: Giesel Investigation
Previous BSAA Operations:
1) European Theater (4)
2) South American Theater (3)
3) North American Theater (2)
4) South African Theater (8)

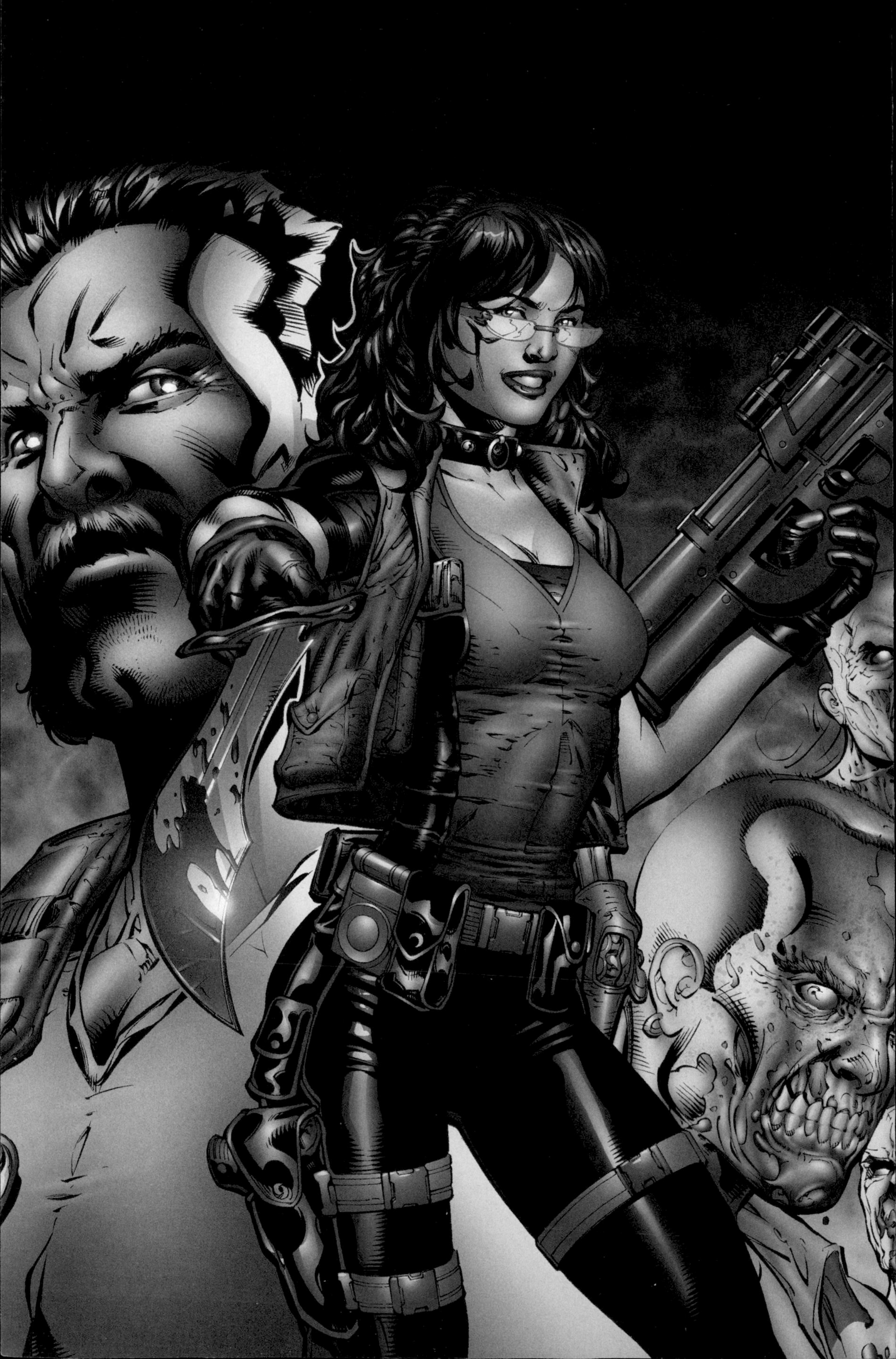

RESIDENT EVIL 4
Cover by Kevin Sharpe

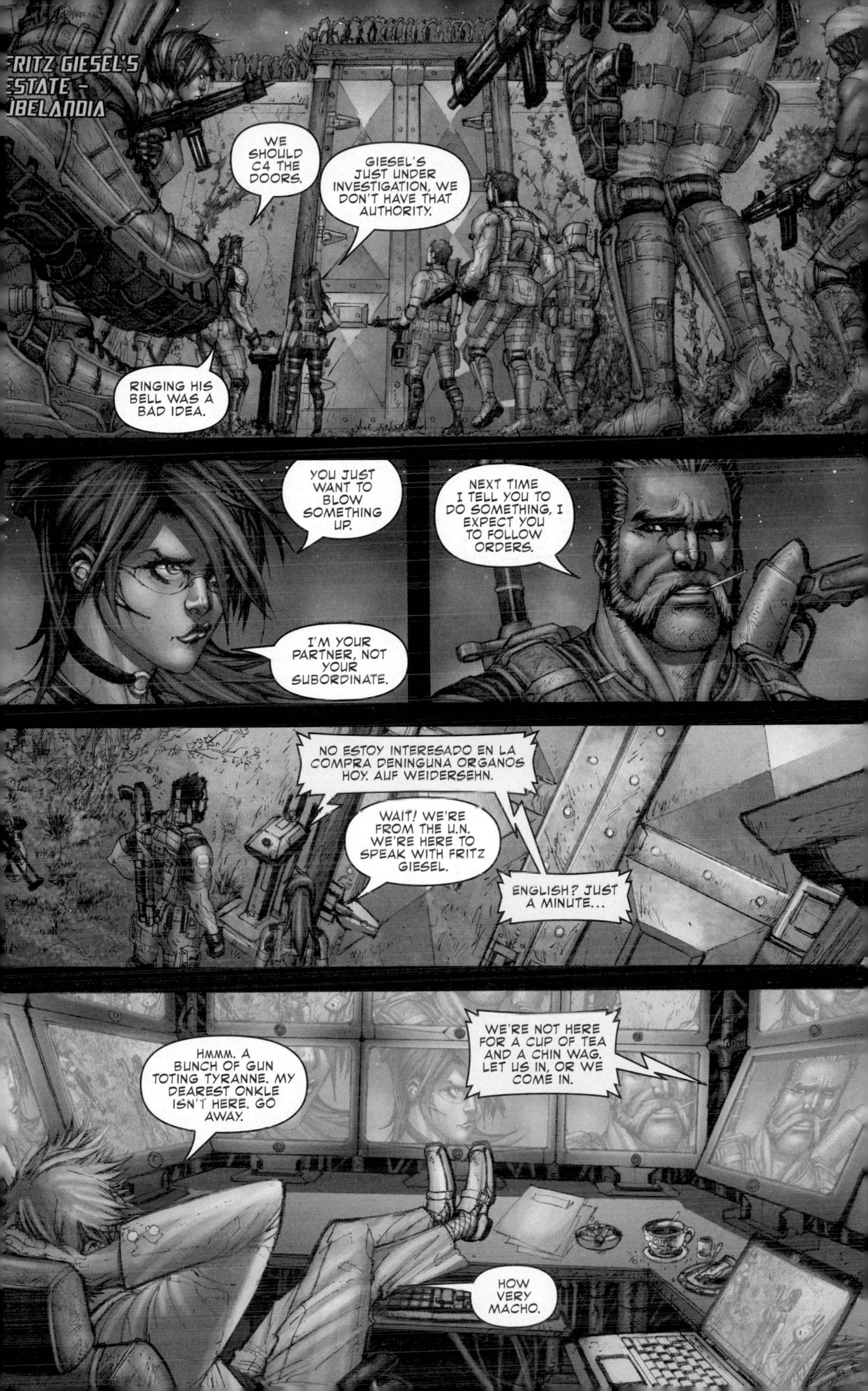
FRITZ GIESEL'S ESTATE – UBELANDIA
WE SHOULD C4 THE DOORS.
GIESEL'S JUST UNDER INVESTIGATION, WE DON'T HAVE THAT AUTHORITY.
RINGING HIS BELL WAS A BAD IDEA.
YOU JUST WANT TO BLOW SOMETHING UP.
NEXT TIME I TELL YOU TO DO SOMETHING, I EXPECT YOU TO FOLLOW ORDERS.
I'M YOUR PARTNER, NOT YOUR SUBORDINATE.
NO ESTOY INTERESADO EN LA COMPRA DENINGUNA ORGANOS HOY. AUF WEIDERSEHN.
WAIT! WE'RE FROM THE U.N. WE'RE HERE TO SPEAK WITH FRITZ GIESEL.
ENGLISH? JUST A MINUTE...
HMMM. A BUNCH OF GUN TOTING TYRANNE. MY DEAREST ONKLE ISN'T HERE. GO AWAY.
WE'RE NOT HERE FOR A CUP OF TEA AND A CHIN WAG. LET US IN, OR WE COME IN.
HOW VERY MACHO.

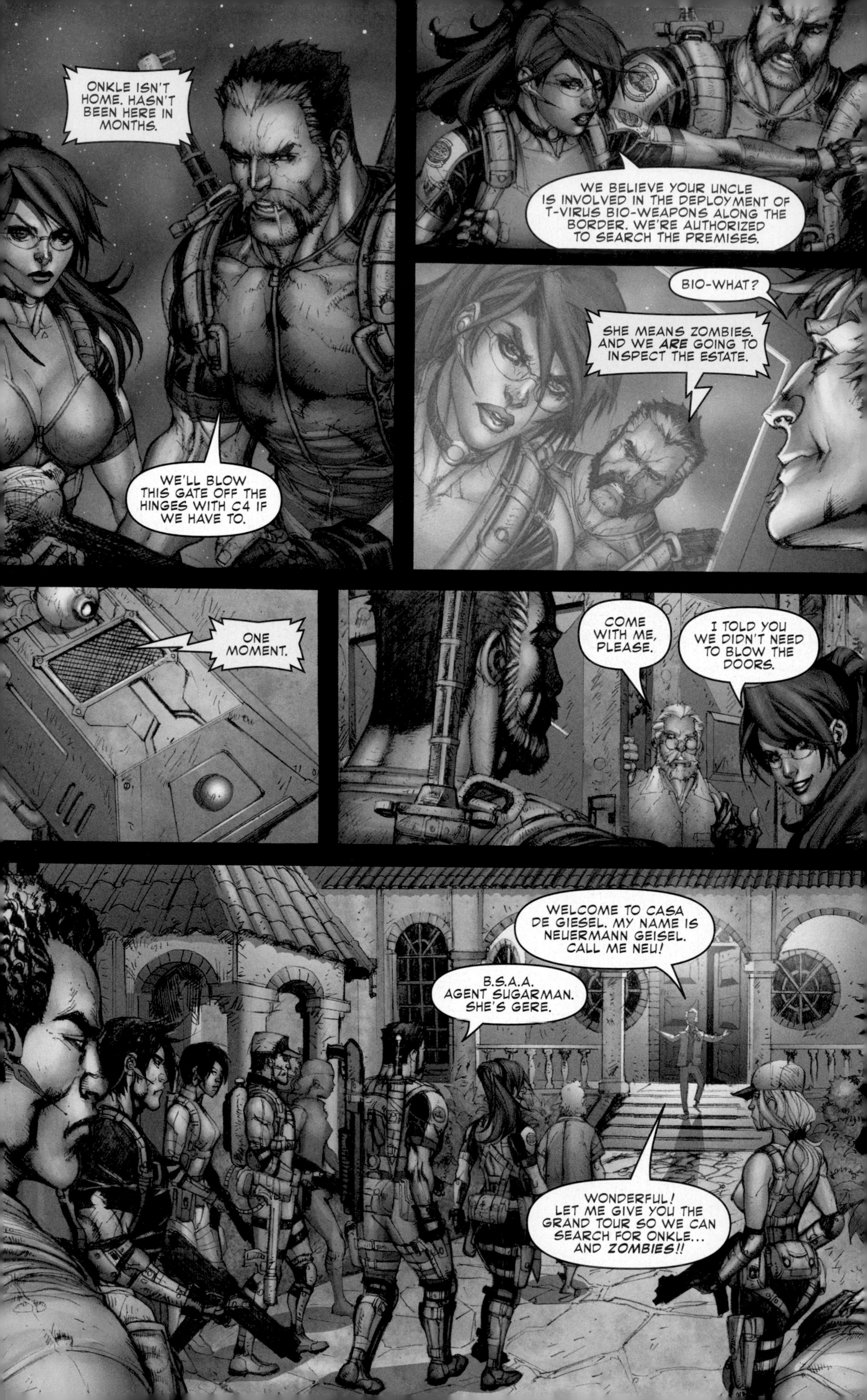

ONKLE ISN'T HOME. HASN'T BEEN HERE IN MONTHS.
WE'LL BLOW THIS GATE OFF THE HINGES WITH C4 IF WE HAVE TO.
WE BELIEVE YOUR UNCLE IS INVOLVED IN THE DEPLOYMENT OF T-VIRUS BIO-WEAPONS ALONG THE BORDER. WE'RE AUTHORIZED TO SEARCH THE PREMISES.
BIO-WHAT?
SHE MEANS ZOMBIES. AND WE ARE GOING TO INSPECT THE ESTATE.
ONE MOMENT.
COME WITH ME, PLEASE.
I TOLD YOU WE DIDN'T NEED TO BLOW THE DOORS.
WELCOME TO CASA DE GIESEL. MY NAME IS NEUERMANN GEISEL. CALL ME NEU!
B.S.A.A. AGENT SUGARMAN. SHE'S GERE.
WONDERFUL! LET ME GIVE YOU THE GRAND TOUR SO WE CAN SEARCH FOR ONKLE... AND ZOMBIES!!

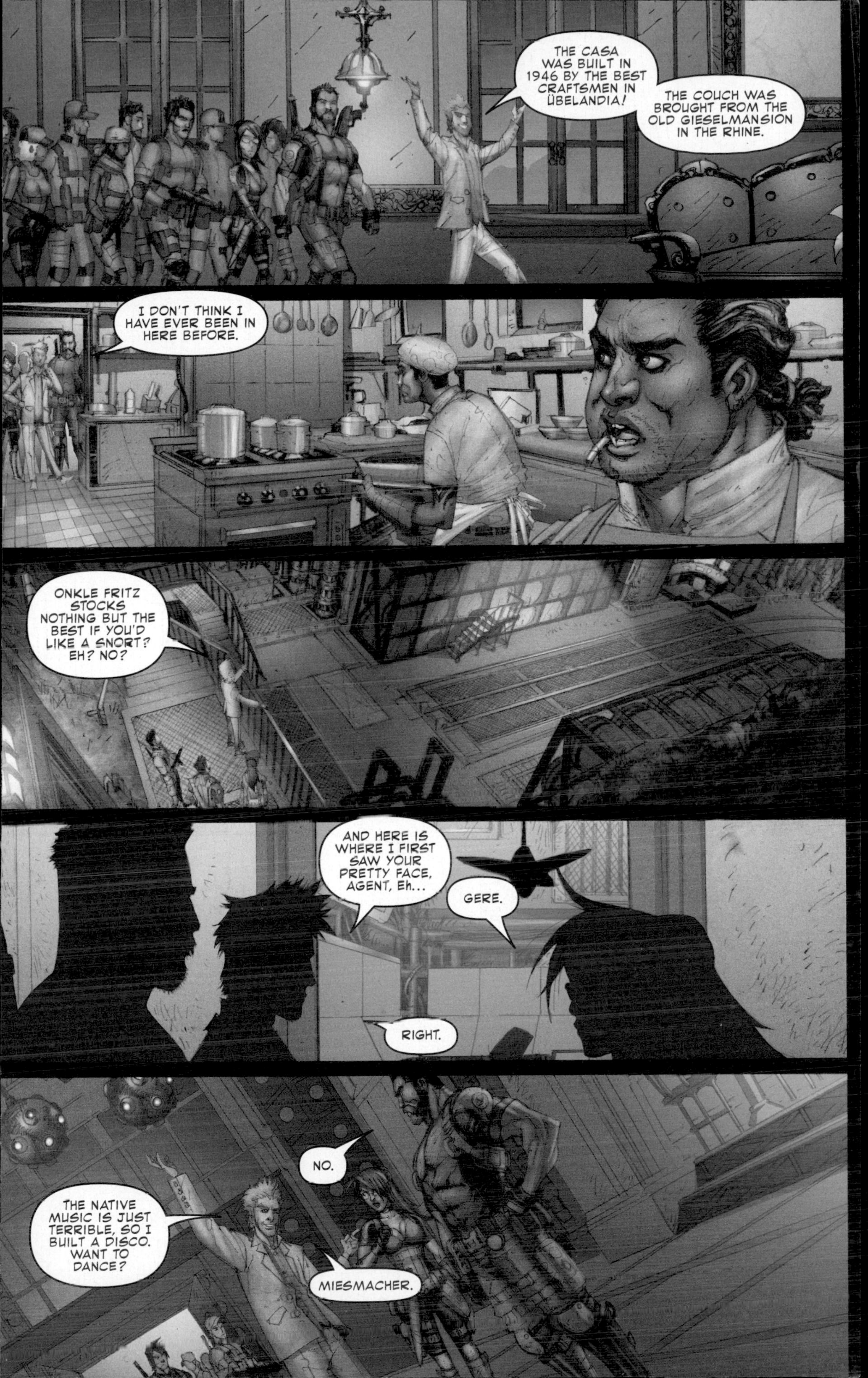
THE CASA WAS BUILT IN 1946 BY THE BEST CRAFTSMEN IN ÜBELANDIA!
THE COUCH WAS BROUGHT FROM THE OLD GIESELMANSION IN THE RHINE.
I DON'T THINK I HAVE EVER BEEN IN HERE BEFORE.
ONKLE FRITZ STOCKS NOTHING BUT THE BEST IF YOU'D LIKE A SNORT? EH? NO?
AND HERE IS WHERE I FIRST SAW YOUR PRETTY FACE, AGENT, Eh...
GERE.
RIGHT.
NO.
THE NATIVE MUSIC IS JUST TERRIBLE, SO I BUILT A DISCO. WANT TO DANCE?
MIESMACHER.

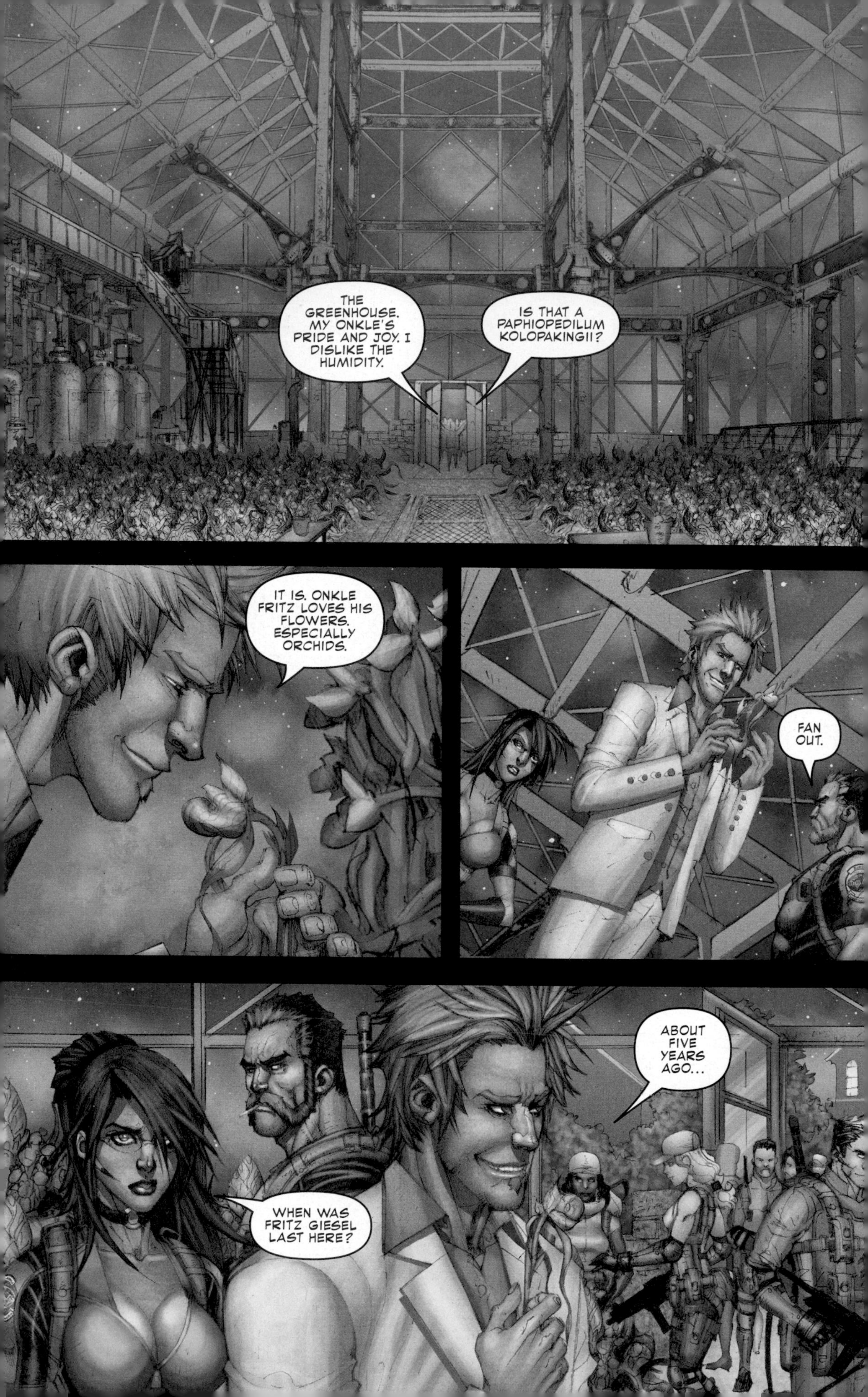
THE GREENHOUSE. MY ONKLE'S PRIDE AND JOY. I DISLIKE THE HUMIDITY.
IS THAT A PAPHIOPEDILUM KOLOPAKINGII?
IT IS. ONKLE FRITZ LOVES HIS FLOWERS. ESPECIALLY ORCHIDS.
FAN OUT.
WHEN WAS FRITZ GIESEL LAST HERE?
ABOUT FIVE YEARS AGO...

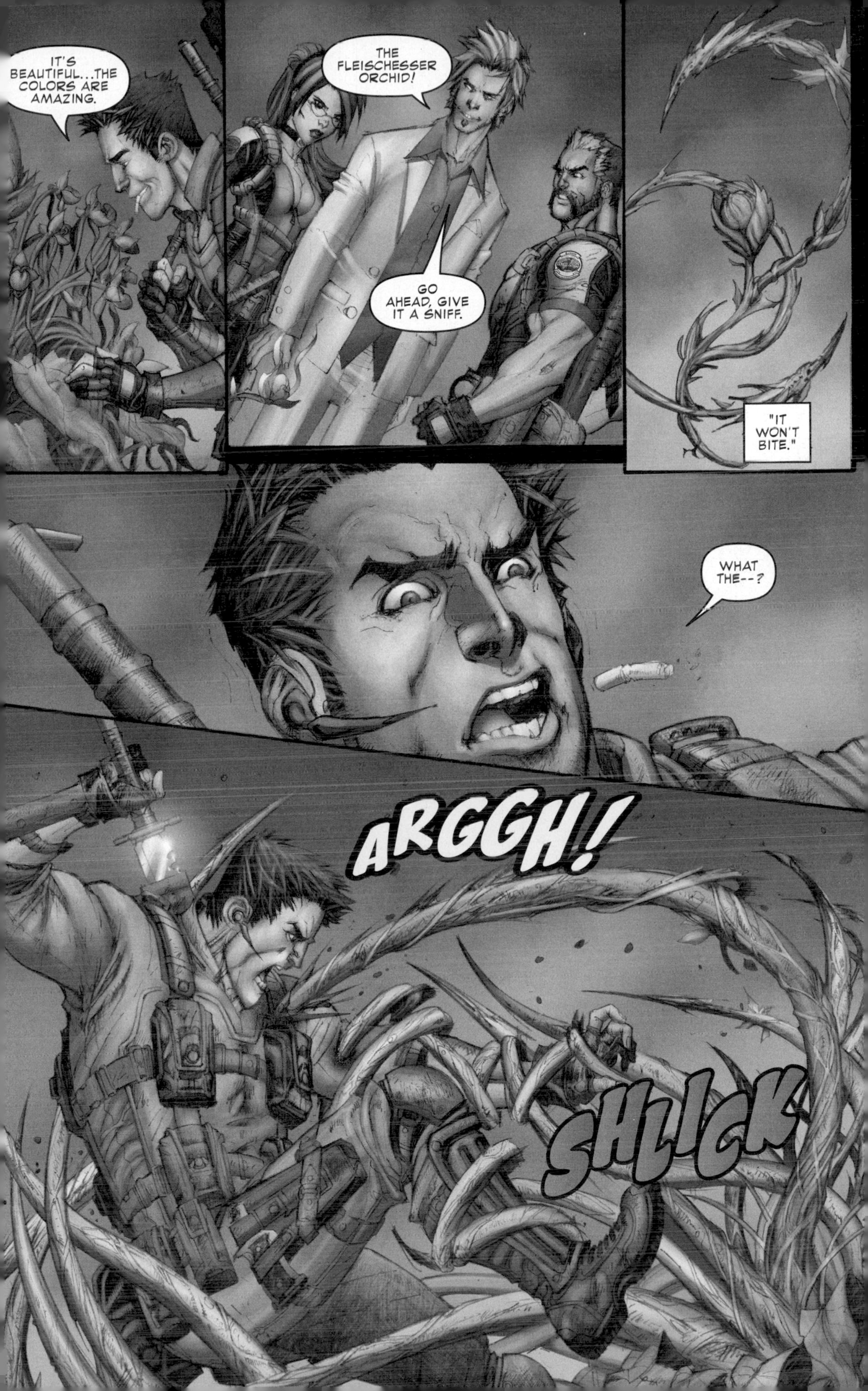
IT'S BEAUTIFUL...THE COLORS ARE AMAZING.
THE FLEISCHESSER ORCHID!
GO AHEAD, GIVE IT A SNIFF.
"IT WON'T BITE."
WHAT THE--?
ARGGH!
SHLICK

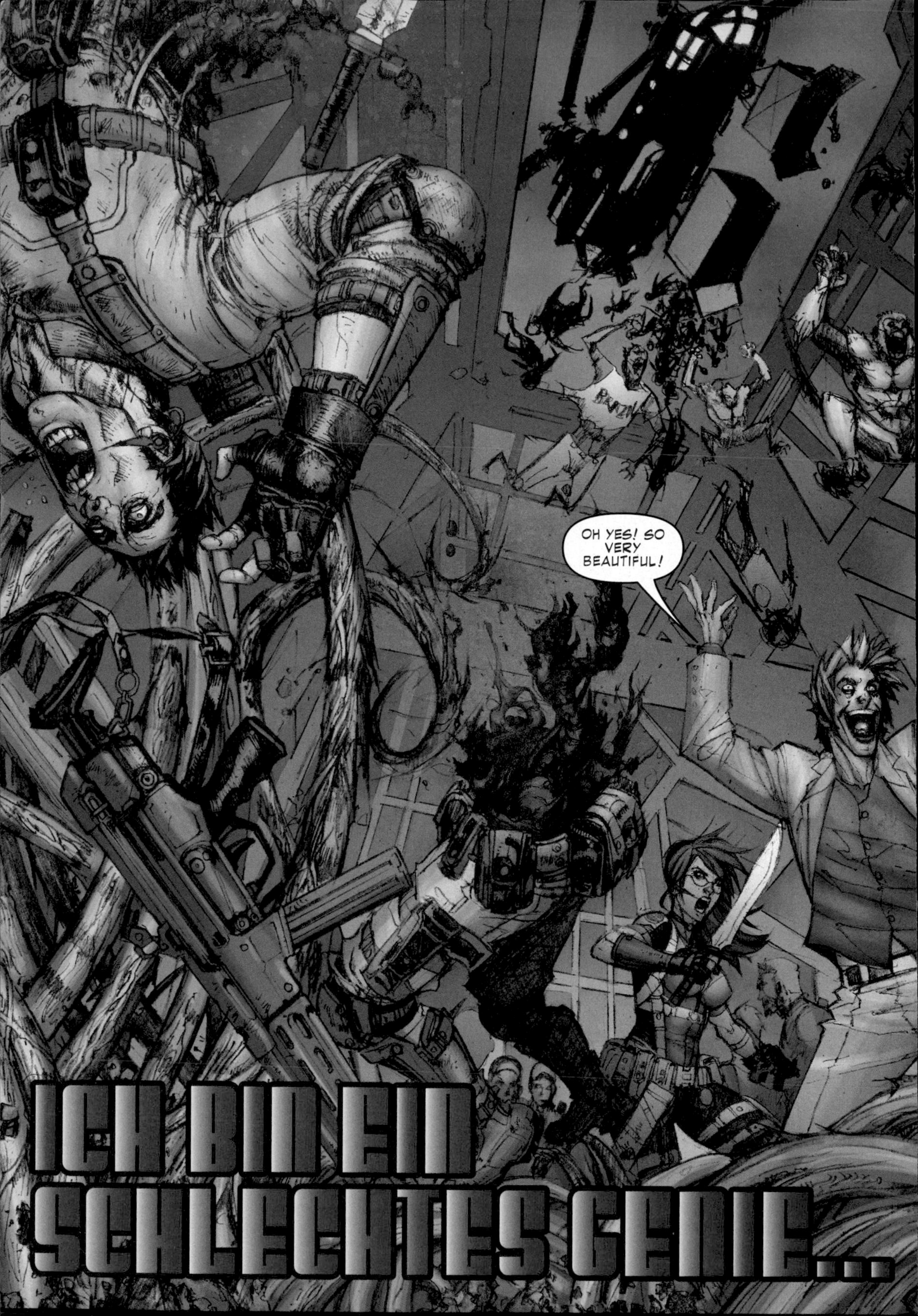
OH YES! SO VERY BEAUTIFUL!
ICH BIN EIN SCHLECHTES GENIE...

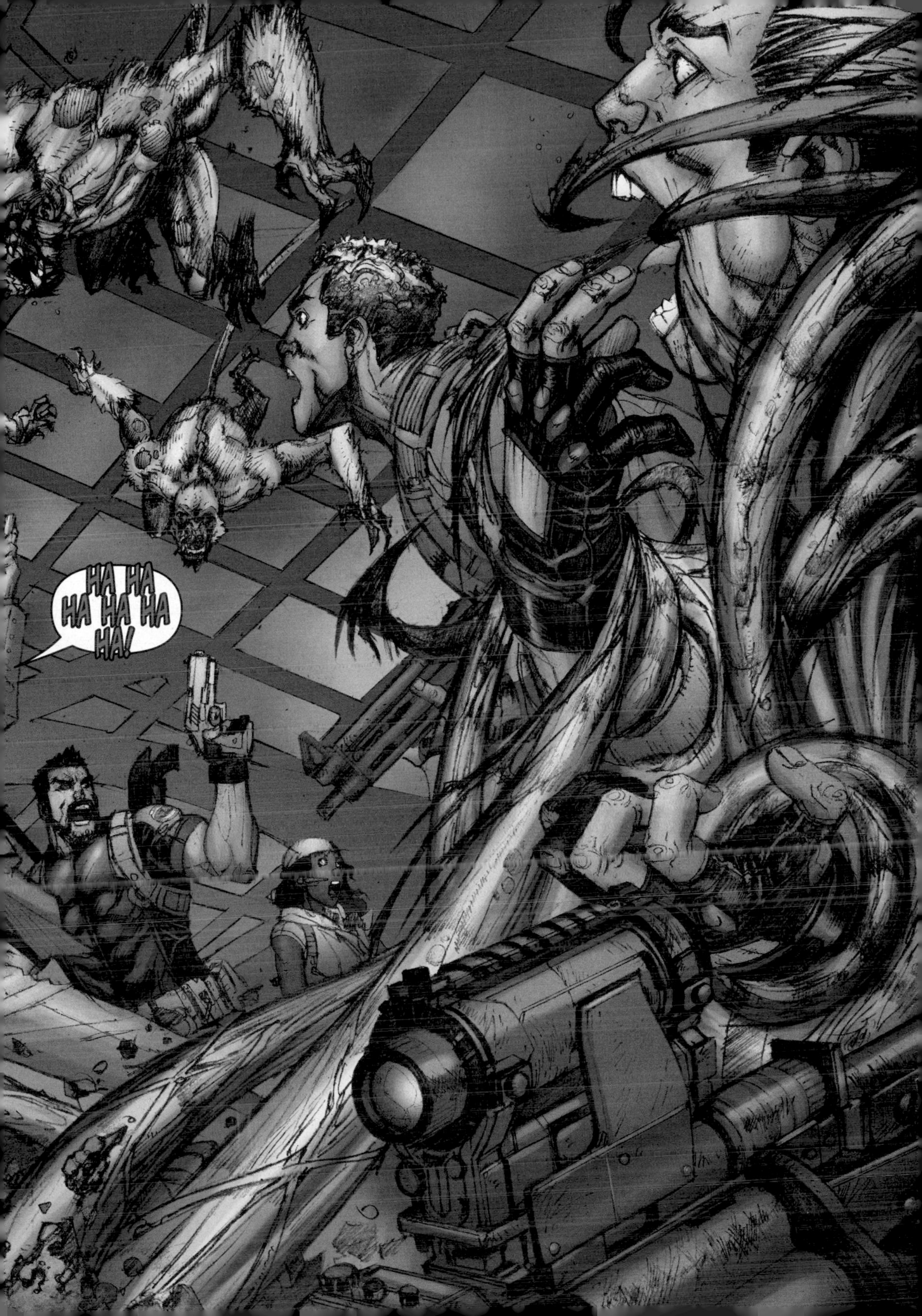
HA HA HA HA HA HA!

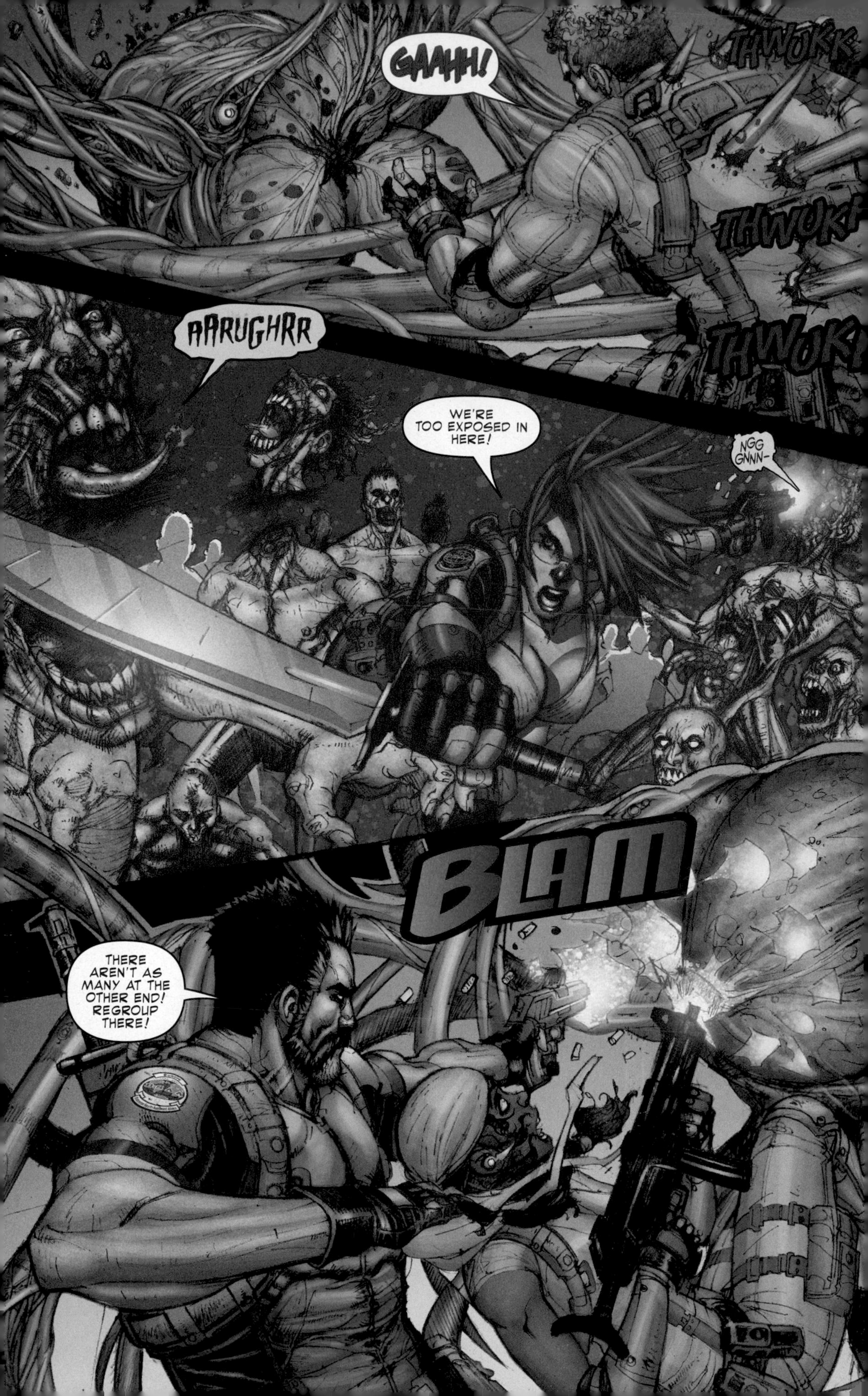
GAAHH!
THWUKK
THWUKK
THWUKK
AARUGHRR
WE'RE TOO EXPOSED IN HERE!
NGG GNNN-
BLAM
THERE AREN'T AS MANY AT THE OTHER END! REGROUP THERE!

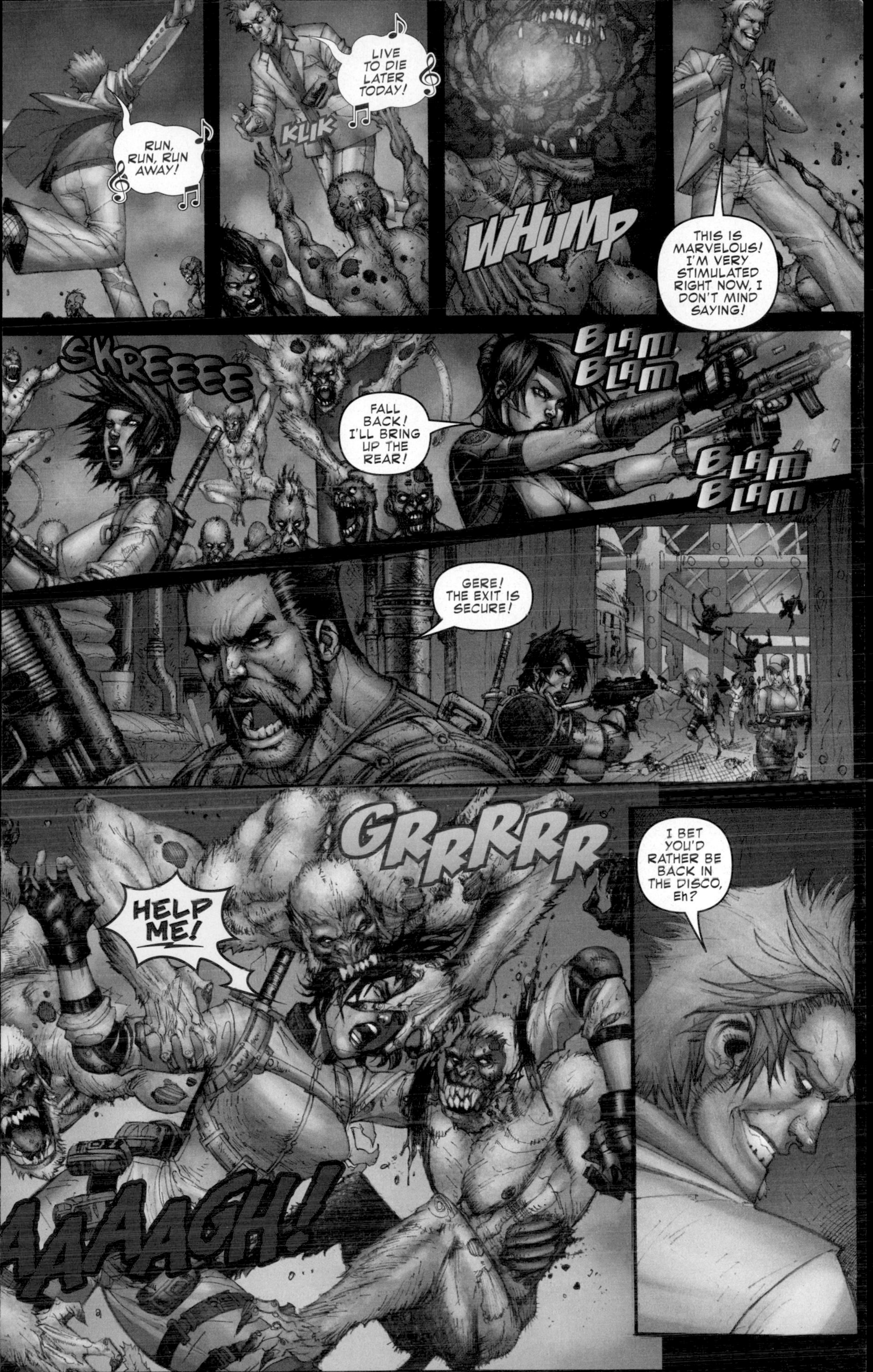

RUN, RUN, RUN AWAY!
KLIK
LIVE TO DIE LATER TODAY!
WHUMP
THIS IS MARVELOUS! I'M VERY STIMULATED RIGHT NOW, I DON'T MIND SAYING!
SKREEEE
BLAM BLAM
FALL BACK! I'LL BRING UP THE REAR!
BLAM BLAM
GERE! THE EXIT IS SECURE!
GRRRRR
HELP ME!
I BET YOU'D RATHER BE BACK IN THE DISCO, Eh?
AAAAGH!

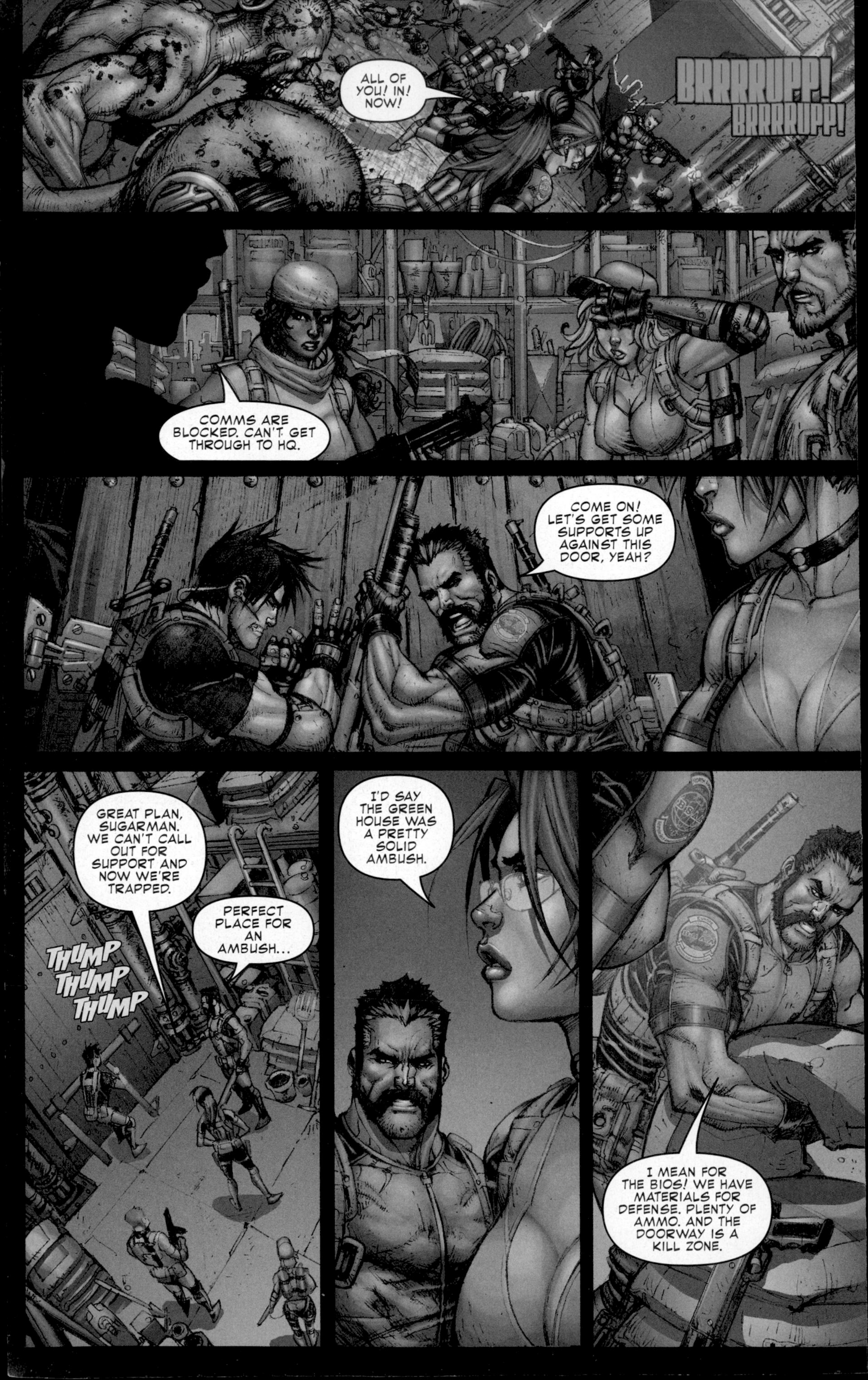
ALL OF YOU! IN! NOW!
BRRRRUPP! BRRRRUPP!
COMMS ARE BLOCKED. CAN'T GET THROUGH TO HQ.
COME ON! LET'S GET SOME SUPPORTS UP AGAINST THIS DOOR, YEAH?
GREAT PLAN, SUGARMAN. WE CAN'T CALL OUT FOR SUPPORT AND NOW WE'RE TRAPPED.
PERFECT PLACE FOR AN AMBUSH...
THUMP THUMP THUMP
I'D SAY THE GREEN HOUSE WAS A PRETTY SOLID AMBUSH.
I MEAN FOR THE BIOS! WE HAVE MATERIALS FOR DEFENSE. PLENTY OF AMMO. AND THE DOORWAY IS A KILL ZONE.

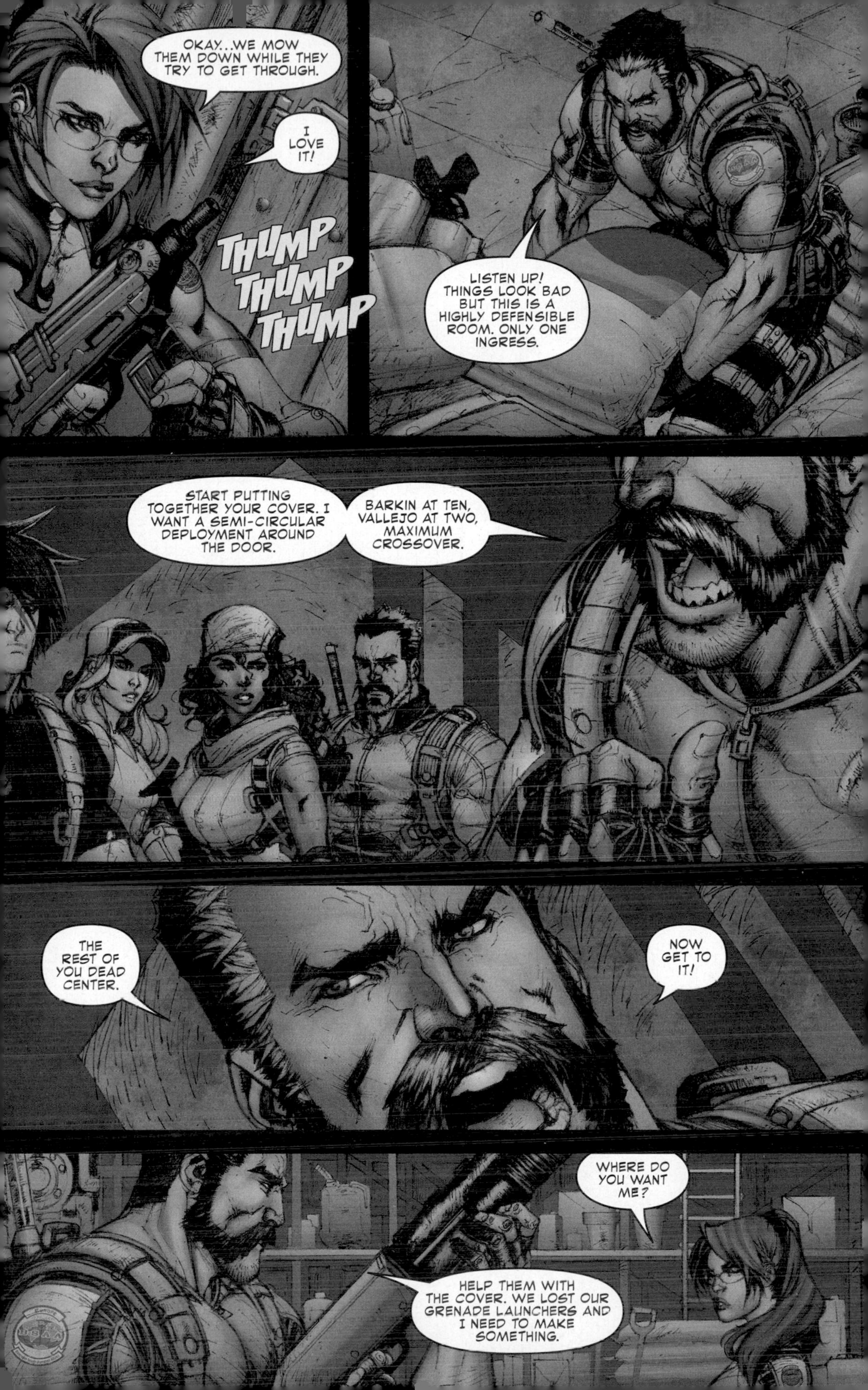
OKAY...WE MOW THEM DOWN WHILE THEY TRY TO GET THROUGH.
I LOVE IT!
THUMP THUMP THUMP
LISTEN UP! THINGS LOOK BAD BUT THIS IS A HIGHLY DEFENSIBLE ROOM. ONLY ONE INGRESS.
START PUTTING TOGETHER YOUR COVER. I WANT A SEMI-CIRCULAR DEPLOYMENT AROUND THE DOOR.
BARKIN AT TEN, VALLEJO AT TWO, MAXIMUM CROSSOVER.
THE REST OF YOU DEAD CENTER.
NOW GET TO IT!
WHERE DO YOU WANT ME?
HELP THEM WITH THE COVER. WE LOST OUR GRENADE LAUNCHERS AND I NEED TO MAKE SOMETHING.

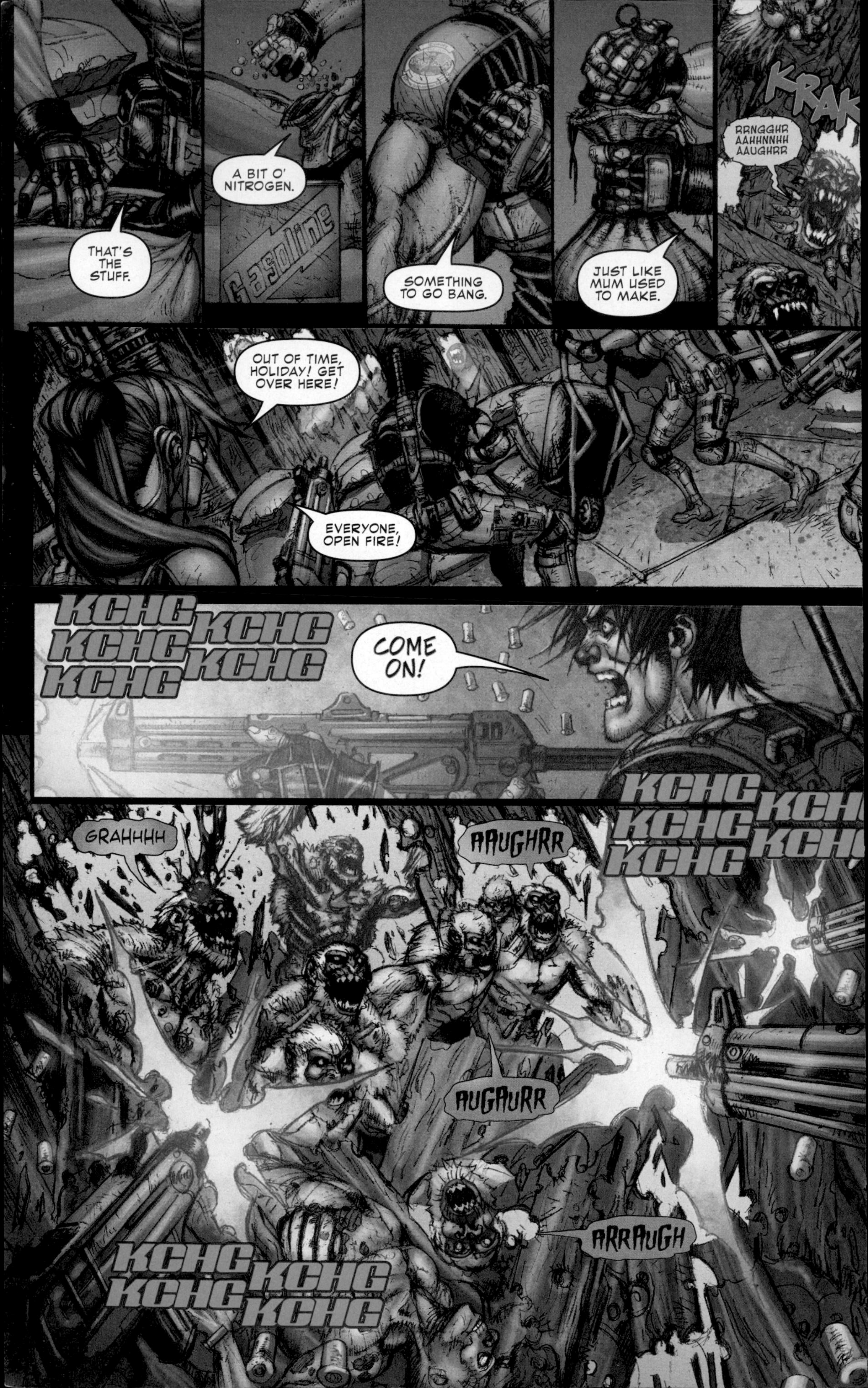

THAT'S THE STUFF.
A BIT O' NITROGEN.
SOMETHING TO GO BANG.
JUST LIKE MUM USED TO MAKE.
KRAK
RRNGGHR AAHHNNNH AAUGHRR
OUT OF TIME, HOLIDAY! GET OVER HERE!
EVERYONE, OPEN FIRE!
KCHG KCHG KCHG KCHG KCHG
COME ON!
KCHG KCHG KCHG
GRAHHHH
AAUGHRR
AUGAURR
ARRAUGH
KCHG KCHG KCHG KCHG

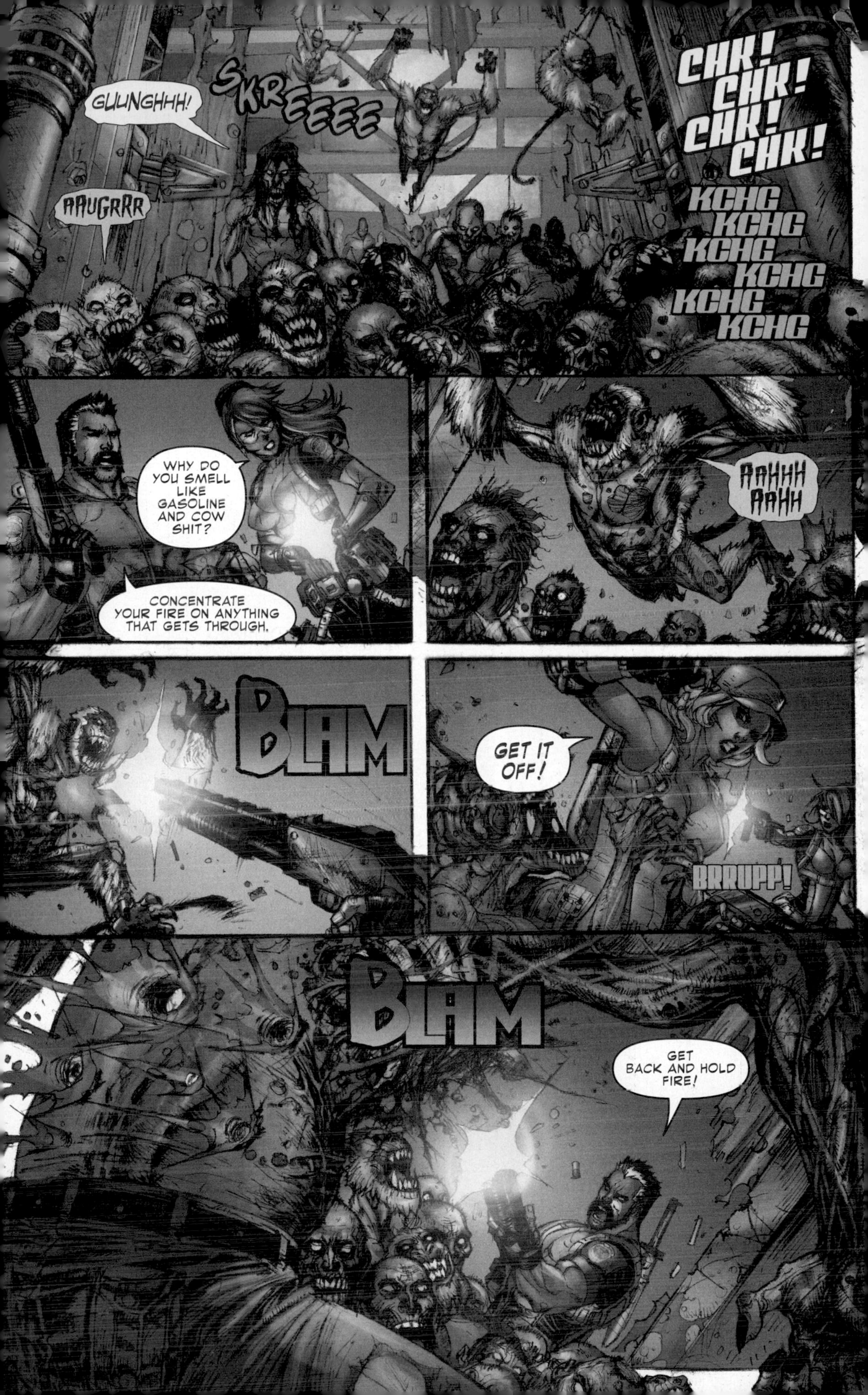
GUUNGHHH!
SKREEEEE
AAUGRRR
CHK! CHK! CHK! CHK!
KCHG KCHG KCHG KCHG KCHG KCHG
WHY DO YOU SMELL LIKE GASOLINE AND COW SHIT?
CONCENTRATE YOUR FIRE ON ANYTHING THAT GETS THROUGH.
AAHHH AAHH
BLAM
GET IT OFF!
BRRUPP!
BLAM
GET BACK AND HOLD FIRE!

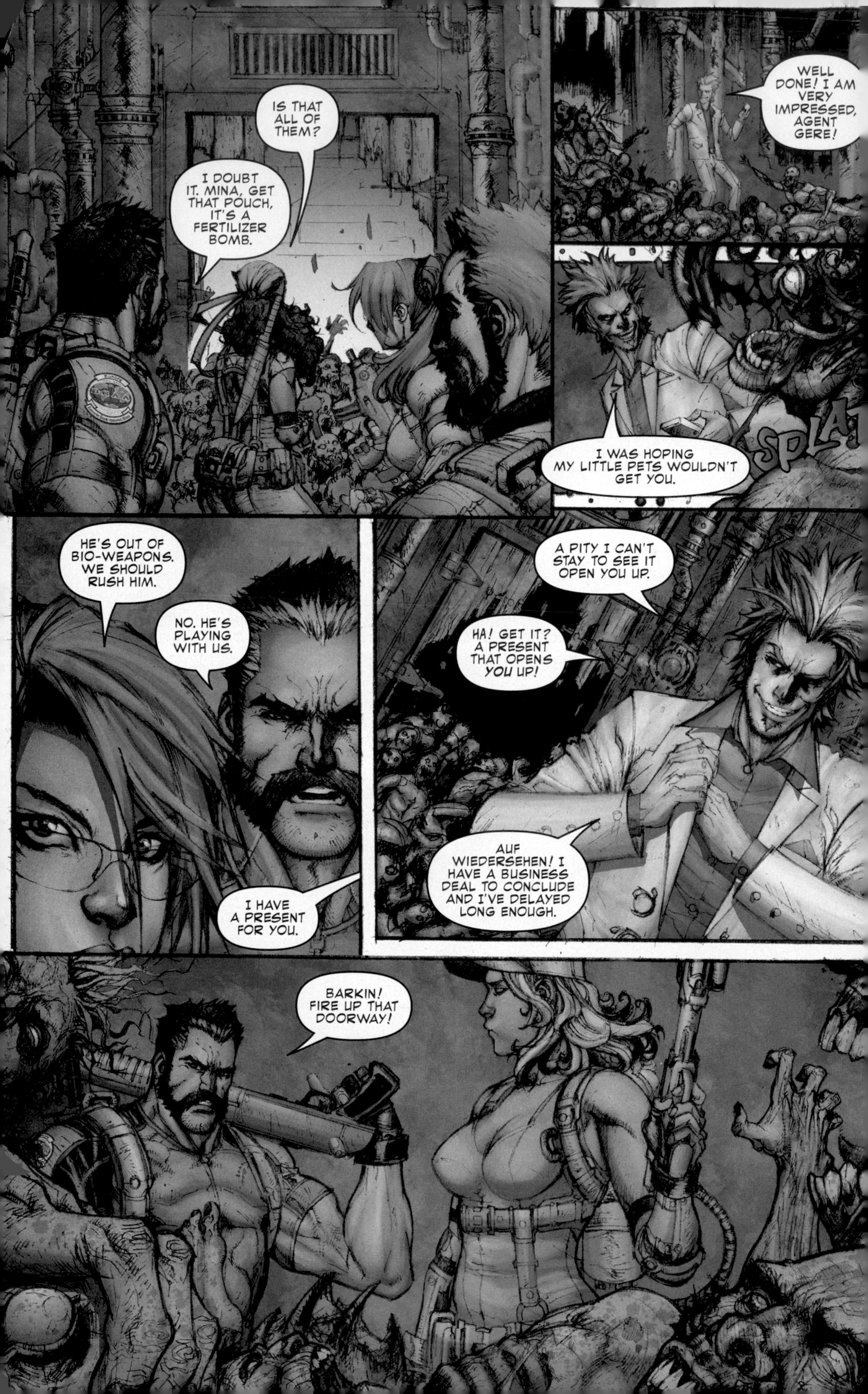
IS THAT ALL OF THEM?
I DOUBT IT. MINA, GET THAT POUCH, IT'S A FERTILIZER BOMB.
WELL DONE! I AM VERY IMPRESSED, AGENT GERE!
I WAS HOPING MY LITTLE PETS WOULDN'T GET YOU.
SPLAT
HE'S OUT OF BIO-WEAPONS. WE SHOULD RUSH HIM.
NO. HE'S PLAYING WITH US.
I HAVE A PRESENT FOR YOU.
A PITY I CAN'T STAY TO SEE IT OPEN YOU UP.
HA! GET IT? A PRESENT THAT OPENS *YOU* UP!
AUF WIEDERSEHEN! I HAVE A BUSINESS DEAL TO CONCLUDE AND I'VE DELAYED LONG ENOUGH.
BARKIN! FIRE UP THAT DOORWAY!

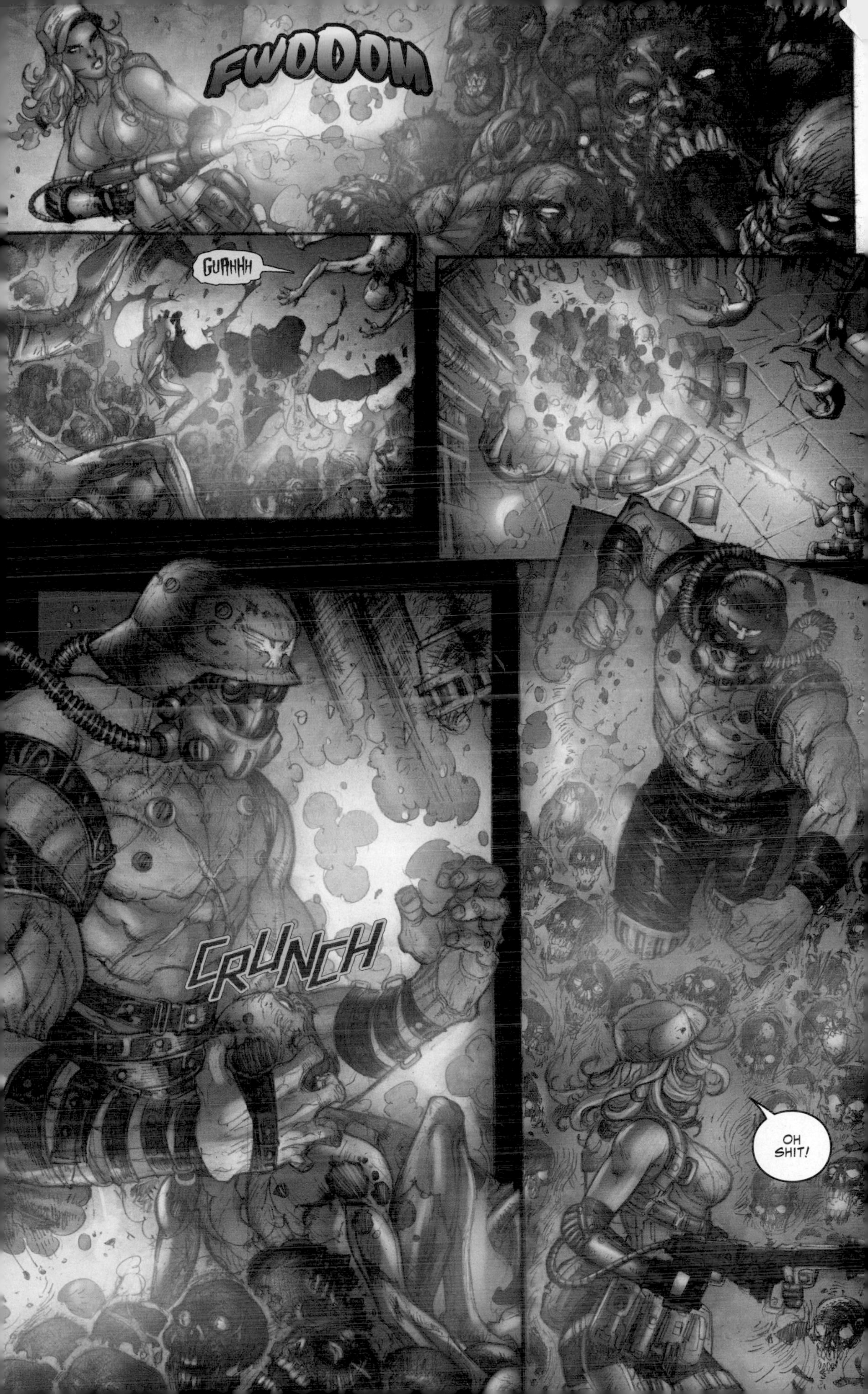
FWOOOM
GUAHHH
CRUNCH
OH SHIT!

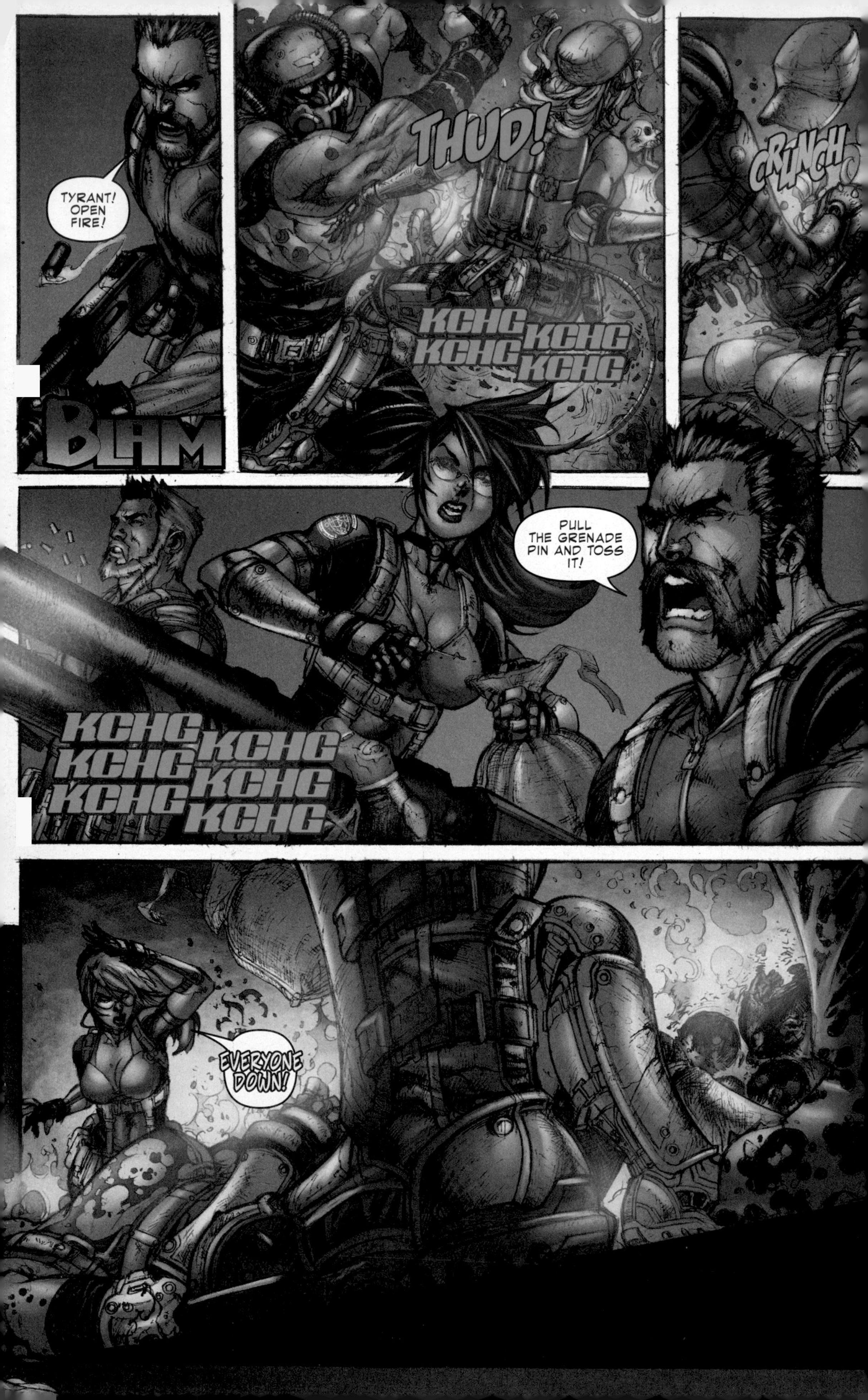
TYRANT! OPEN FIRE!
BLAM
THUD!
KCHG KCHG KCHG KCHG
CRUNCH
PULL THE GRENADE PIN AND TOSS IT!
KCHG KCHG KCHG KCHG KCHG KCHG
EVERYONE DOWN!

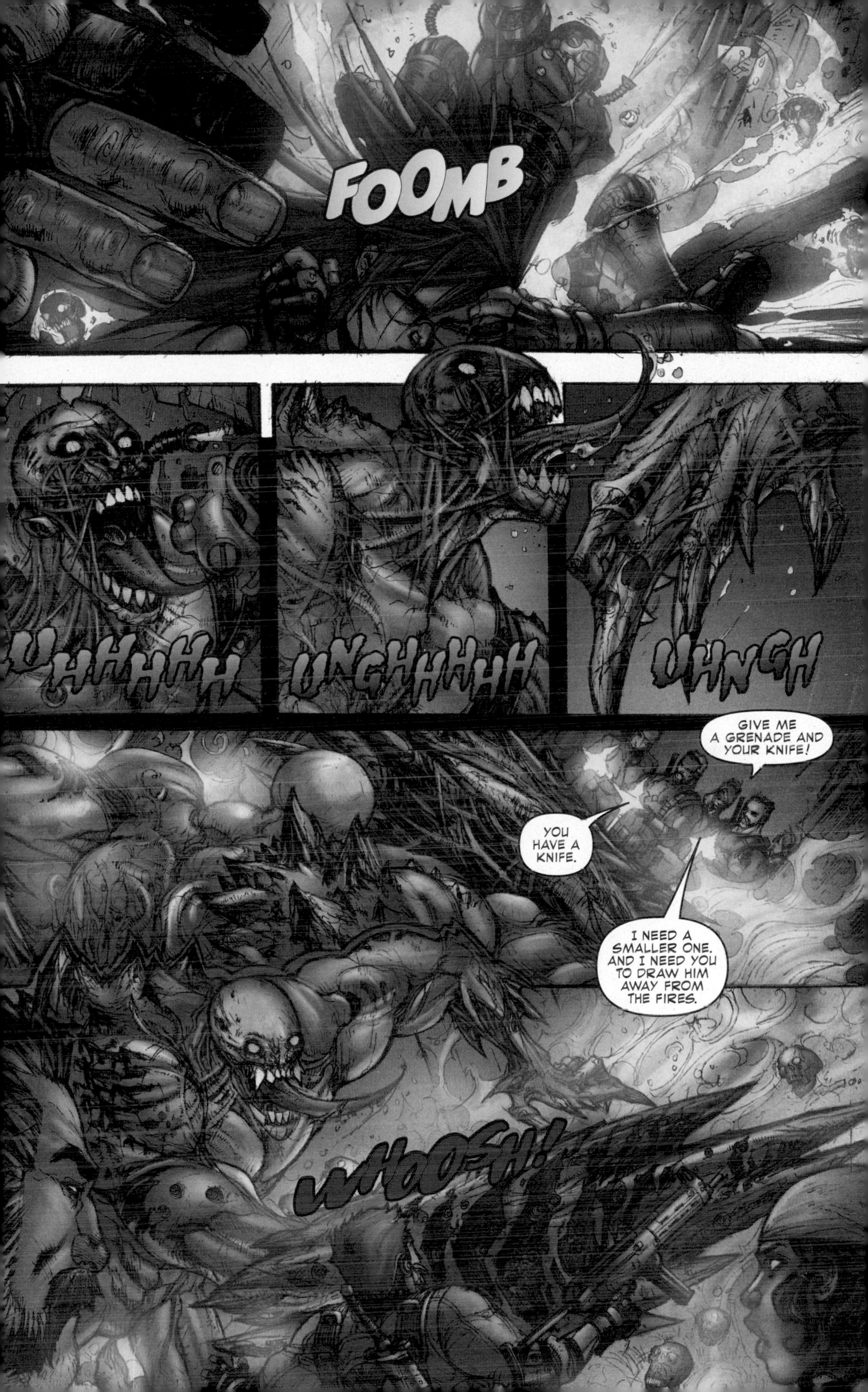
FOOMB
UHHHHH
UNGHHHHH
UHNGH
GIVE ME A GRENADE AND YOUR KNIFE!
YOU HAVE A KNIFE.
I NEED A SMALLER ONE. AND I NEED YOU TO DRAW HIM AWAY FROM THE FIRES.
WHOOSH!

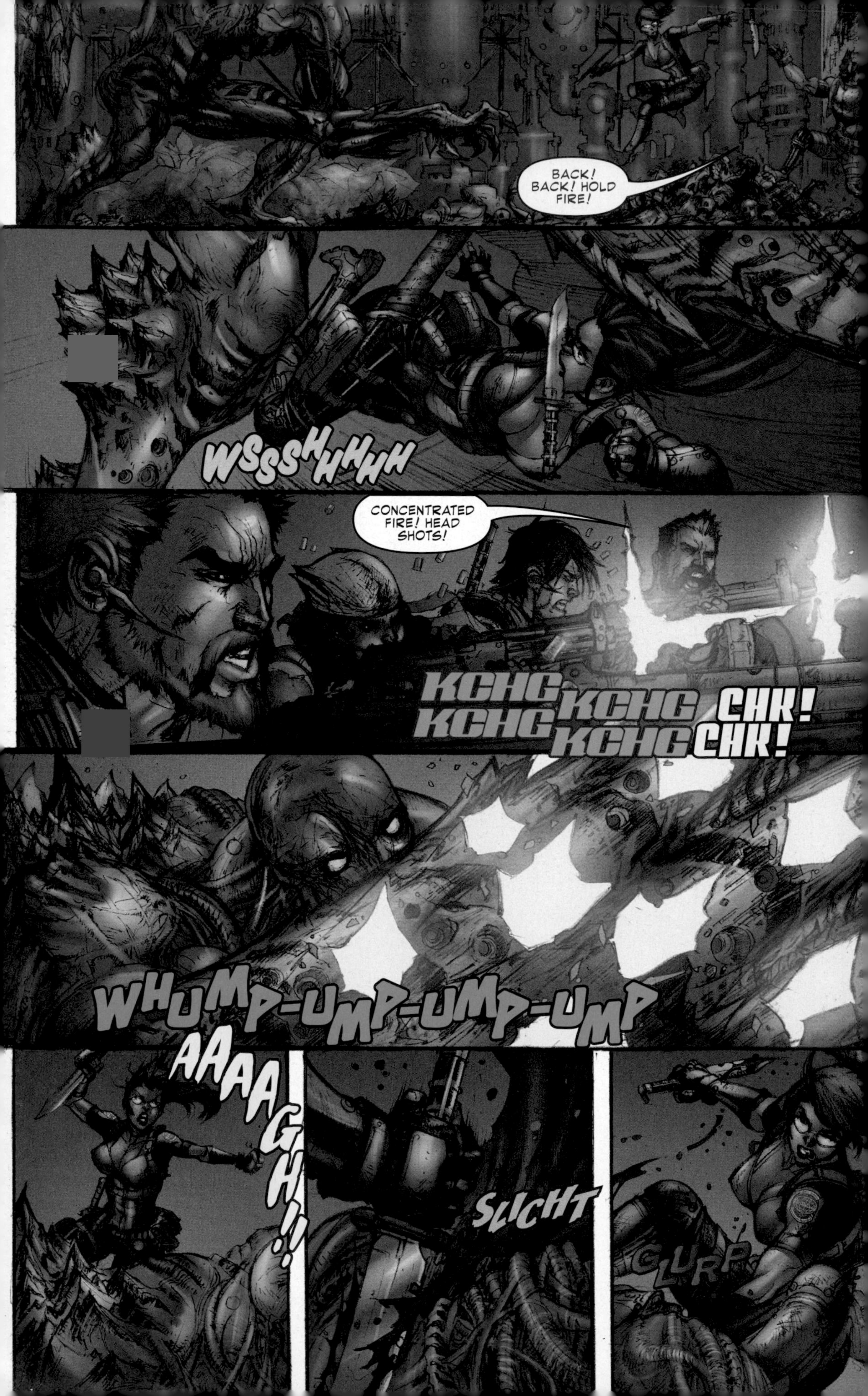

BACK! BACK! HOLD FIRE!
WSSSHHHHH
CONCENTRATED FIRE! HEAD SHOTS!
KCHG KCHG KCHG KCHG
CHK! CHK!
WHUMP-UMP-UMP-UMP
AAAAAGH!!!
SLICHT
GLURP

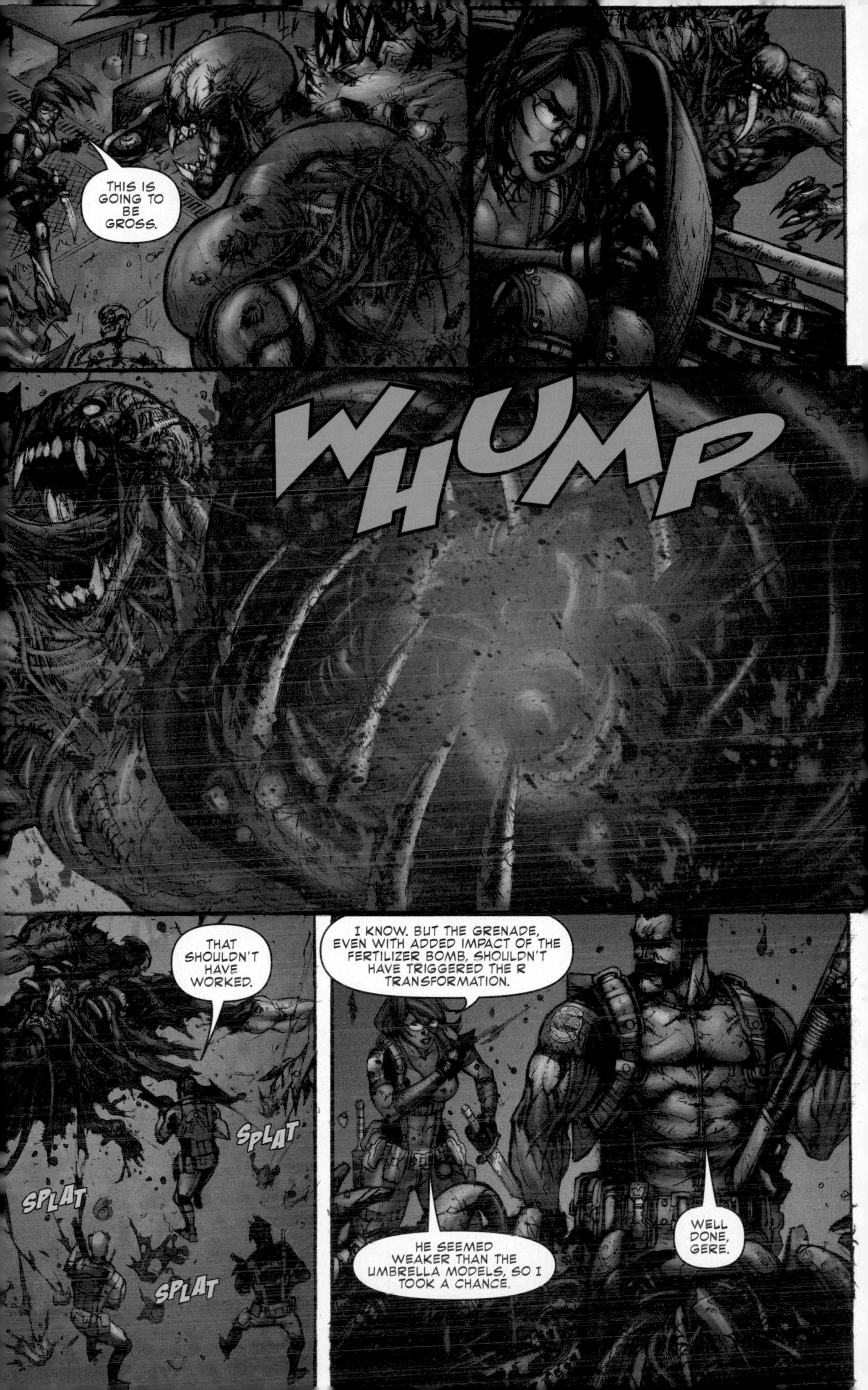
THIS IS GOING TO BE GROSS.
WHUMP
THAT SHOULDN'T HAVE WORKED.
SPLAT
SPLAT
SPLAT
I KNOW. BUT THE GRENADE, EVEN WITH ADDED IMPACT OF THE FERTILIZER BOMB, SHOULDN'T HAVE TRIGGERED THE R TRANSFORMATION.
HE SEEMED WEAKER THAN THE UMBRELLA MODELS, SO I TOOK A CHANCE.
WELL DONE, GERE.

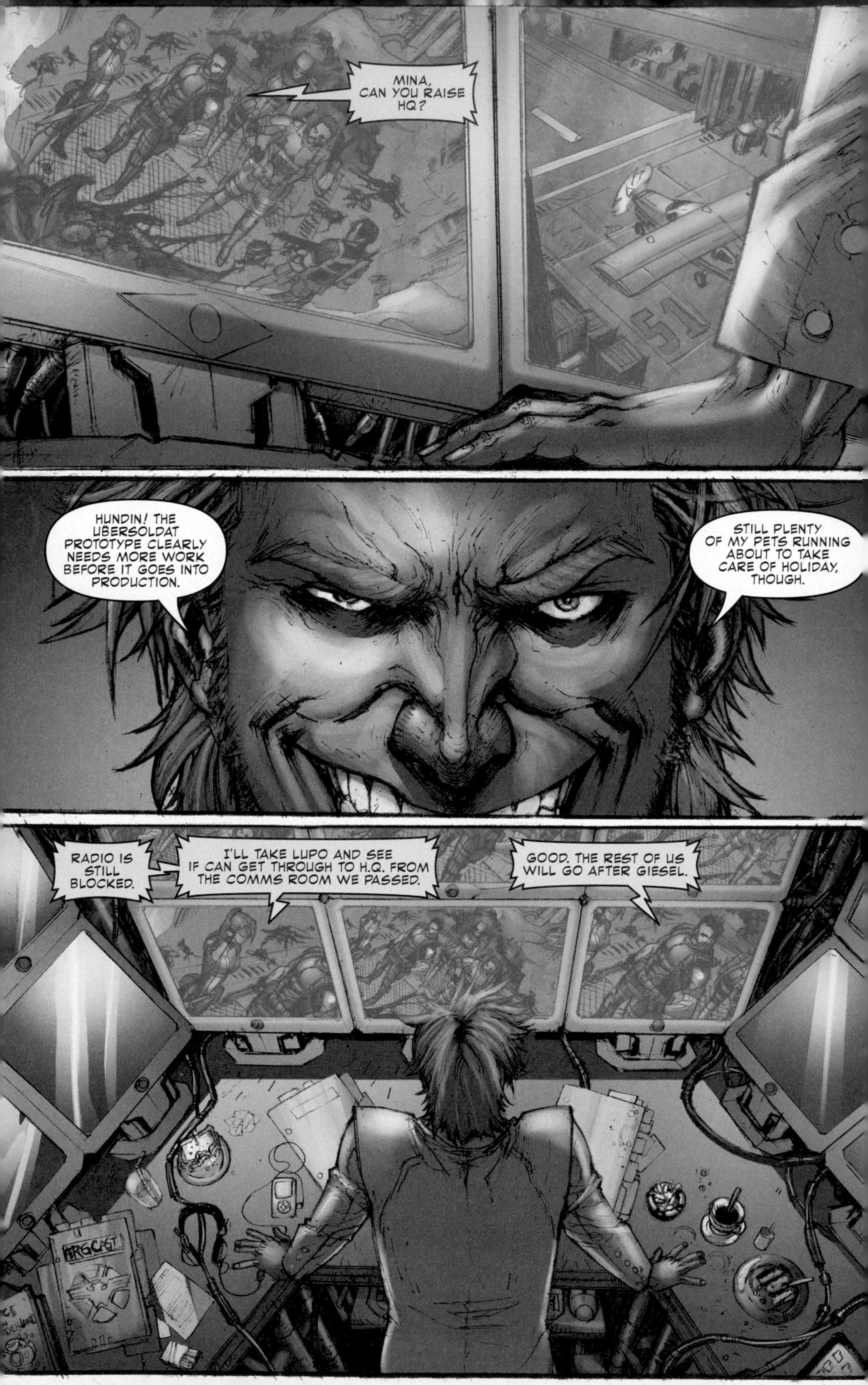
MINA, CAN YOU RAISE HQ?
HUNDIN! THE ÜBERSOLDAT PROTOTYPE CLEARLY NEEDS MORE WORK BEFORE IT GOES INTO PRODUCTION.
STILL PLENTY OF MY PETS RUNNING ABOUT TO TAKE CARE OF HOLIDAY, THOUGH.
RADIO IS STILL BLOCKED.
I'LL TAKE LUPO AND SEE IF CAN GET THROUGH TO H.Q. FROM THE COMMS ROOM WE PASSED.
GOOD. THE REST OF US WILL GO AFTER GIESEL.
ARG CAST

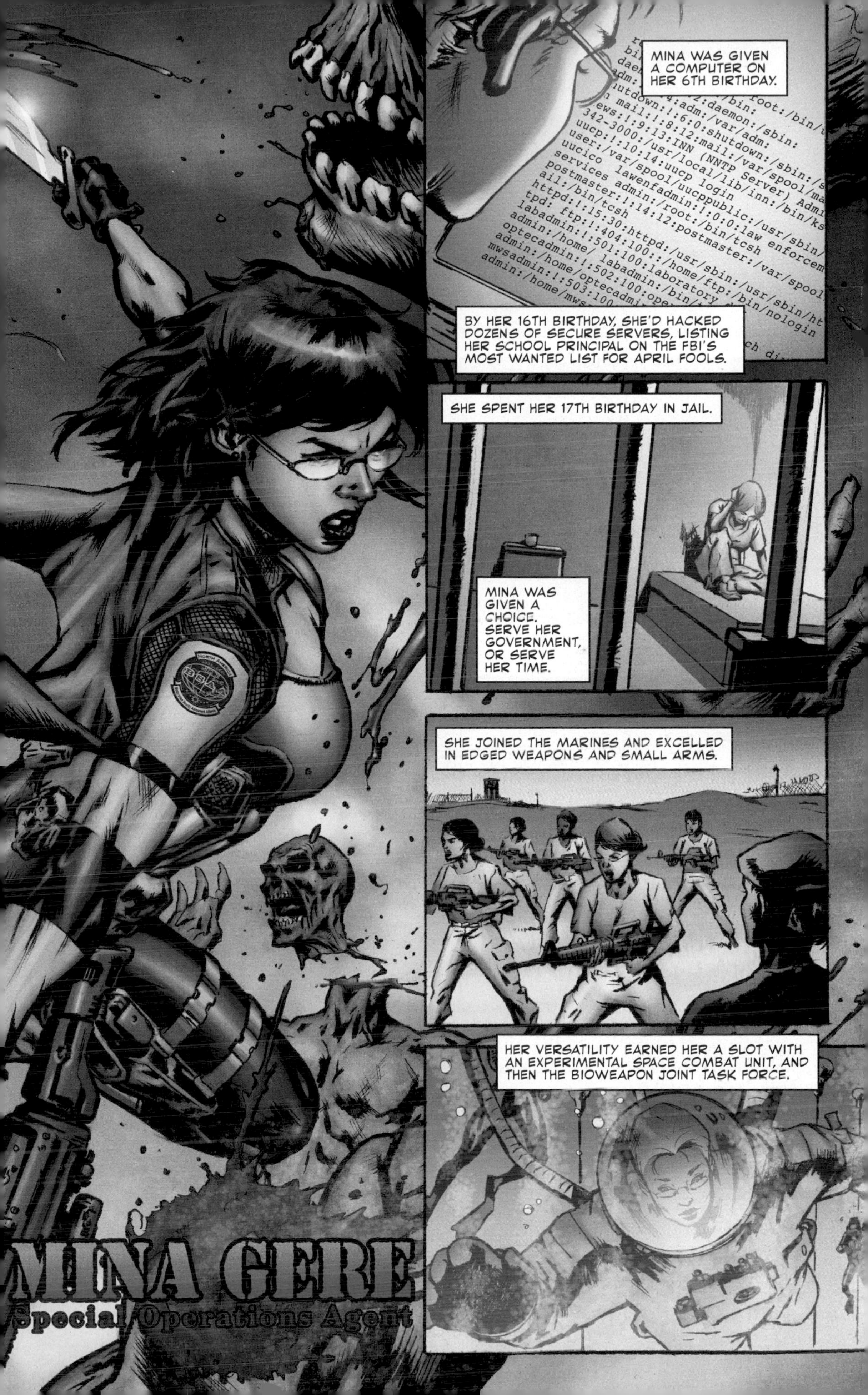
MINA WAS GIVEN A COMPUTER ON HER 6TH BIRTHDAY.
BY HER 16TH BIRTHDAY, SHE'D HACKED DOZENS OF SECURE SERVERS, LISTING HER SCHOOL PRINCIPAL ON THE FBI'S MOST WANTED LIST FOR APRIL FOOLS.
SHE SPENT HER 17TH BIRTHDAY IN JAIL.
MINA WAS GIVEN A CHOICE. SERVE HER GOVERNMENT, OR SERVE HER TIME.
SHE JOINED THE MARINES AND EXCELLED IN EDGED WEAPONS AND SMALL ARMS.
HER VERSATILITY EARNED HER A SLOT WITH AN EXPERIMENTAL SPACE COMBAT UNIT, AND THEN THE BIOWEAPON JOINT TASK FORCE.
MINA GERE
Special Operations Agent

WHEN THE B.S.A.A. RE-FORMED AS A U.N. SPECIAL FORCES UNIT, MINA TRANSFERRED IN AND TRAINED AS A SPECIAL OPERATIONS AGENT.

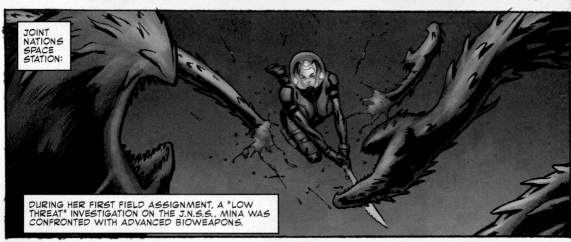

JOINT NATIONS SPACE STATION:

DURING HER FIRST FIELD ASSIGNMENT, A "LOW THREAT" INVESTIGATION ON THE J.N.S.S., MINA WAS CONFRONTED WITH ADVANCED BIOWEAPONS.

THE STATION WAS LOST, BUT MINA ELIMINATED THE BOW THREAT AND WAS REWARDED WITH A PARTNER AND THE INVESTIGATION INTO GIESEL INDUSTRIES.

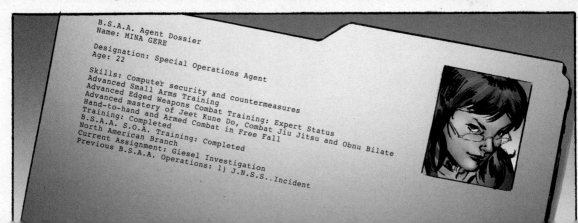

B.S.A.A. Agent Dossier
Name: MINA GERE

Designation: Special Operations Agent
Age: 22

Skills: Computer security and countermeasures
Advanced Small Arms Training
Advanced Edged Weapons Combat Training: Expert Status
Advanced mastery of Jeet Kune Do, Combat Jiu Jitsu and Obnu Bilate
Hand-to-hand and Armed Combat in Free Fall
Training: Completed
B.S.A.A. S.O.A. Training: Completed
North American Branch
Current Assignment: Giesel Investigation
Previous B.S.A.A. Operations: 1) J.N.S.S..Incident

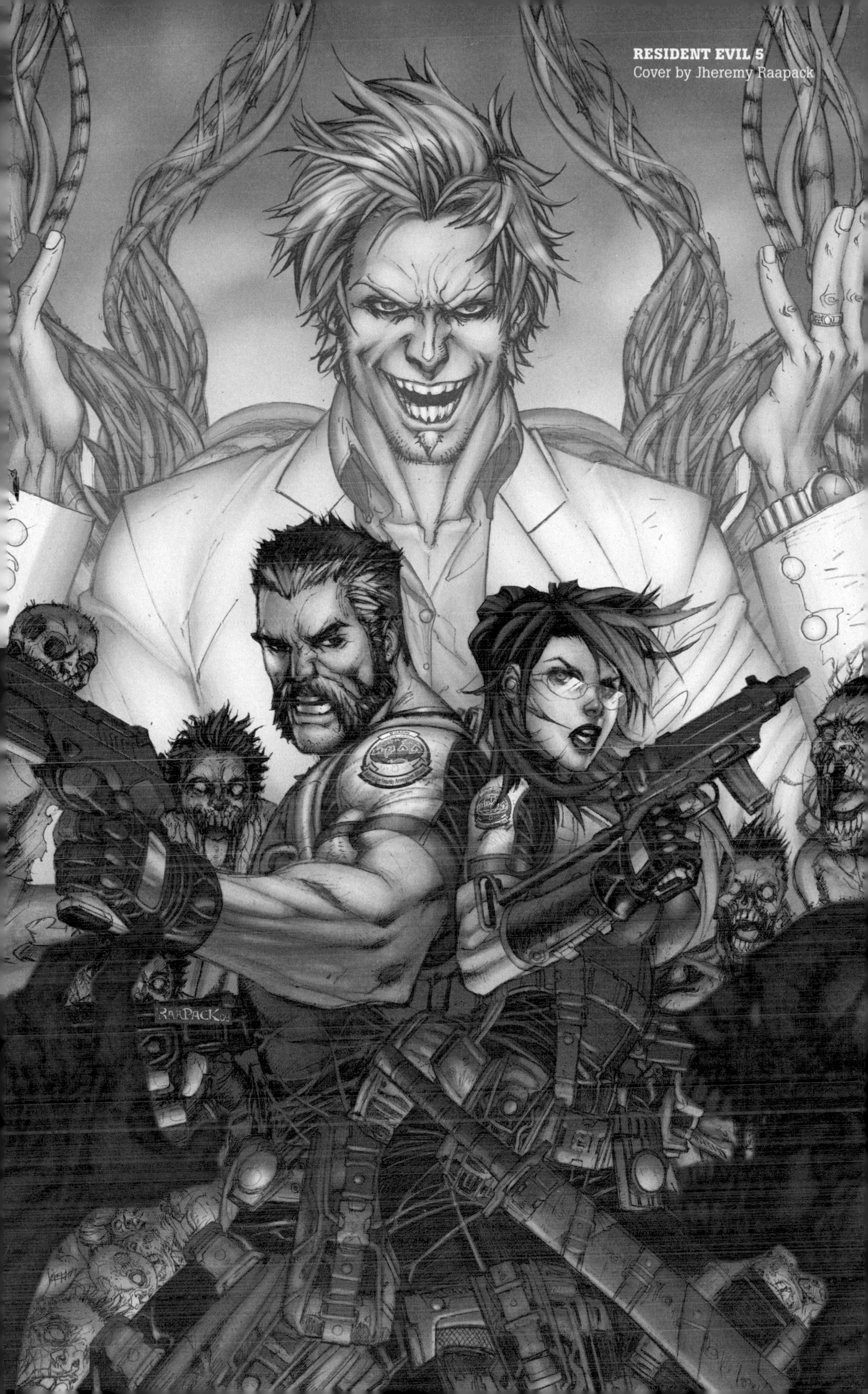

RESIDENT EVIL 5
Cover by Jheremy Raapack

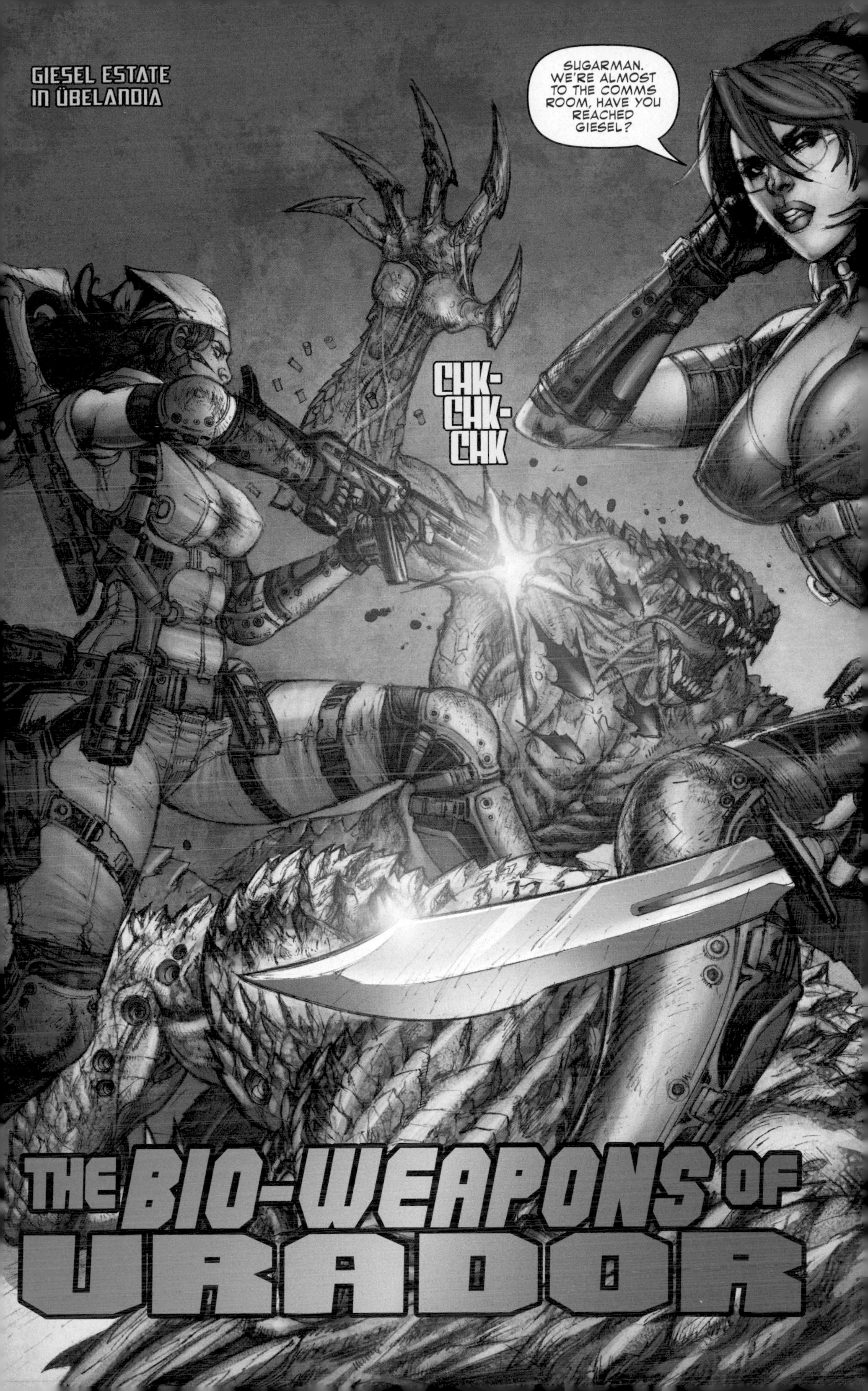

GIESEL ESTATE IN ÜBELANDIA
SUGARMAN. WE'RE ALMOST TO THE COMMS ROOM, HAVE YOU REACHED GIESEL?
CHK-CHK-CHK
THE BIO-WEAPONS OF URADOR

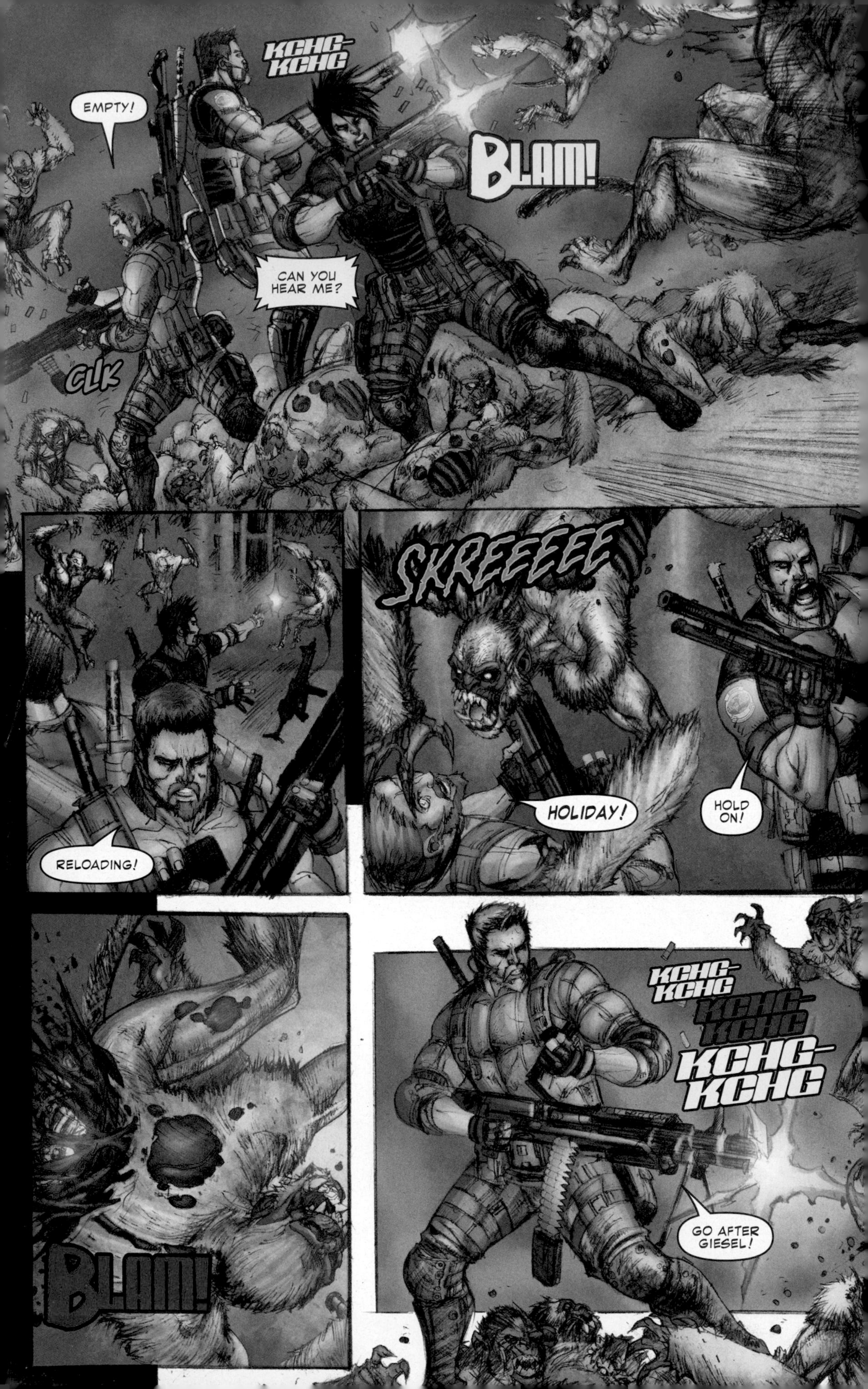
KCHG-KCHG
EMPTY!
BLAM!
CAN YOU HEAR ME?
CLIK
RELOADING!
SKREEEEEE
HOLIDAY!
HOLD ON!
BLAM!
KCHG-KCHG
KCHG-KCHG
KCHG-KCHG
GO AFTER GIESEL!

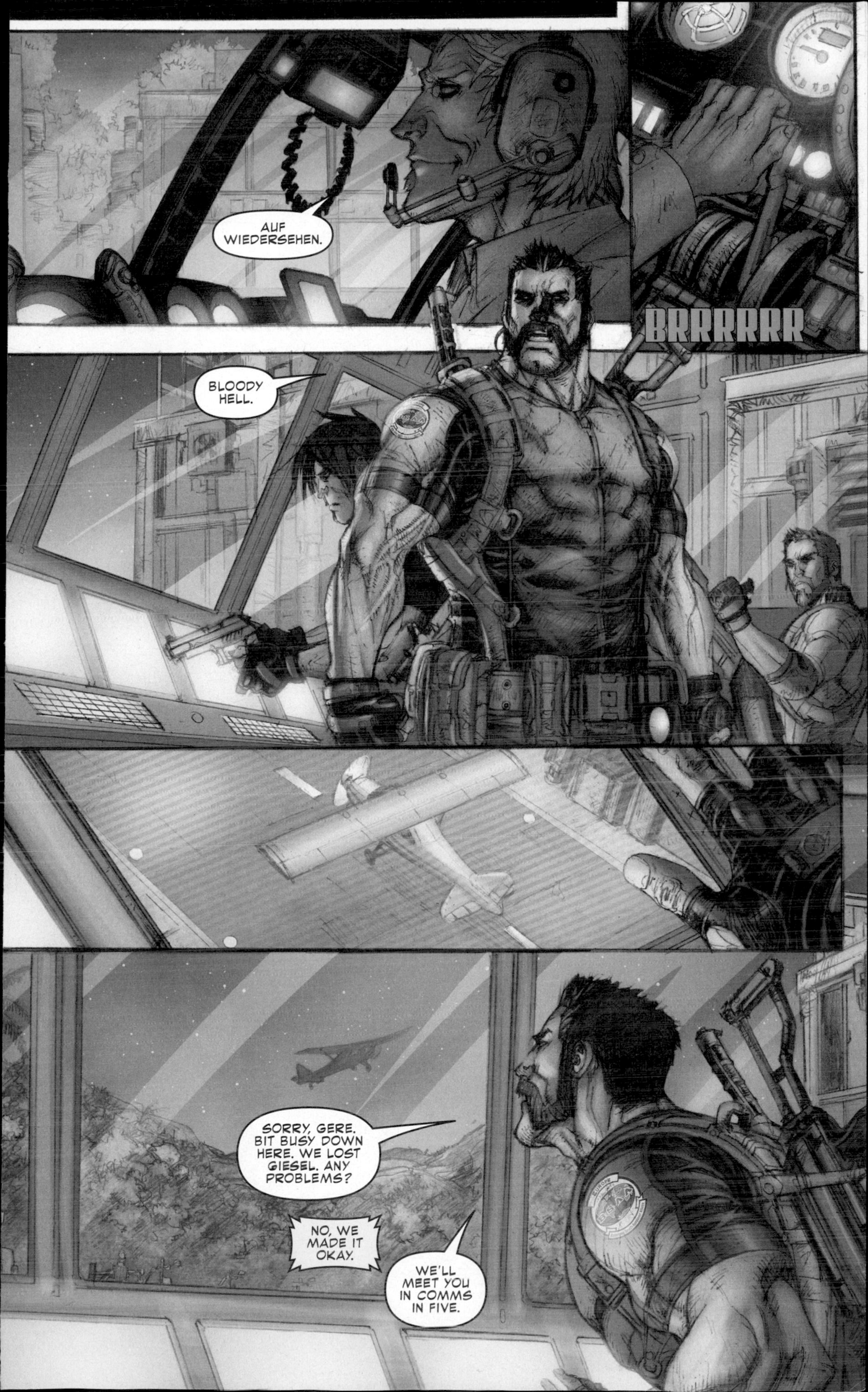
AUF WIEDERSEHEN.
BRRRRRRR
BLOODY HELL.
SORRY, GERE. BIT BUSY DOWN HERE. WE LOST GIESEL. ANY PROBLEMS?
NO, WE MADE IT OKAY.
WE'LL MEET YOU IN COMMS IN FIVE.

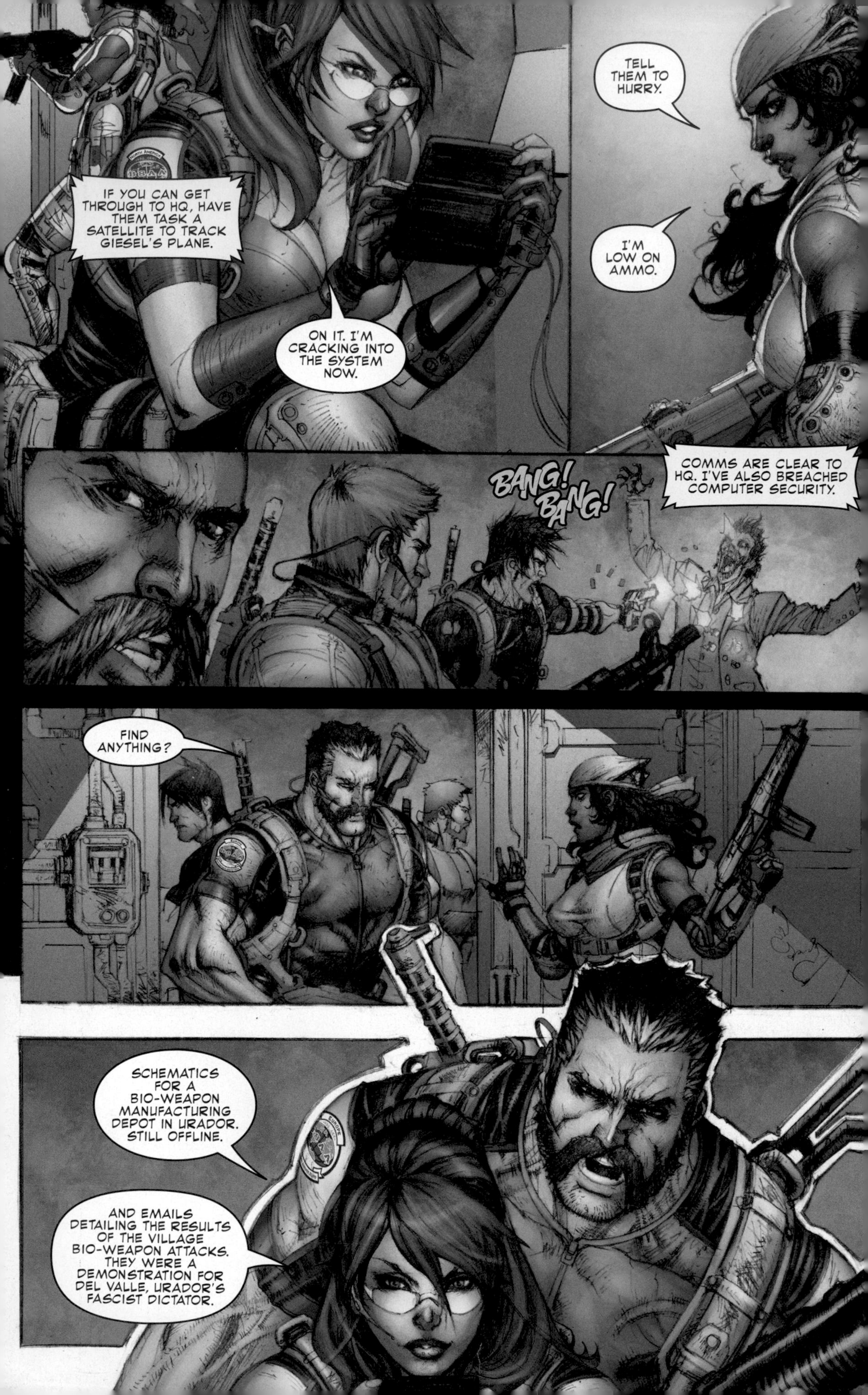
IF YOU CAN GET THROUGH TO HQ, HAVE THEM TASK A SATELLITE TO TRACK GIESEL'S PLANE.
ON IT. I'M CRACKING INTO THE SYSTEM NOW.
TELL THEM TO HURRY.
I'M LOW ON AMMO.
BANG! BANG!
COMMS ARE CLEAR TO HQ. I'VE ALSO BREACHED COMPUTER SECURITY.
FIND ANYTHING?
SCHEMATICS FOR A BIO-WEAPON MANUFACTURING DEPOT IN URADOR. STILL OFFLINE.
AND EMAILS DETAILING THE RESULTS OF THE VILLAGE BIO-WEAPON ATTACKS. THEY WERE A DEMONSTRATION FOR DEL VALLE, URADOR'S FASCIST DICTATOR.

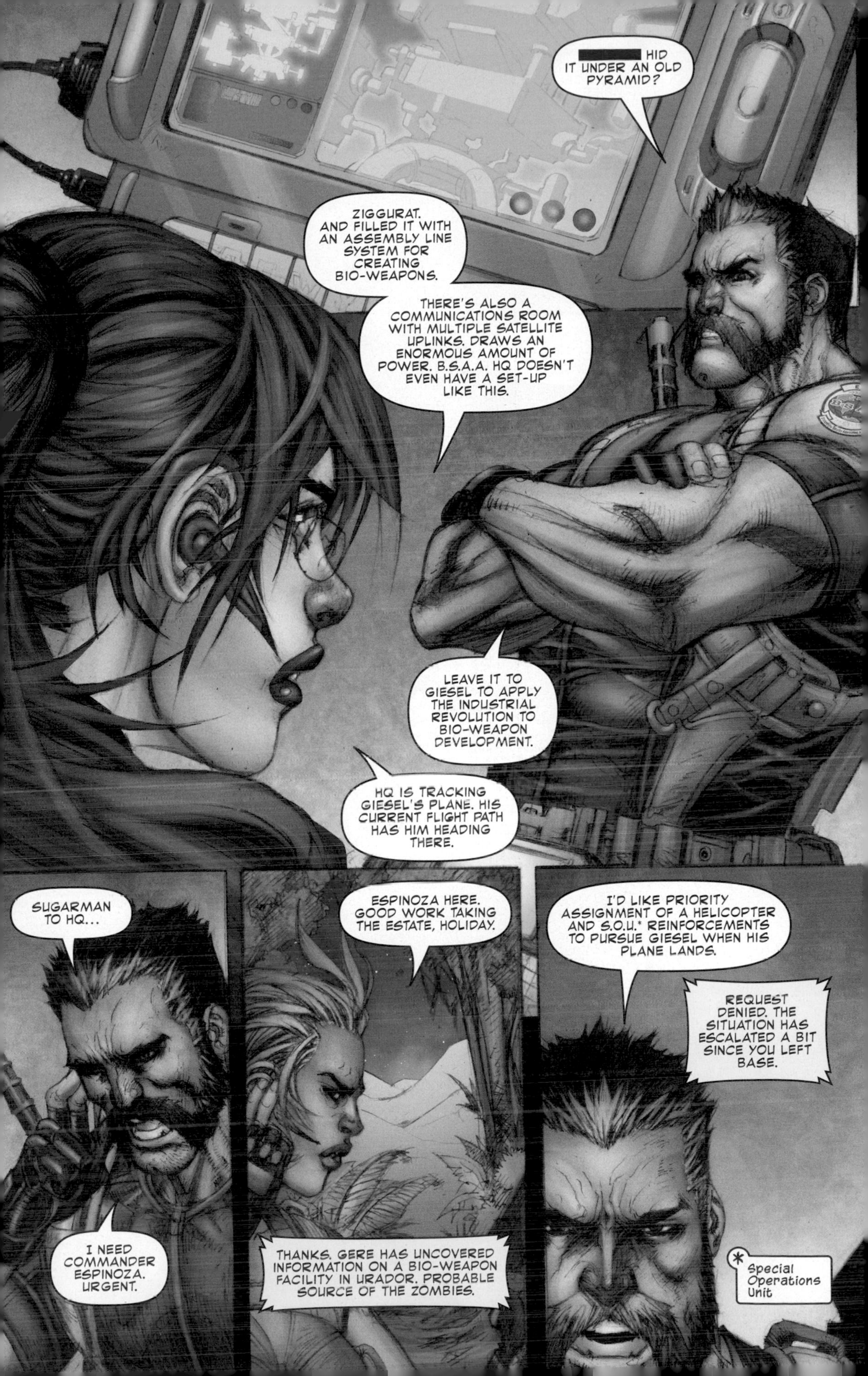
[redacted] HID IT UNDER AN OLD PYRAMID?
ZIGGURAT. AND FILLED IT WITH AN ASSEMBLY LINE SYSTEM FOR CREATING BIO-WEAPONS.
THERE'S ALSO A COMMUNICATIONS ROOM WITH MULTIPLE SATELLITE UPLINKS. DRAWS AN ENORMOUS AMOUNT OF POWER. B.S.A.A. HQ DOESN'T EVEN HAVE A SET-UP LIKE THIS.
LEAVE IT TO GIESEL TO APPLY THE INDUSTRIAL REVOLUTION TO BIO-WEAPON DEVELOPMENT.
HQ IS TRACKING GIESEL'S PLANE. HIS CURRENT FLIGHT PATH HAS HIM HEADING THERE.
SUGARMAN TO HQ...
I NEED COMMANDER ESPINOZA. URGENT.
ESPINOZA HERE. GOOD WORK TAKING THE ESTATE, HOLIDAY.
THANKS. GERE HAS UNCOVERED INFORMATION ON A BIO-WEAPON FACILITY IN URADOR. PROBABLE SOURCE OF THE ZOMBIES.
I'D LIKE PRIORITY ASSIGNMENT OF A HELICOPTER AND S.O.U.* REINFORCEMENTS TO PURSUE GIESEL WHEN HIS PLANE LANDS.
REQUEST DENIED. THE SITUATION HAS ESCALATED A BIT SINCE YOU LEFT BASE.
* Special Operations Unit

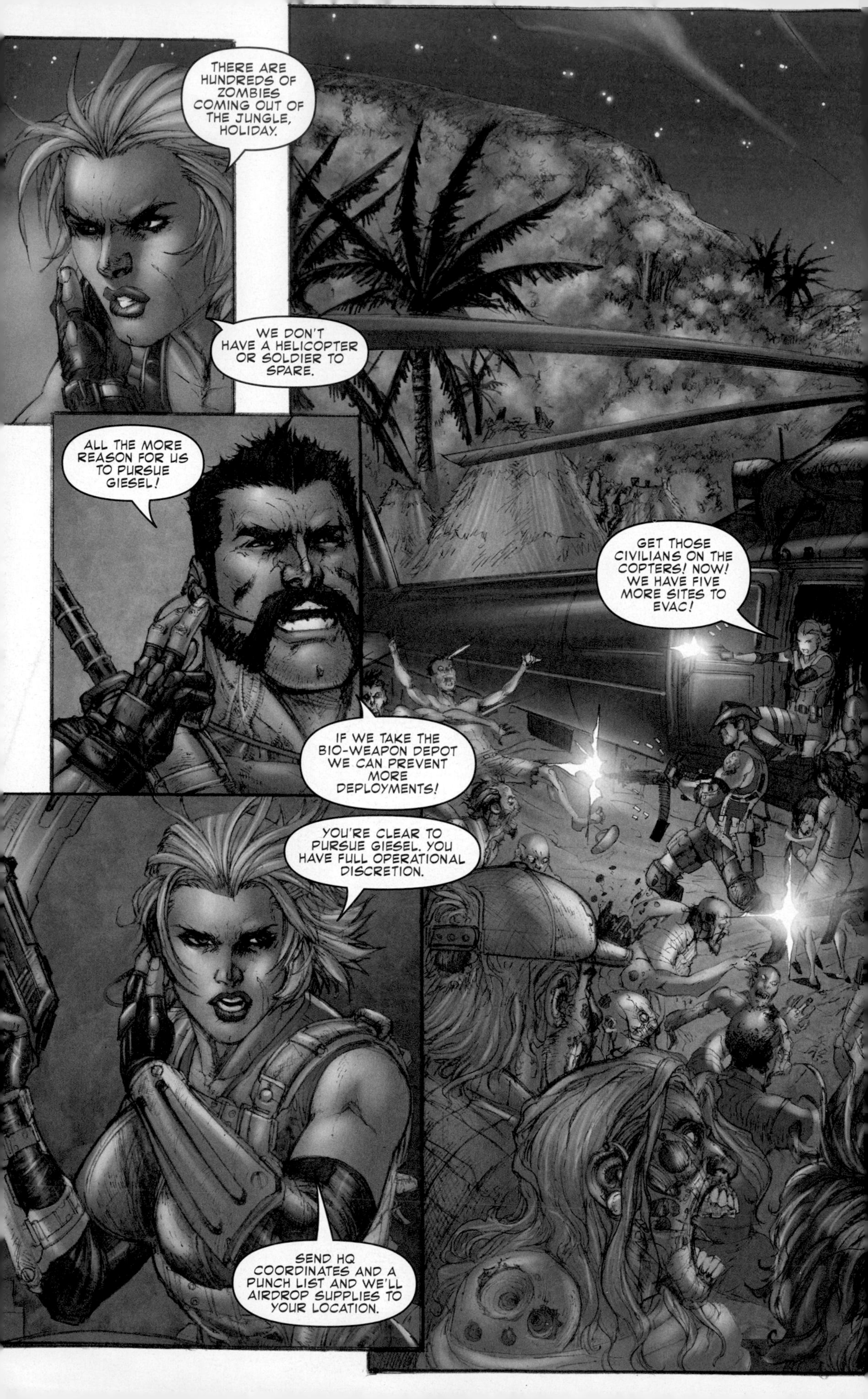
THERE ARE HUNDREDS OF ZOMBIES COMING OUT OF THE JUNGLE, HOLIDAY.
WE DON'T HAVE A HELICOPTER OR SOLDIER TO SPARE.
ALL THE MORE REASON FOR US TO PURSUE GIESEL!
IF WE TAKE THE BIO-WEAPON DEPOT WE CAN PREVENT MORE DEPLOYMENTS!
GET THOSE CIVILIANS ON THE COPTERS! NOW! WE HAVE FIVE MORE SITES TO EVAC!
YOU'RE CLEAR TO PURSUE GIESEL. YOU HAVE FULL OPERATIONAL DISCRETION.
SEND HQ COORDINATES AND A PUNCH LIST AND WE'LL AIRDROP SUPPLIES TO YOUR LOCATION.

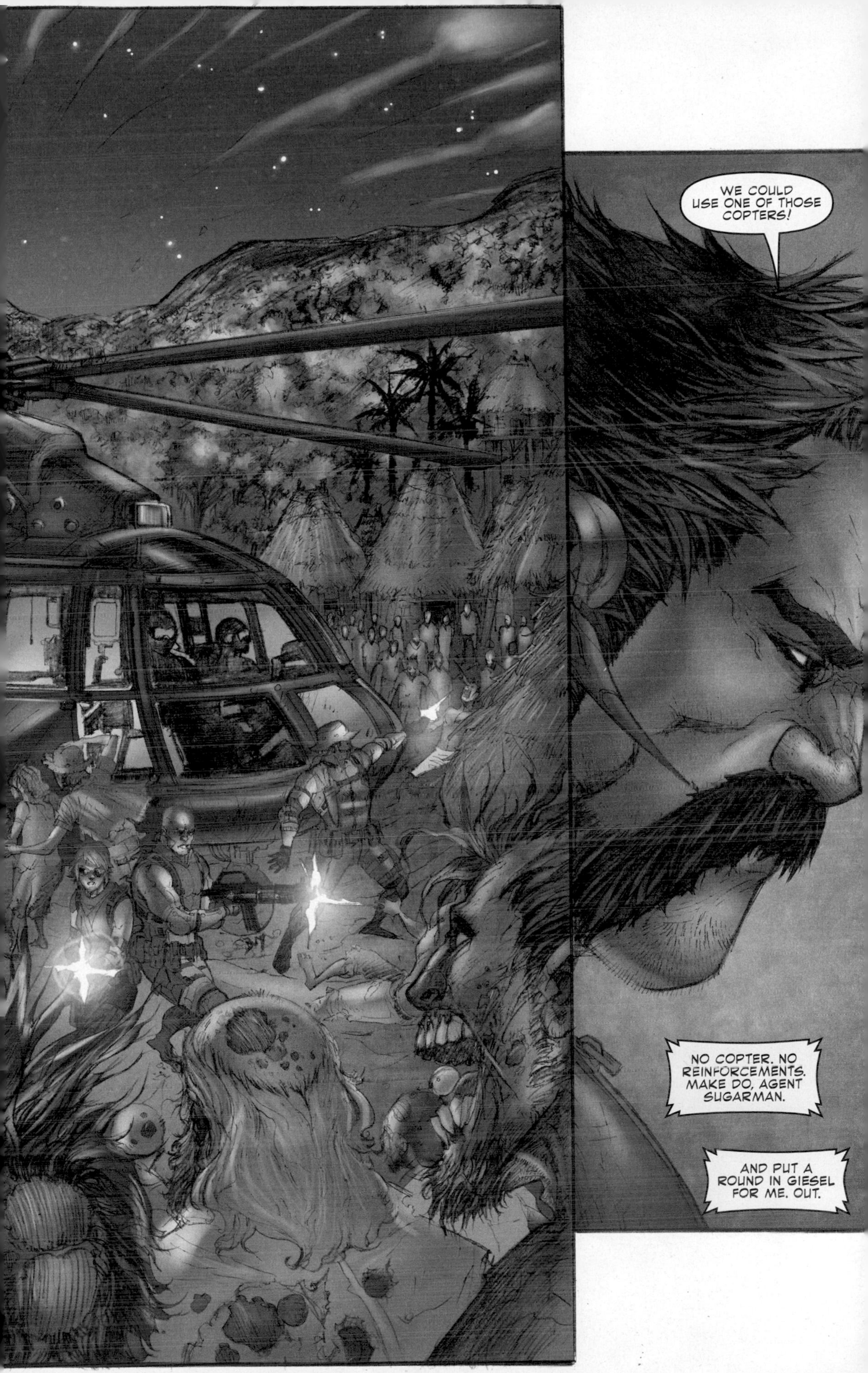
WE COULD USE ONE OF THOSE COPTERS!
NO COPTER. NO REINFORCEMENTS. MAKE DO, AGENT SUGARMAN.
AND PUT A ROUND IN GIESEL FOR ME. OUT.

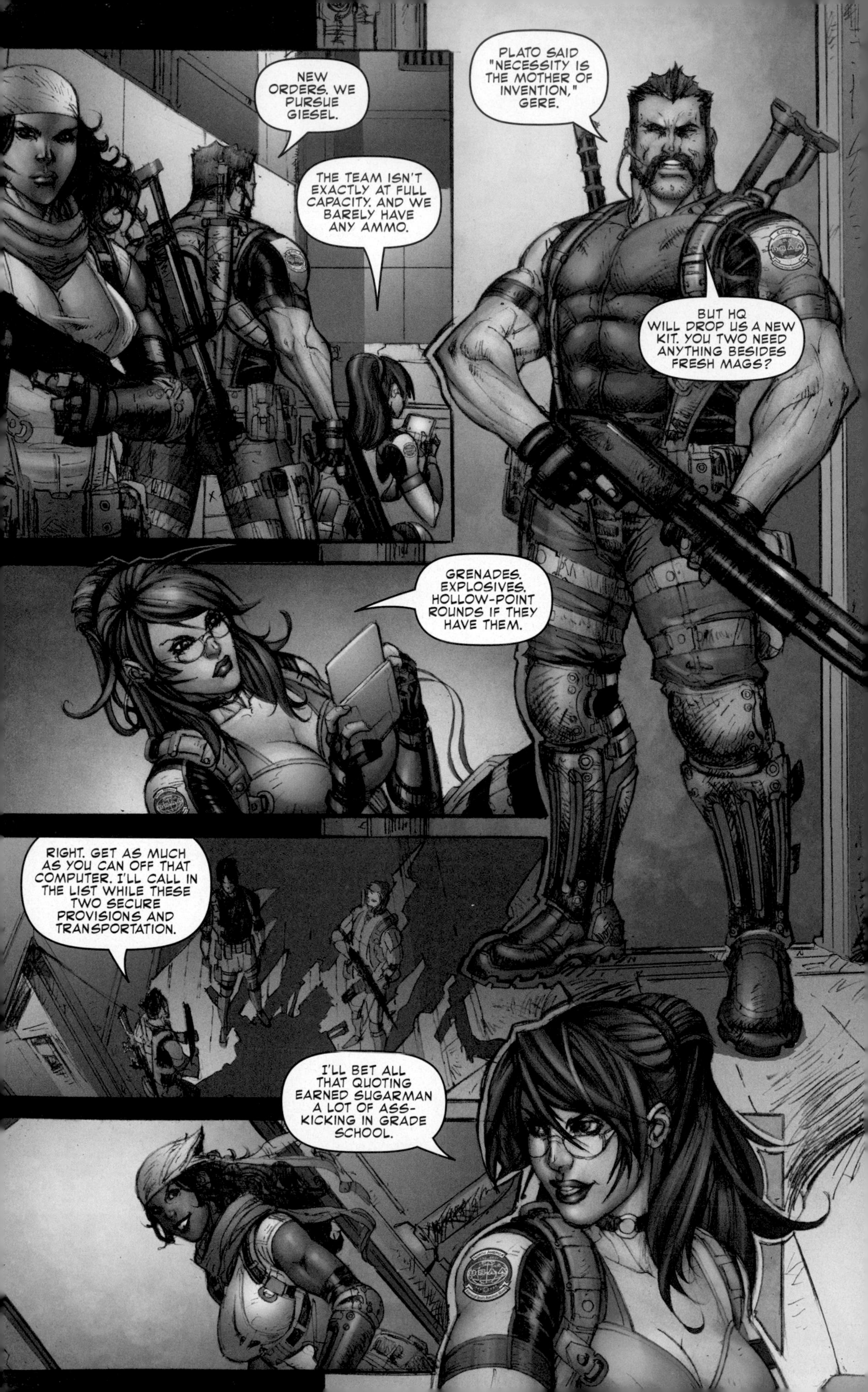
NEW ORDERS. WE PURSUE GIESEL.
THE TEAM ISN'T EXACTLY AT FULL CAPACITY. AND WE BARELY HAVE ANY AMMO.
PLATO SAID "NECESSITY IS THE MOTHER OF INVENTION," GERE.
BUT HQ WILL DROP US A NEW KIT. YOU TWO NEED ANYTHING BESIDES FRESH MAGS?
GRENADES. EXPLOSIVES. HOLLOW-POINT ROUNDS IF THEY HAVE THEM.
RIGHT. GET AS MUCH AS YOU CAN OFF THAT COMPUTER. I'LL CALL IN THE LIST WHILE THESE TWO SECURE PROVISIONS AND TRANSPORTATION.
I'LL BET ALL THAT QUOTING EARNED SUGARMAN A LOT OF ASS-KICKING IN GRADE SCHOOL.

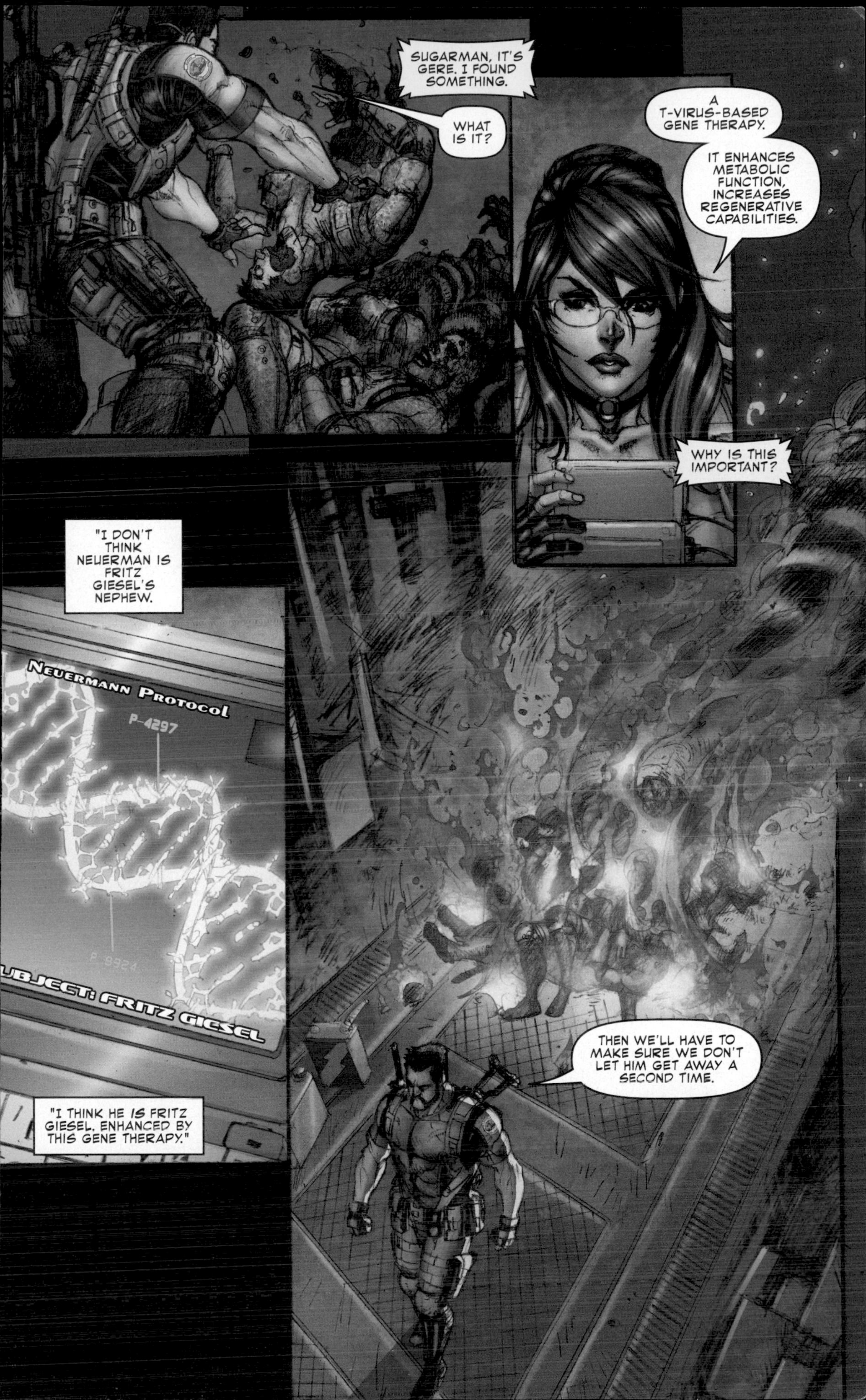
SUGARMAN, IT'S GERE. I FOUND SOMETHING.
WHAT IS IT?
A T-VIRUS-BASED GENE THERAPY.
IT ENHANCES METABOLIC FUNCTION, INCREASES REGENERATIVE CAPABILITIES.
WHY IS THIS IMPORTANT?
"I DON'T THINK NEUERMAN IS FRITZ GIESEL'S NEPHEW.
NEUERMANN PROTOCOL
P-4297
P-8924
SUBJECT: FRITZ GIESEL
"I THINK HE IS FRITZ GIESEL, ENHANCED BY THIS GENE THERAPY."
THEN WE'LL HAVE TO MAKE SURE WE DON'T LET HIM GET AWAY A SECOND TIME.

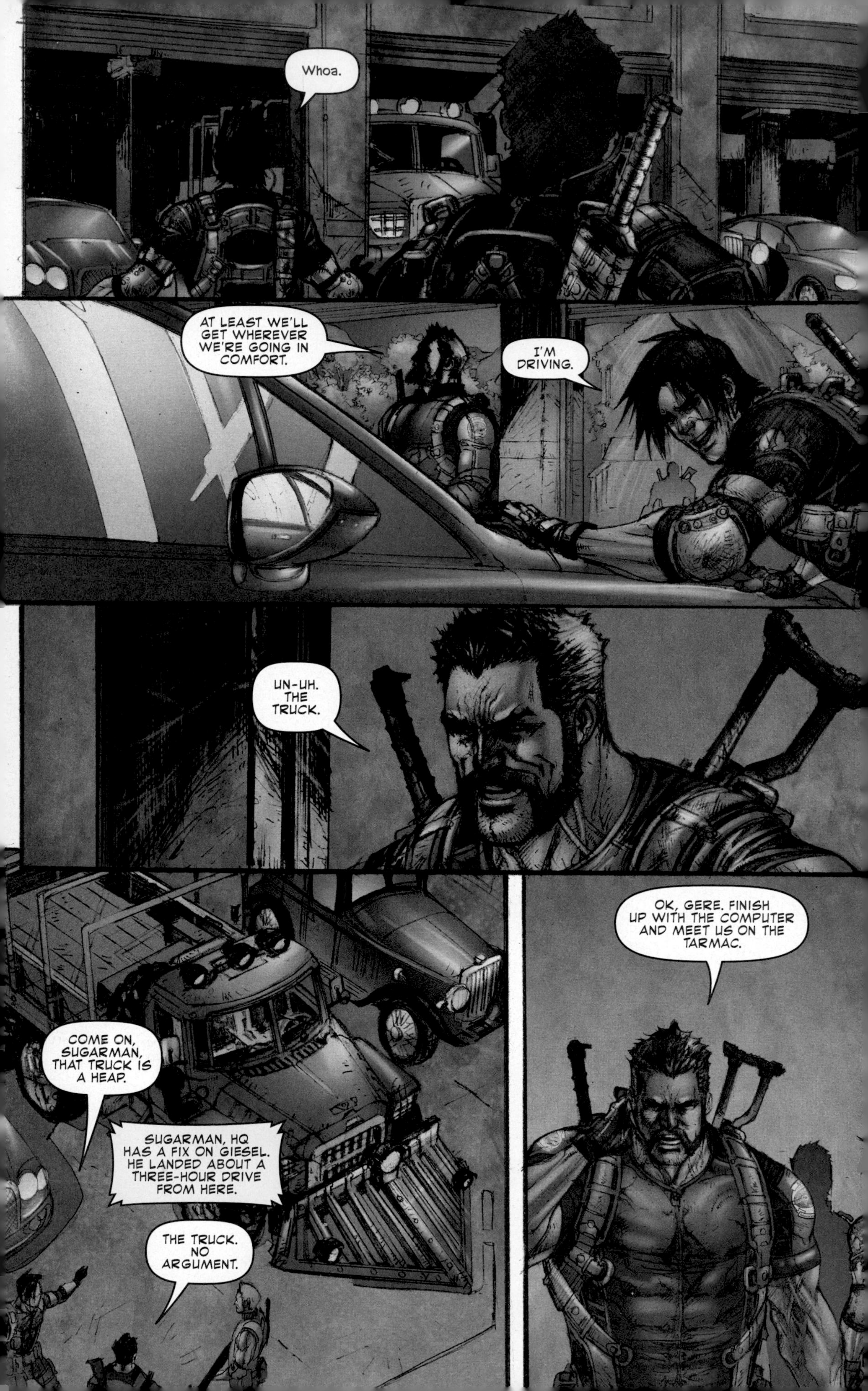
Whoa.
AT LEAST WE'LL GET WHEREVER WE'RE GOING IN COMFORT.
I'M DRIVING.
UN-UH. THE TRUCK.
COME ON, SUGARMAN, THAT TRUCK IS A HEAP.
SUGARMAN, HQ HAS A FIX ON GIESEL. HE LANDED ABOUT A THREE-HOUR DRIVE FROM HERE.
THE TRUCK. NO ARGUMENT.
OK, GERE. FINISH UP WITH THE COMPUTER AND MEET US ON THE TARMAC.

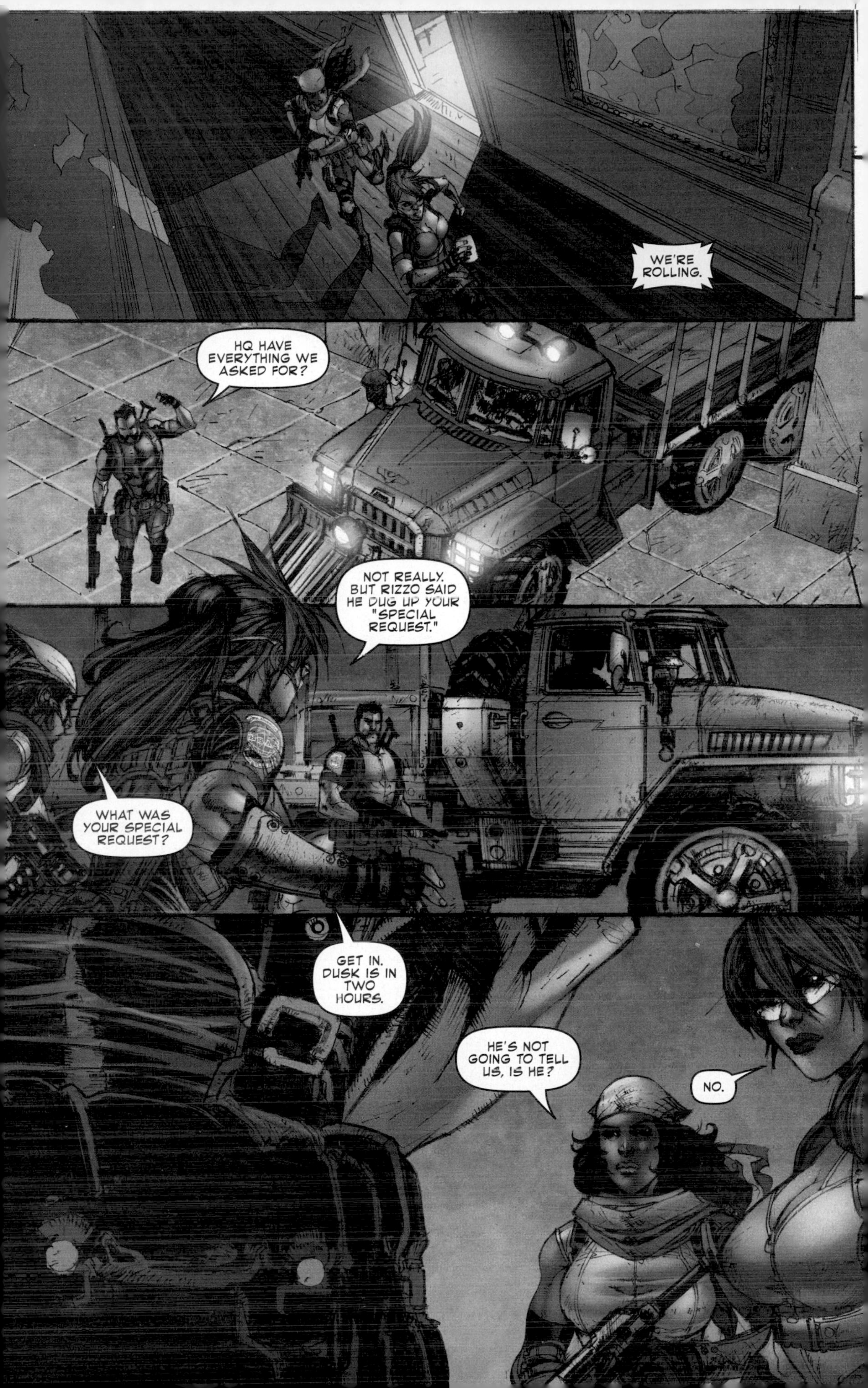
WE'RE ROLLING.
HQ HAVE EVERYTHING WE ASKED FOR?
NOT REALLY. BUT RIZZO SAID HE DUG UP YOUR "SPECIAL REQUEST."
WHAT WAS YOUR SPECIAL REQUEST?
GET IN. DUSK IS IN TWO HOURS.
HE'S NOT GOING TO TELL US, IS HE?
NO.

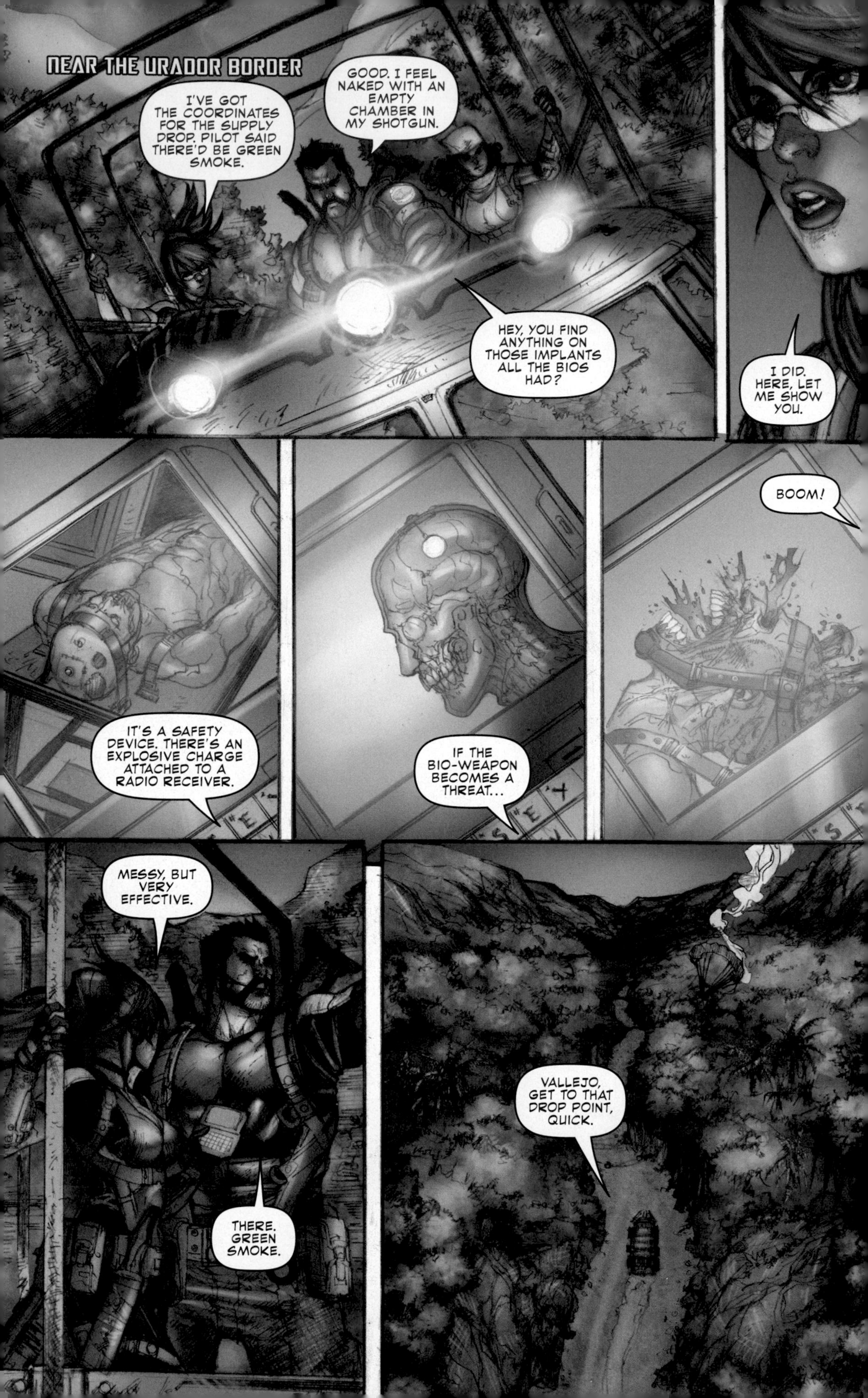
NEAR THE URADOR BORDER
I'VE GOT THE COORDINATES FOR THE SUPPLY DROP. PILOT SAID THERE'D BE GREEN SMOKE.
GOOD. I FEEL NAKED WITH AN EMPTY CHAMBER IN MY SHOTGUN.
HEY, YOU FIND ANYTHING ON THOSE IMPLANTS ALL THE BIOS HAD?
I DID. HERE, LET ME SHOW YOU.
IT'S A SAFETY DEVICE. THERE'S AN EXPLOSIVE CHARGE ATTACHED TO A RADIO RECEIVER.
IF THE BIO-WEAPON BECOMES A THREAT...
BOOM!
MESSY, BUT VERY EFFECTIVE.
THERE. GREEN SMOKE.
VALLEJO, GET TO THAT DROP POINT, QUICK.

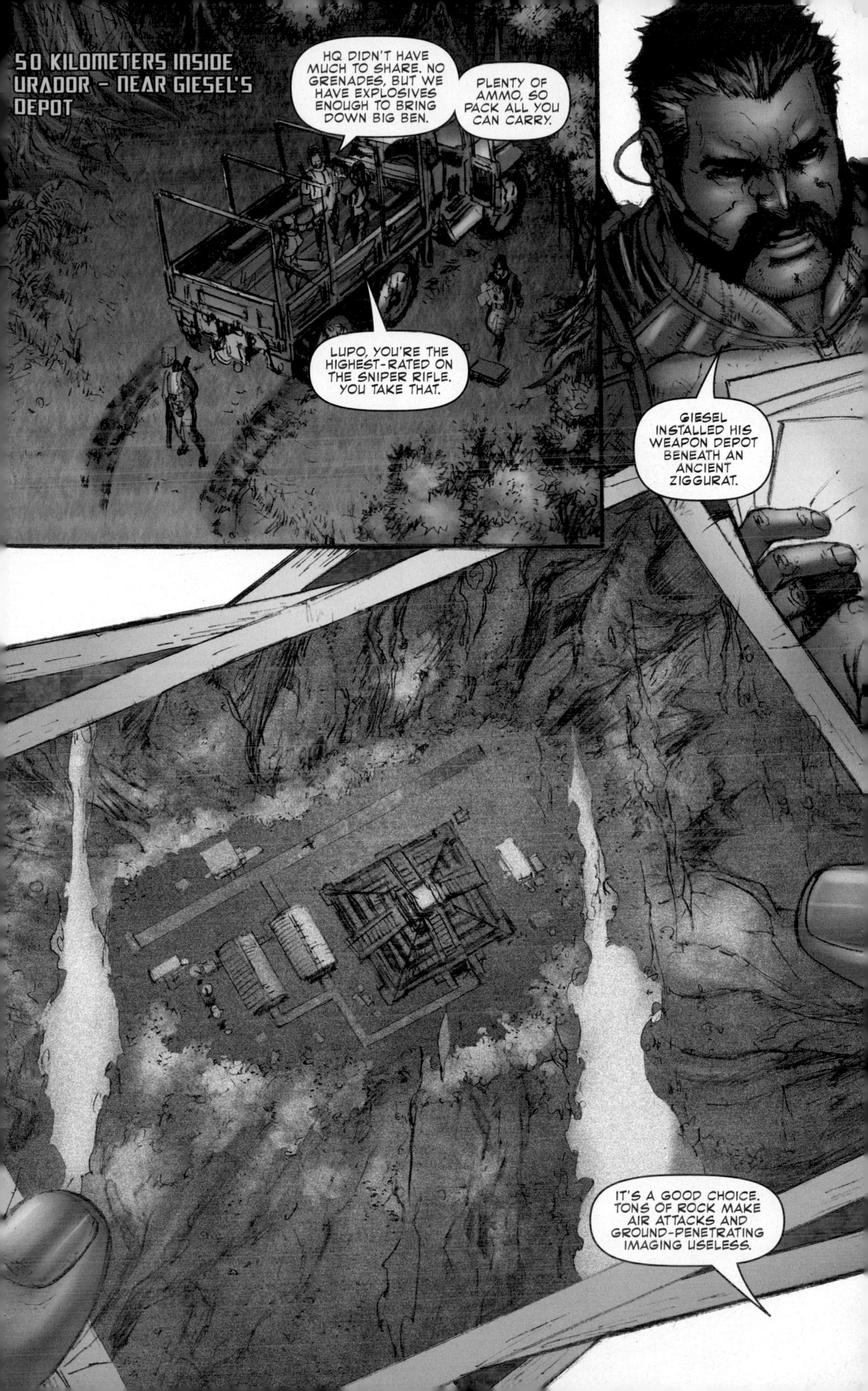
50 KILOMETERS INSIDE URADOR - NEAR GIESEL'S DEPOT
HQ DIDN'T HAVE MUCH TO SHARE. NO GRENADES, BUT WE HAVE EXPLOSIVES ENOUGH TO BRING DOWN BIG BEN.
PLENTY OF AMMO, SO PACK ALL YOU CAN CARRY.
LUPO, YOU'RE THE HIGHEST-RATED ON THE SNIPER RIFLE. YOU TAKE THAT.
GIESEL INSTALLED HIS WEAPON DEPOT BENEATH AN ANCIENT ZIGGURAT.
IT'S A GOOD CHOICE. TONS OF ROCK MAKE AIR ATTACKS AND GROUND-PENETRATING IMAGING USELESS.

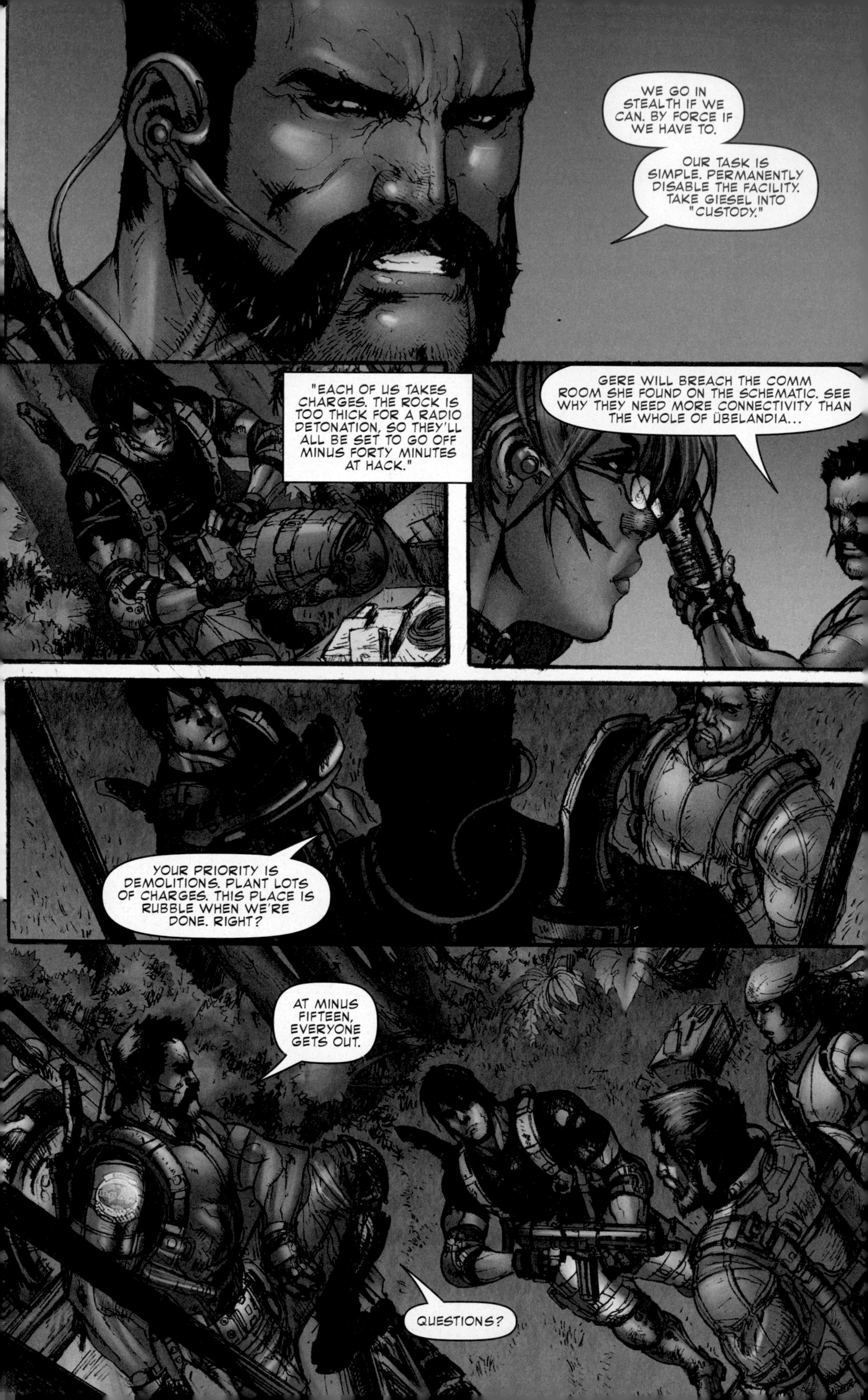
WE GO IN STEALTH IF WE CAN. BY FORCE IF WE HAVE TO.
OUR TASK IS SIMPLE. PERMANENTLY DISABLE THE FACILITY. TAKE GIESEL INTO "CUSTODY."
"EACH OF US TAKES CHARGES. THE ROCK IS TOO THICK FOR A RADIO DETONATION, SO THEY'LL ALL BE SET TO GO OFF MINUS FORTY MINUTES AT HACK."
GERE WILL BREACH THE COMM ROOM SHE FOUND ON THE SCHEMATIC. SEE WHY THEY NEED MORE CONNECTIVITY THAN THE WHOLE OF ÜBELANDIA...
YOUR PRIORITY IS DEMOLITIONS. PLANT LOTS OF CHARGES. THIS PLACE IS RUBBLE WHEN WE'RE DONE. RIGHT?
AT MINUS FIFTEEN, EVERYONE GETS OUT.
QUESTIONS?

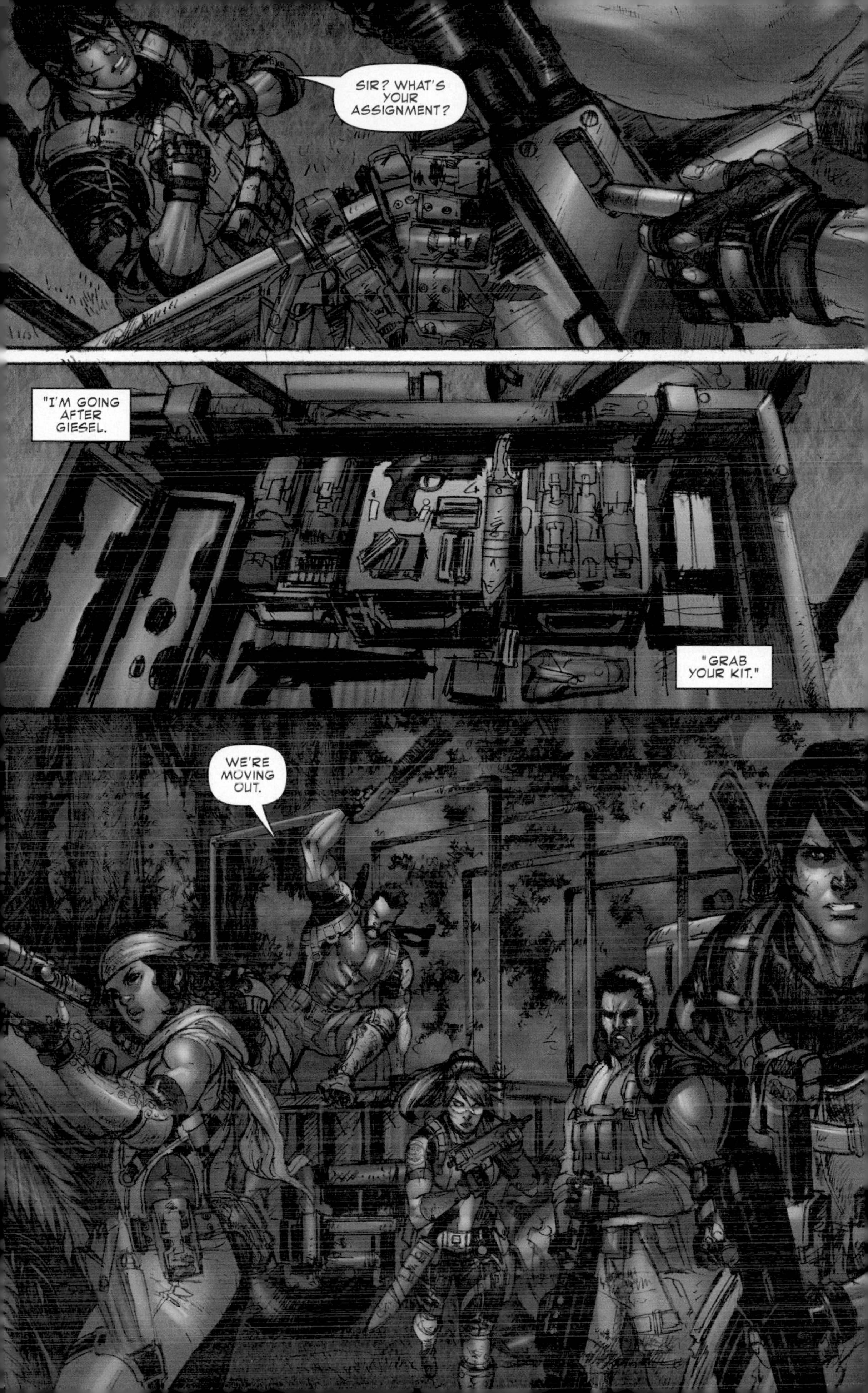
SIR? WHAT'S YOUR ASSIGNMENT?
"I'M GOING AFTER GIESEL.
"GRAB YOUR KIT."
WE'RE MOVING OUT.

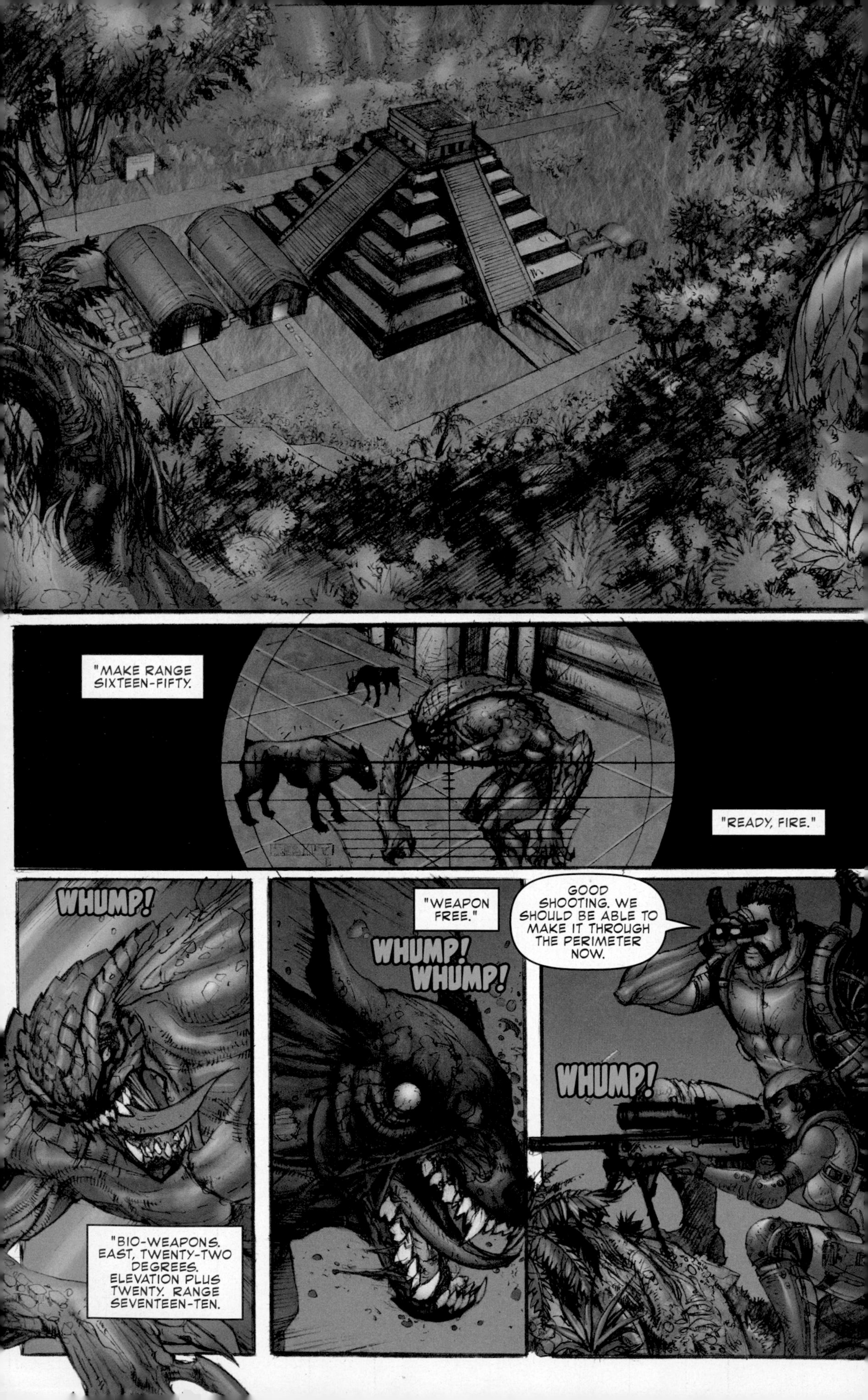
"MAKE RANGE SIXTEEN-FIFTY.
"READY, FIRE."
WHUMP!
"BIO-WEAPONS. EAST, TWENTY-TWO DEGREES. ELEVATION PLUS TWENTY. RANGE SEVENTEEN-TEN.
"WEAPON FREE."
WHUMP! WHUMP!
GOOD SHOOTING. WE SHOULD BE ABLE TO MAKE IT THROUGH THE PERIMETER NOW.
WHUMP!

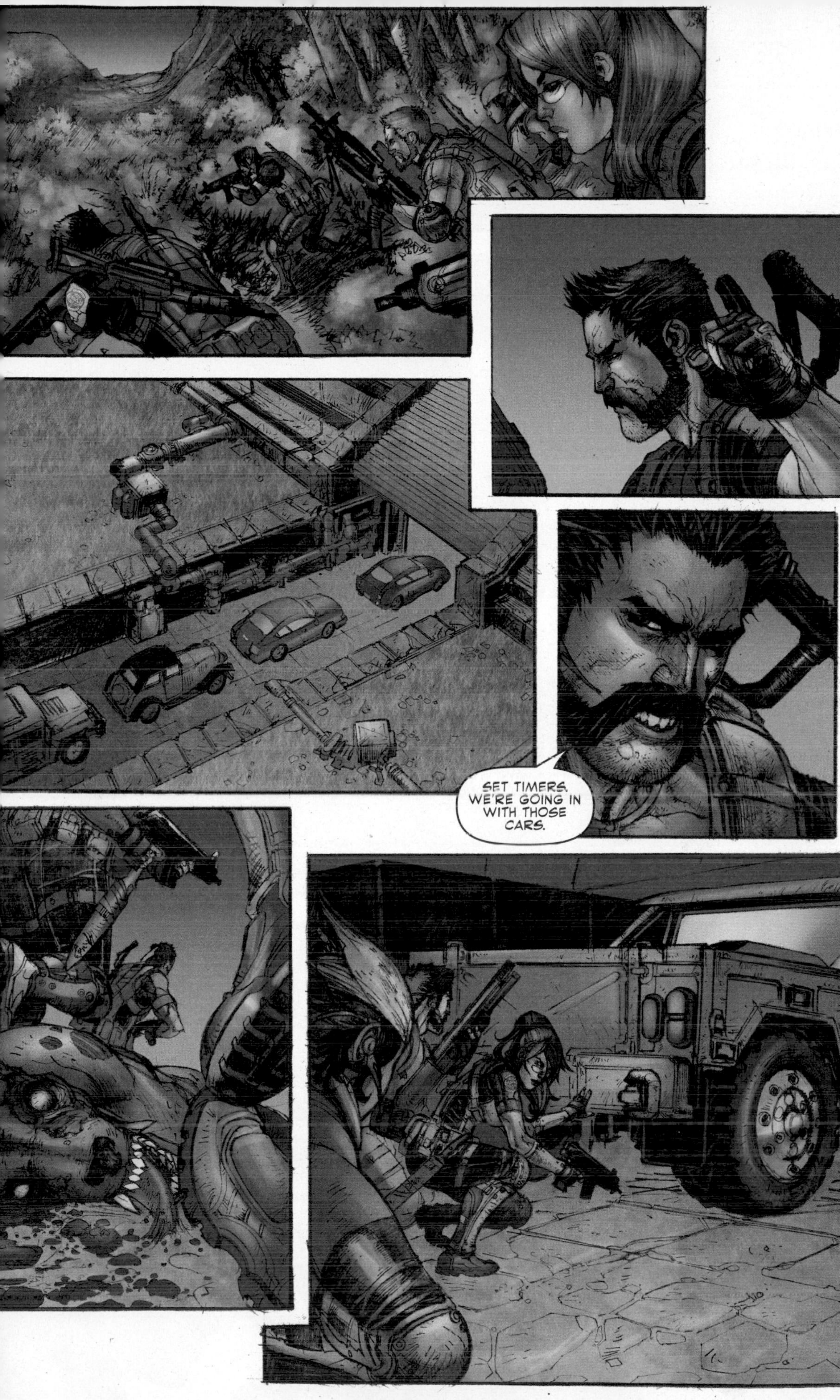
SET TIMERS. WE'RE GOING IN WITH THOSE CARS.

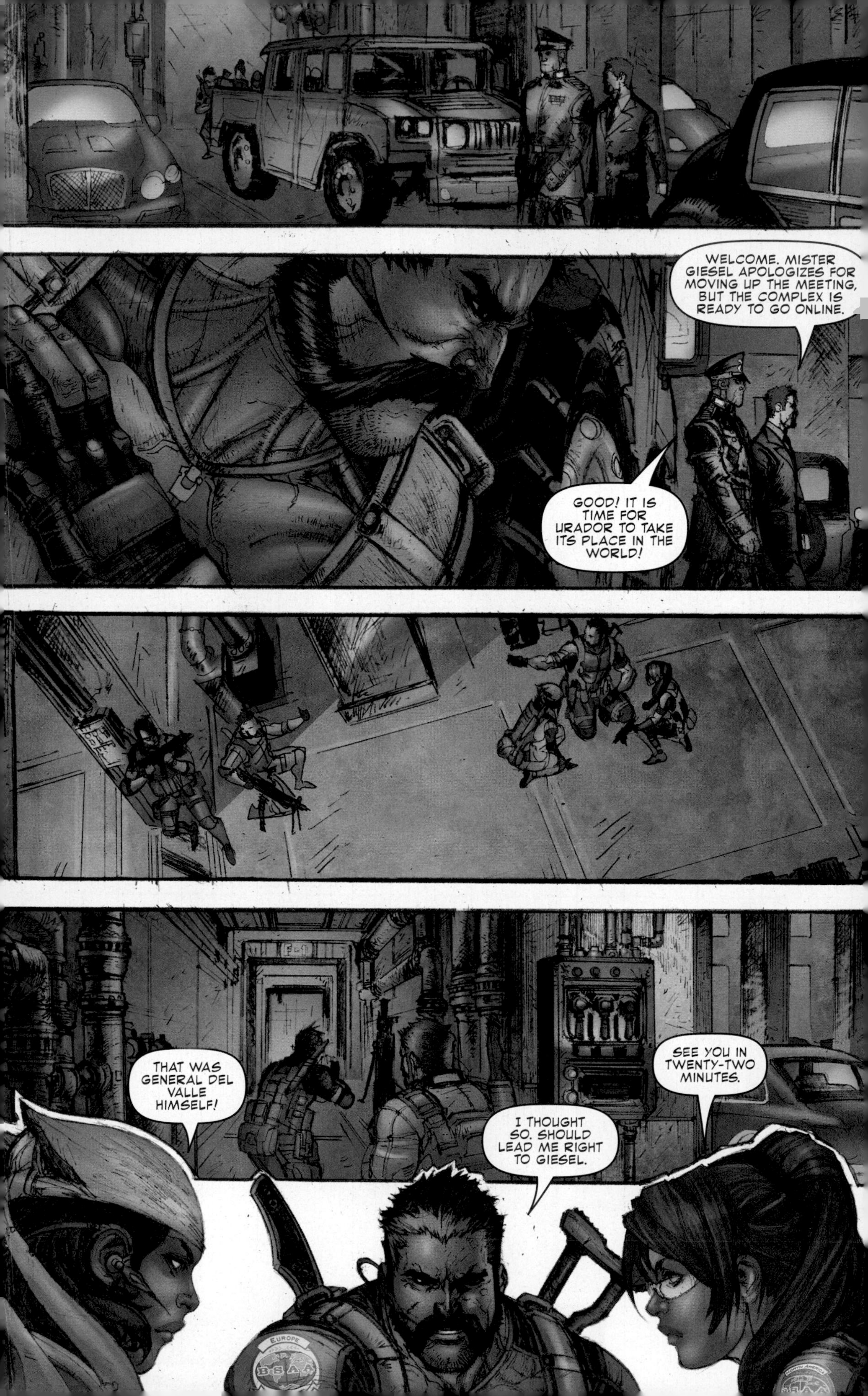
WELCOME. MISTER GIESEL APOLOGIZES FOR MOVING UP THE MEETING, BUT THE COMPLEX IS READY TO GO ONLINE.
GOOD! IT IS TIME FOR URADOR TO TAKE ITS PLACE IN THE WORLD!
THAT WAS GENERAL DEL VALLE HIMSELF!
I THOUGHT SO. SHOULD LEAD ME RIGHT TO GIESEL.
SEE YOU IN TWENTY-TWO MINUTES.
EUROPE
BSAA

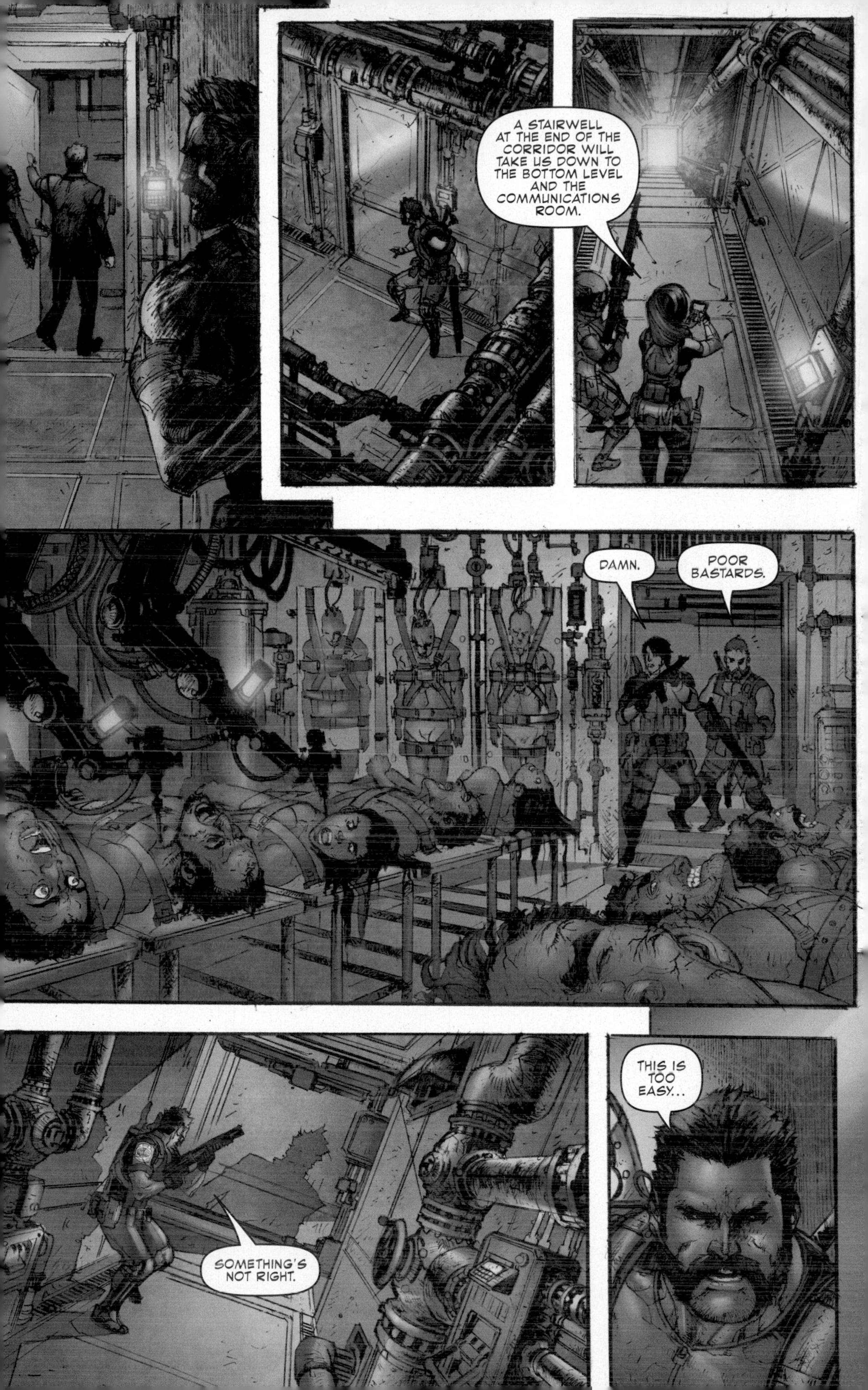
A STAIRWELL AT THE END OF THE CORRIDOR WILL TAKE US DOWN TO THE BOTTOM LEVEL AND THE COMMUNICATIONS ROOM.
DAMN.
POOR BASTARDS.
SOMETHING'S NOT RIGHT.
THIS IS TOO EASY...

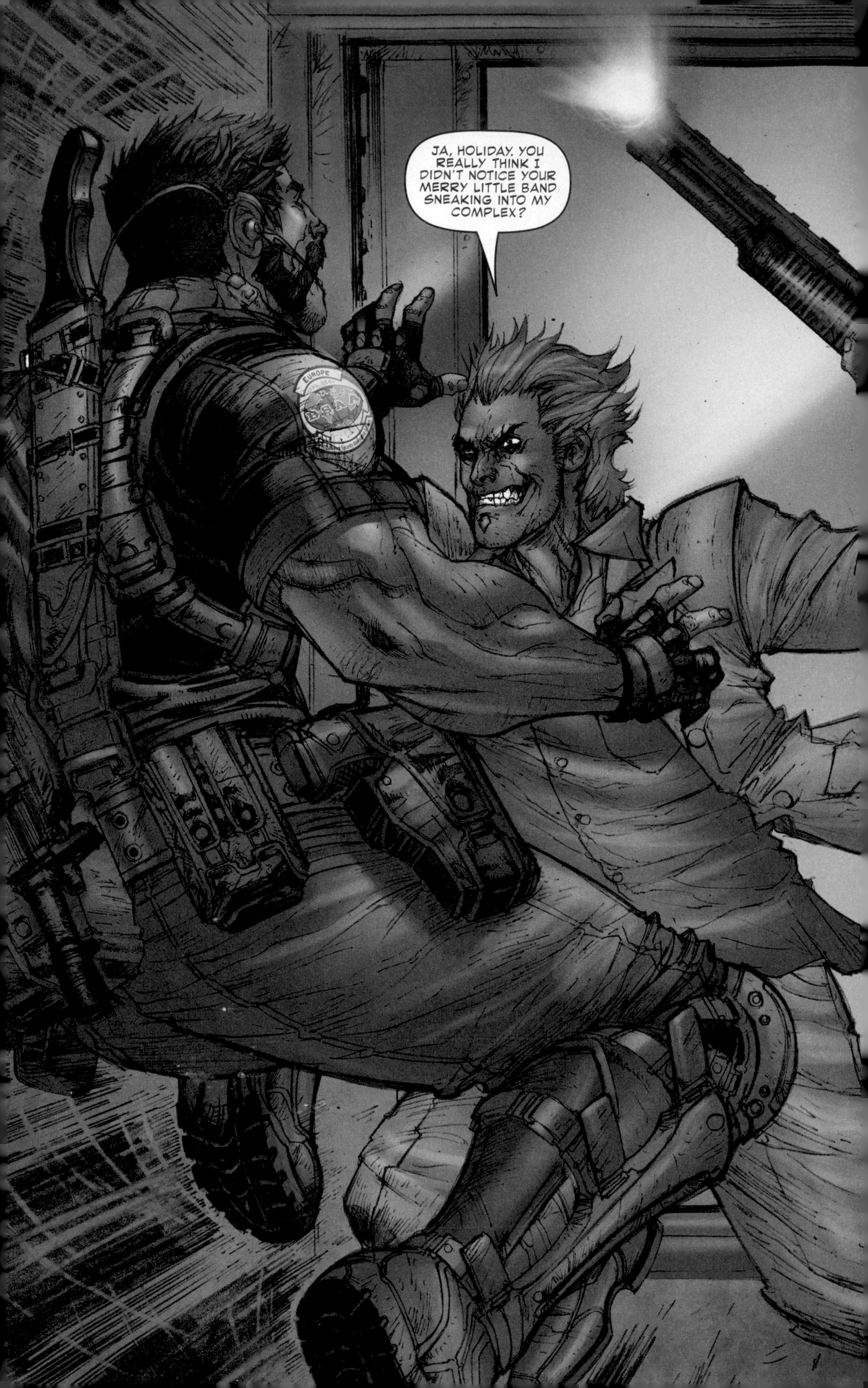
JA, HOLIDAY. YOU REALLY THINK I DIDN'T NOTICE YOUR MERRY LITTLE BAND SNEAKING INTO MY COMPLEX?

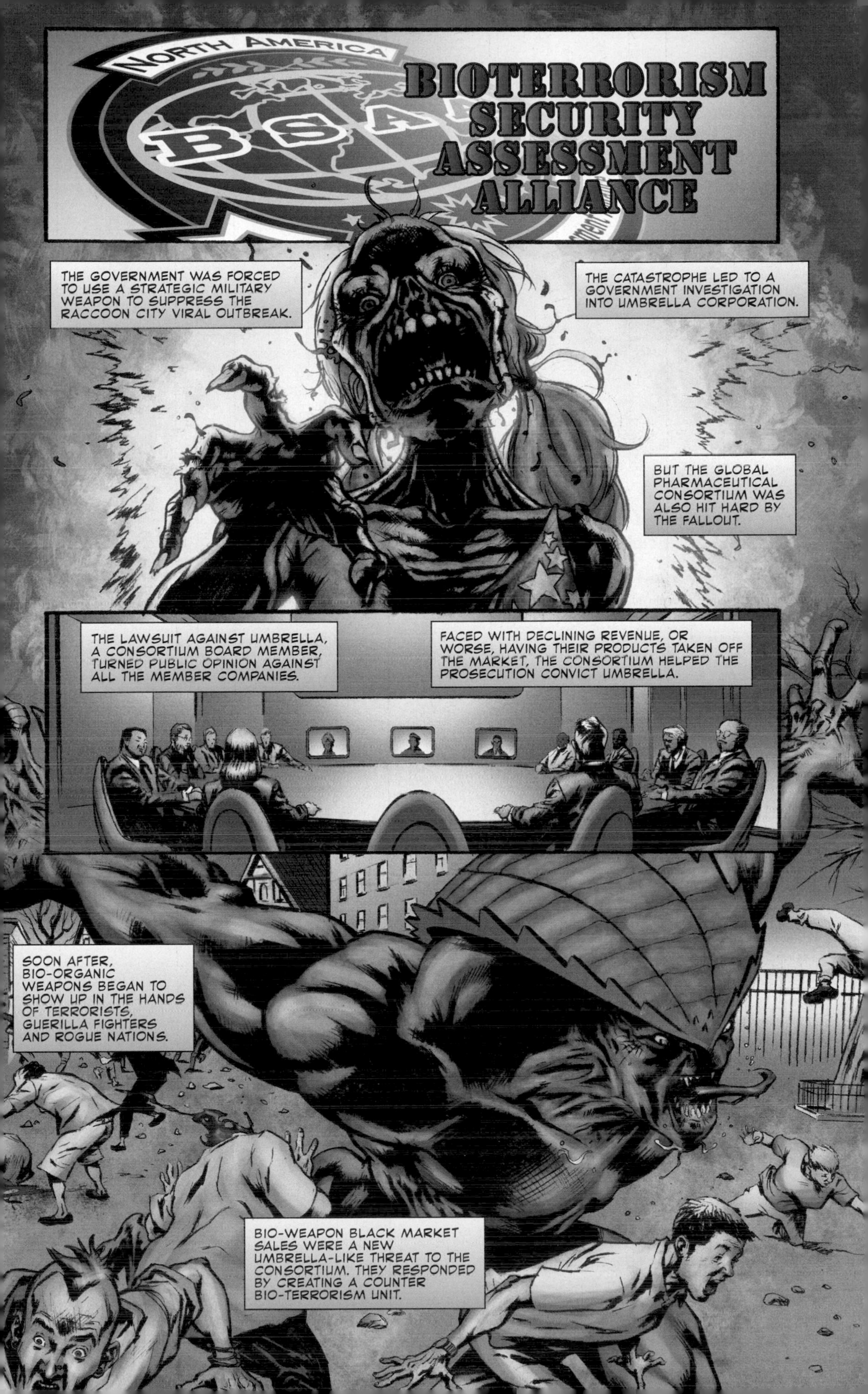
NORTH AMERICA
BSAA
BIOTERRORISM SECURITY ASSESSMENT ALLIANCE
THE GOVERNMENT WAS FORCED TO USE A STRATEGIC MILITARY WEAPON TO SUPPRESS THE RACCOON CITY VIRAL OUTBREAK.
THE CATASTROPHE LED TO A GOVERNMENT INVESTIGATION INTO UMBRELLA CORPORATION.
BUT THE GLOBAL PHARMACEUTICAL CONSORTIUM WAS ALSO HIT HARD BY THE FALLOUT.
THE LAWSUIT AGAINST UMBRELLA, A CONSORTIUM BOARD MEMBER, TURNED PUBLIC OPINION AGAINST ALL THE MEMBER COMPANIES.
FACED WITH DECLINING REVENUE, OR WORSE, HAVING THEIR PRODUCTS TAKEN OFF THE MARKET, THE CONSORTIUM HELPED THE PROSECUTION CONVICT UMBRELLA.
SOON AFTER, BIO-ORGANIC WEAPONS BEGAN TO SHOW UP IN THE HANDS OF TERRORISTS, GUERILLA FIGHTERS AND ROGUE NATIONS.
BIO-WEAPON BLACK MARKET SALES WERE A NEW UMBRELLA-LIKE THREAT TO THE CONSORTIUM. THEY RESPONDED BY CREATING A COUNTER BIO-TERRORISM UNIT.

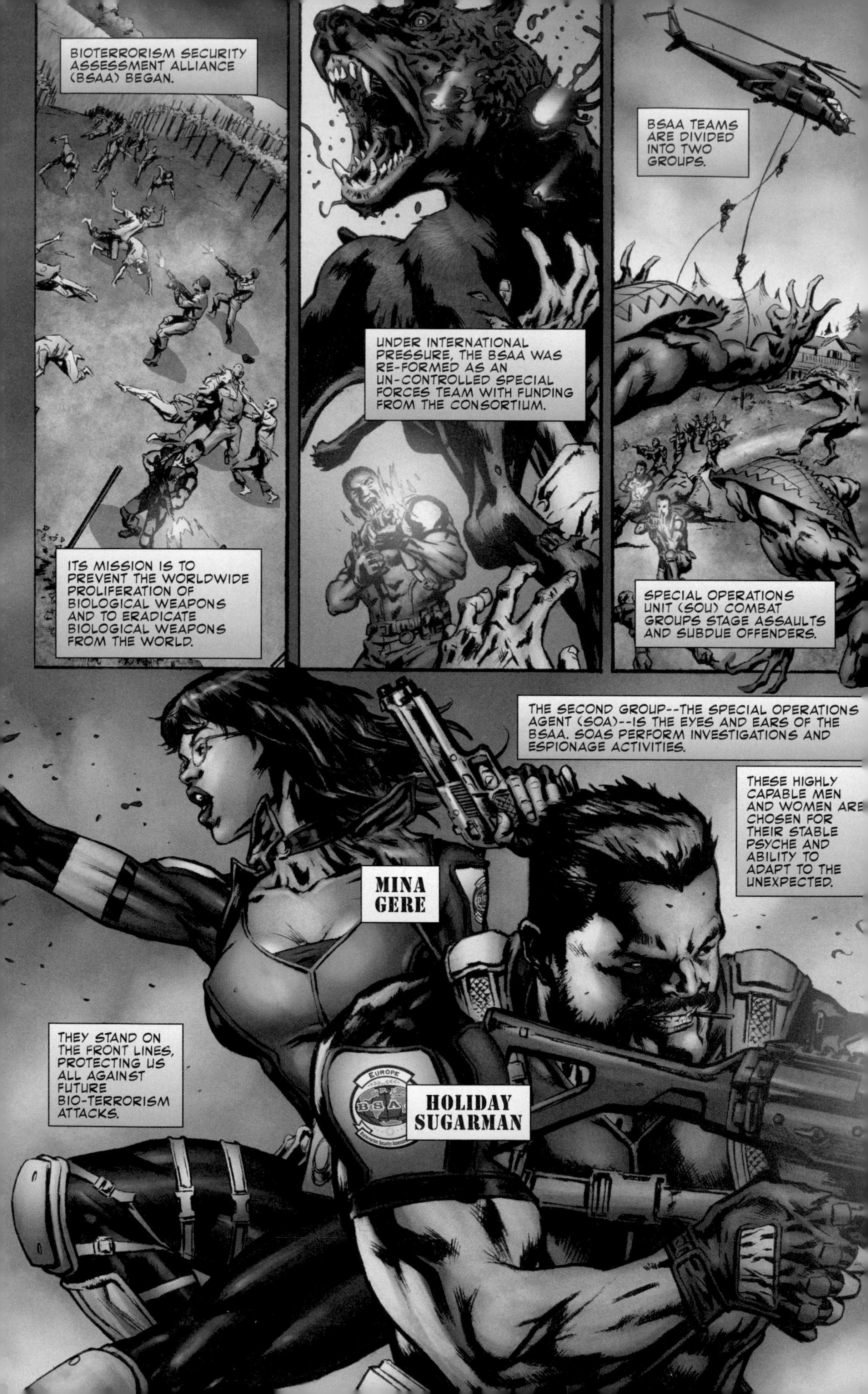
BIOTERRORISM SECURITY ASSESSMENT ALLIANCE (BSAA) BEGAN.
ITS MISSION IS TO PREVENT THE WORLDWIDE PROLIFERATION OF BIOLOGICAL WEAPONS AND TO ERADICATE BIOLOGICAL WEAPONS FROM THE WORLD.
UNDER INTERNATIONAL PRESSURE, THE BSAA WAS RE-FORMED AS AN UN-CONTROLLED SPECIAL FORCES TEAM WITH FUNDING FROM THE CONSORTIUM.
BSAA TEAMS ARE DIVIDED INTO TWO GROUPS.
SPECIAL OPERATIONS UNIT (SOU) COMBAT GROUPS STAGE ASSAULTS AND SUBDUE OFFENDERS.
THE SECOND GROUP--THE SPECIAL OPERATIONS AGENT (SOA)--IS THE EYES AND EARS OF THE BSAA. SOAS PERFORM INVESTIGATIONS AND ESPIONAGE ACTIVITIES.
THESE HIGHLY CAPABLE MEN AND WOMEN ARE CHOSEN FOR THEIR STABLE PSYCHE AND ABILITY TO ADAPT TO THE UNEXPECTED.
MINA GERE
THEY STAND ON THE FRONT LINES, PROTECTING US ALL AGAINST FUTURE BIO-TERRORISM ATTACKS.
EUROPE
BSAA
HOLIDAY SUGARMAN

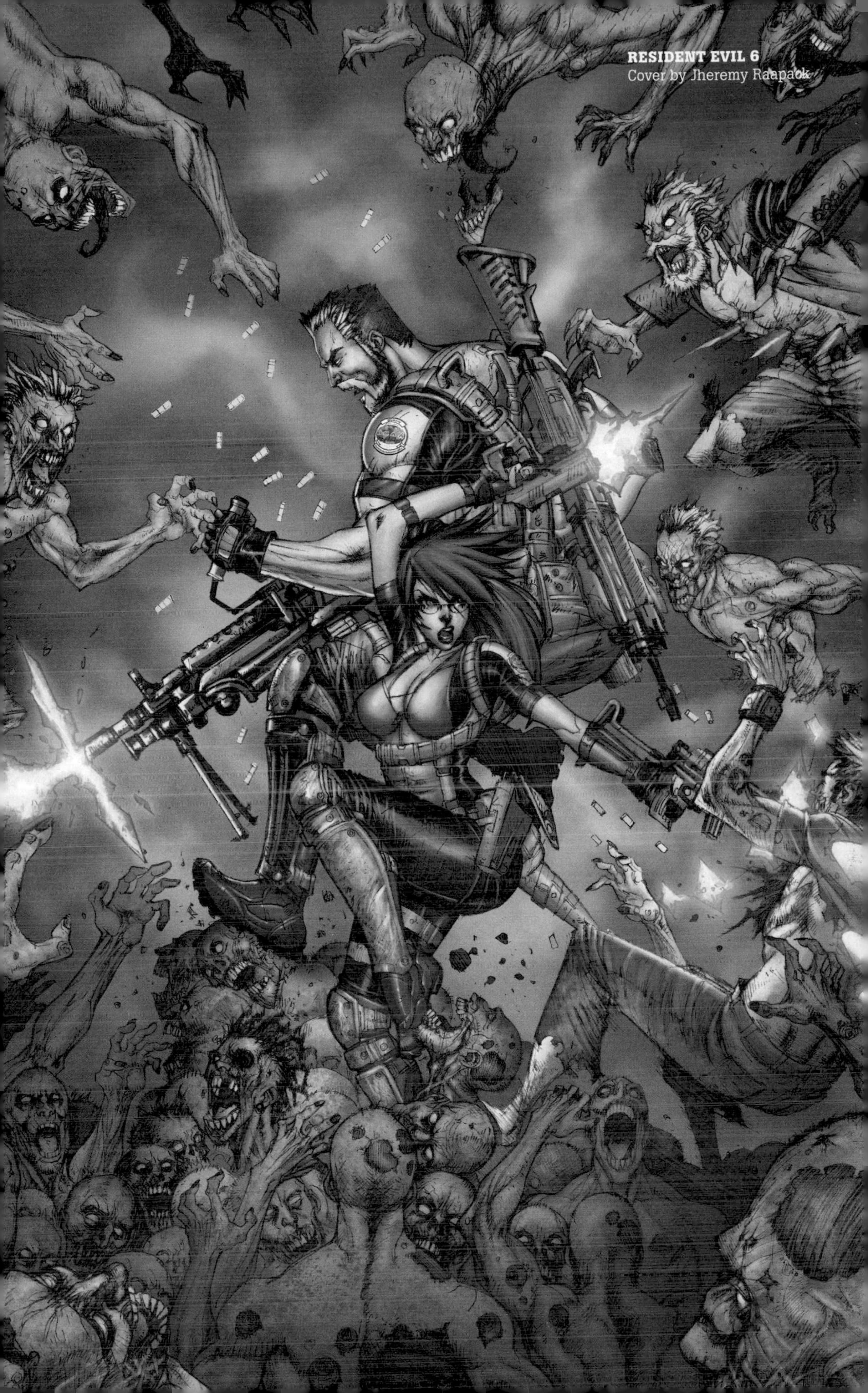

RESIDENT EVIL 6
Cover by Jheremy Raapack

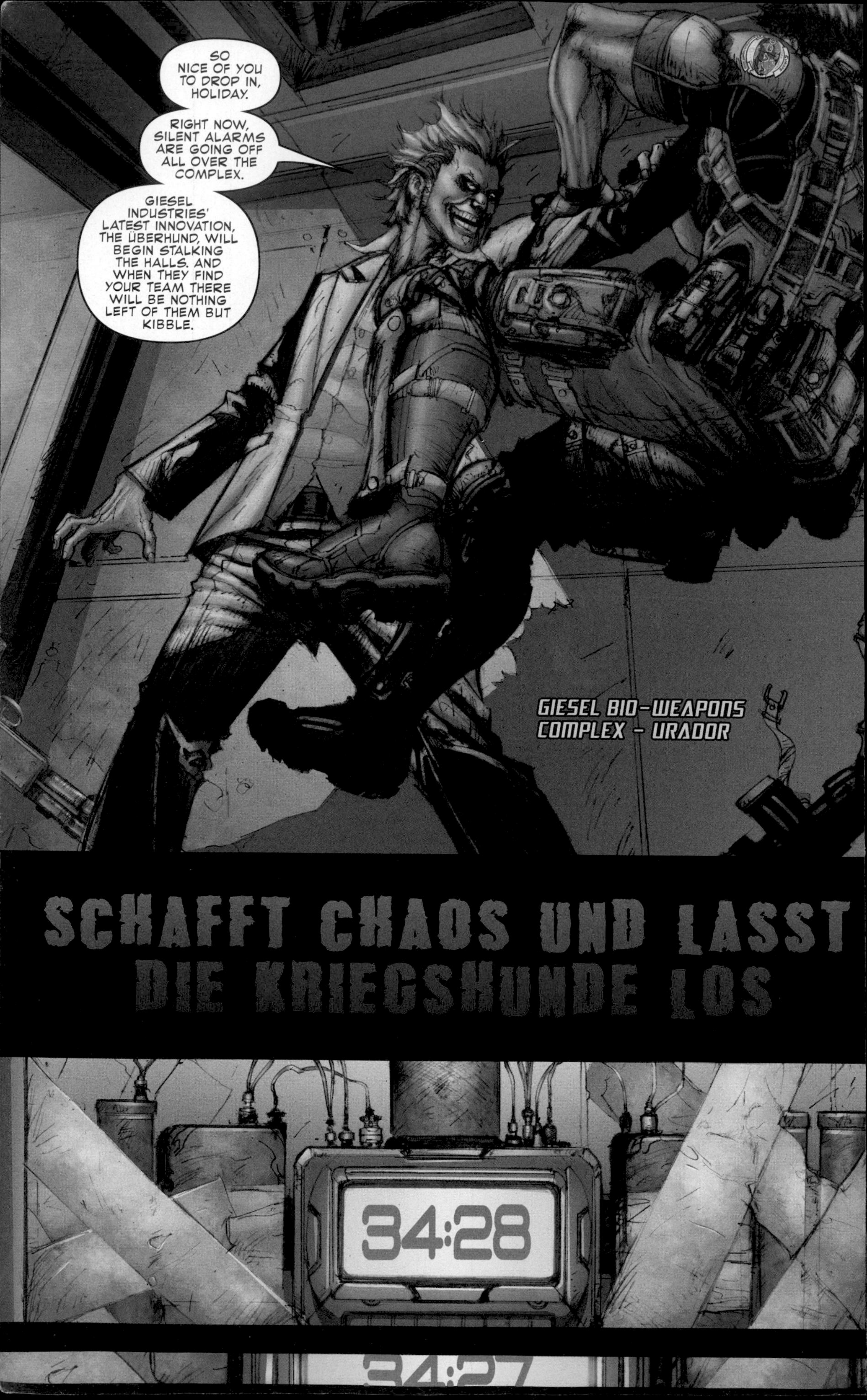
SO NICE OF YOU TO DROP IN, HOLIDAY.
RIGHT NOW, SILENT ALARMS ARE GOING OFF ALL OVER THE COMPLEX.
GIESEL INDUSTRIES' LATEST INNOVATION, THE ÜBERHUND, WILL BEGIN STALKING THE HALLS. AND WHEN THEY FIND YOUR TEAM THERE WILL BE NOTHING LEFT OF THEM BUT KIBBLE.
GIESEL BIO-WEAPONS COMPLEX - URADOR
SCHAFFT CHAOS UND LASST DIE KRIEGSHUNDE LOS
34:28

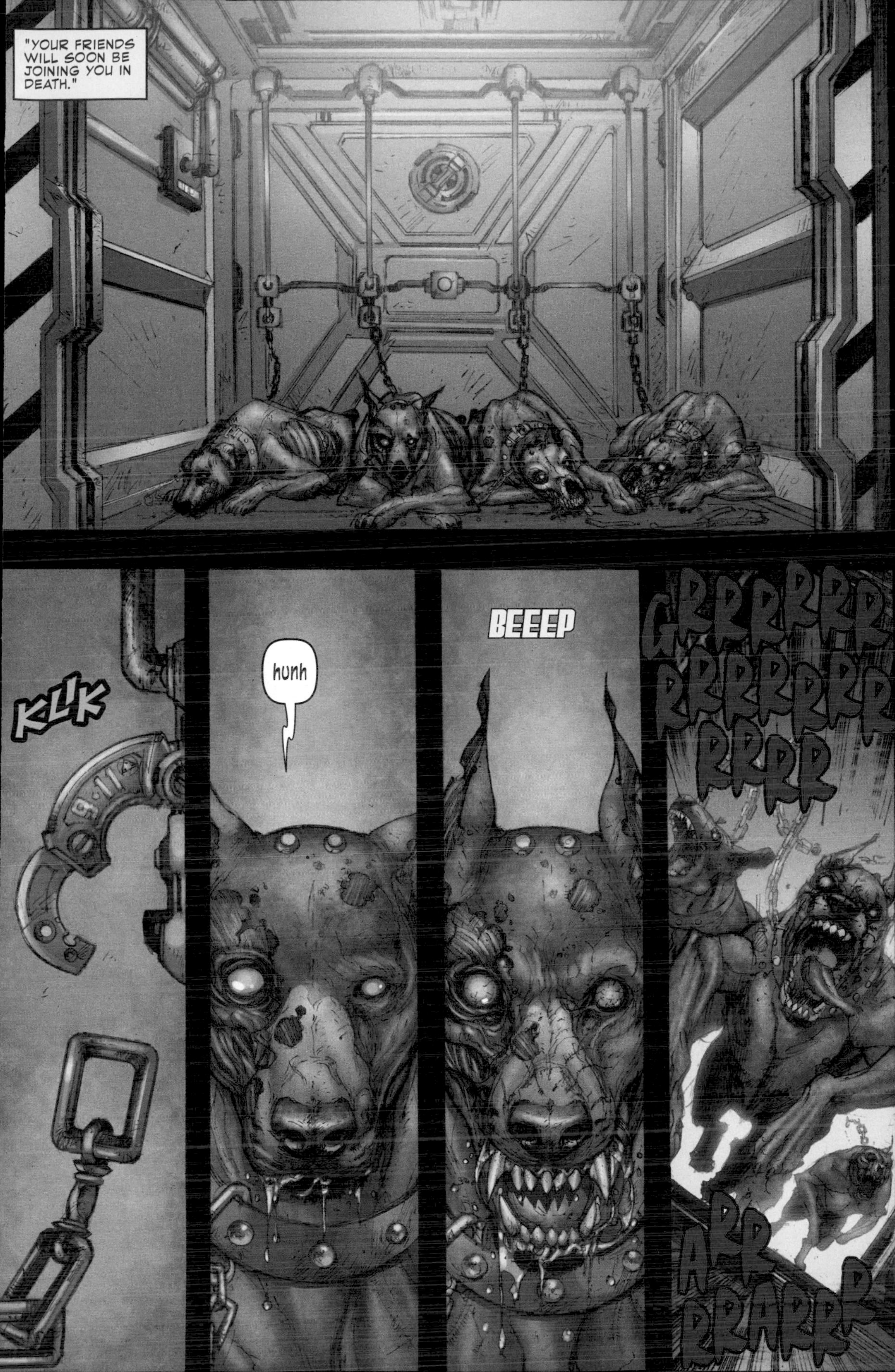
"YOUR FRIENDS WILL SOON BE JOINING YOU IN DEATH."
KLIK
hunh
BEEEP
GRRRRRR RRRRRRR RRRR
ARR RRARRR

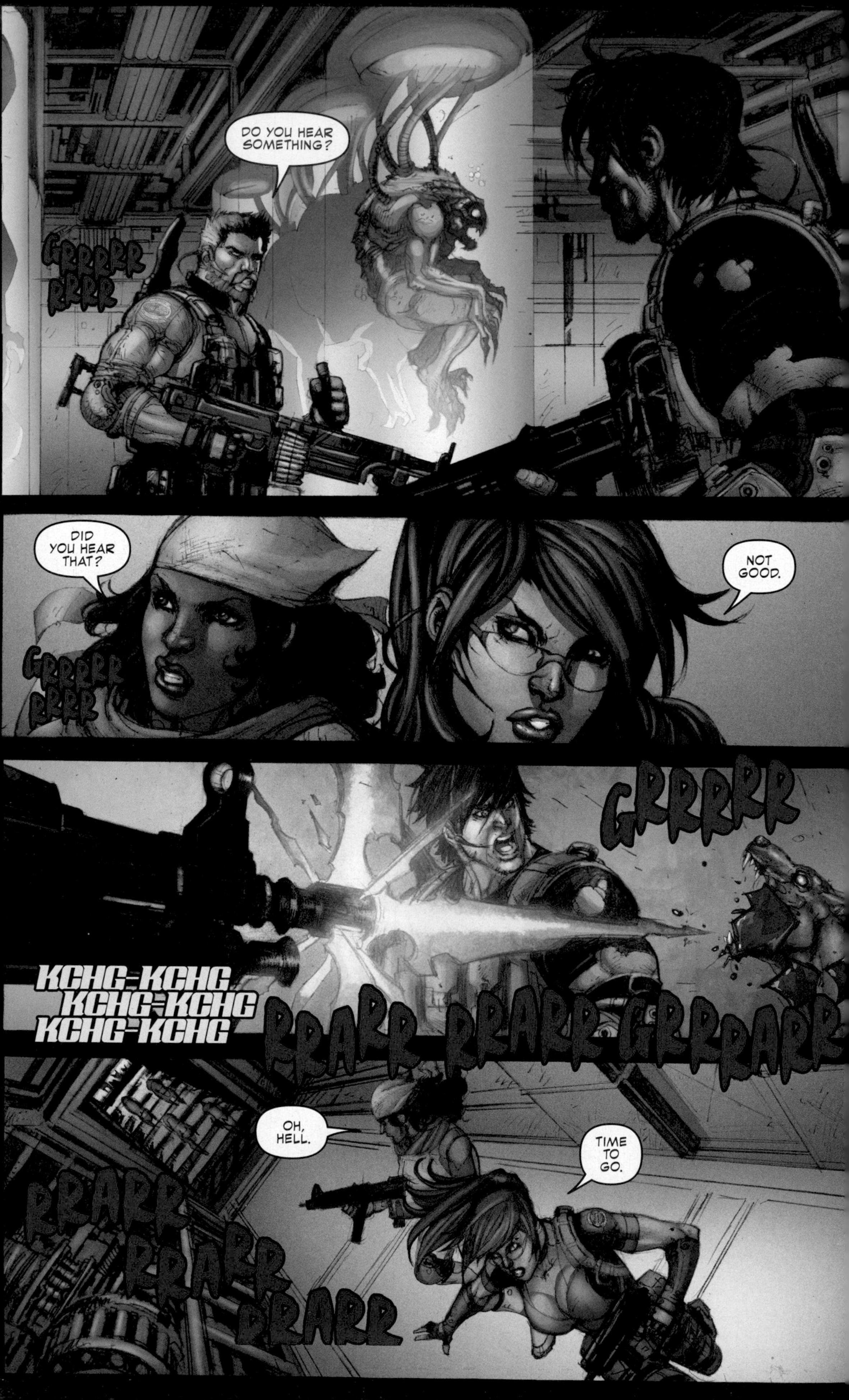
DO YOU HEAR SOMETHING?
GRRRRR RRRR
DID YOU HEAR THAT?
NOT GOOD.
GRRRRR RRRR
GRRRRR
KCHG-KCHG KCHG-KCHG KCHG-KCHG
RRARR RRARR GRRRARR
OH, HELL.
TIME TO GO.
RRARR RRARR RRARR

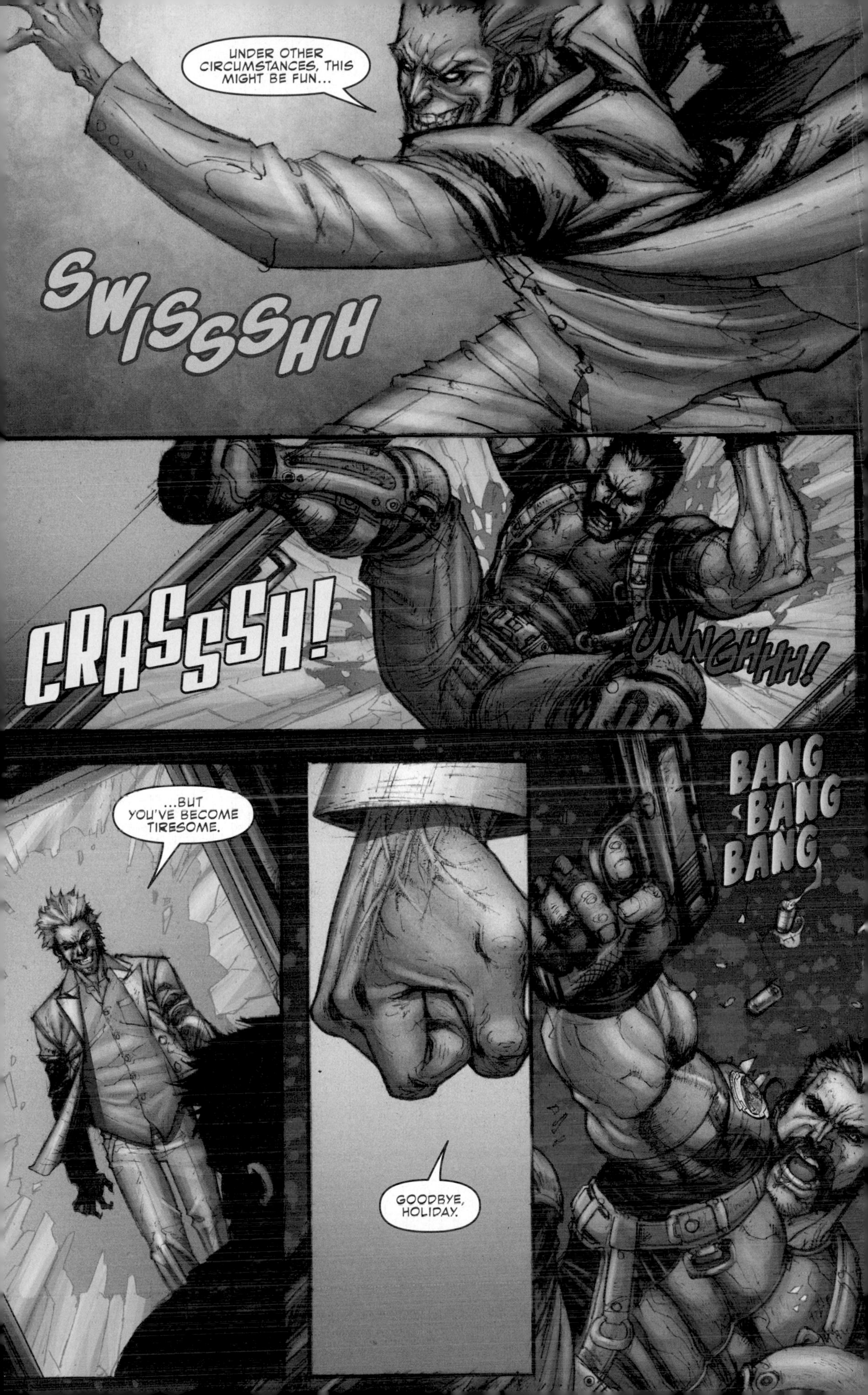
UNDER OTHER CIRCUMSTANCES, THIS MIGHT BE FUN...
SWISSSHH
CRASSSH!
UNNGHHH!
...BUT YOU'VE BECOME TIRESOME.
BANG BANG BANG
GOODBYE, HOLIDAY.

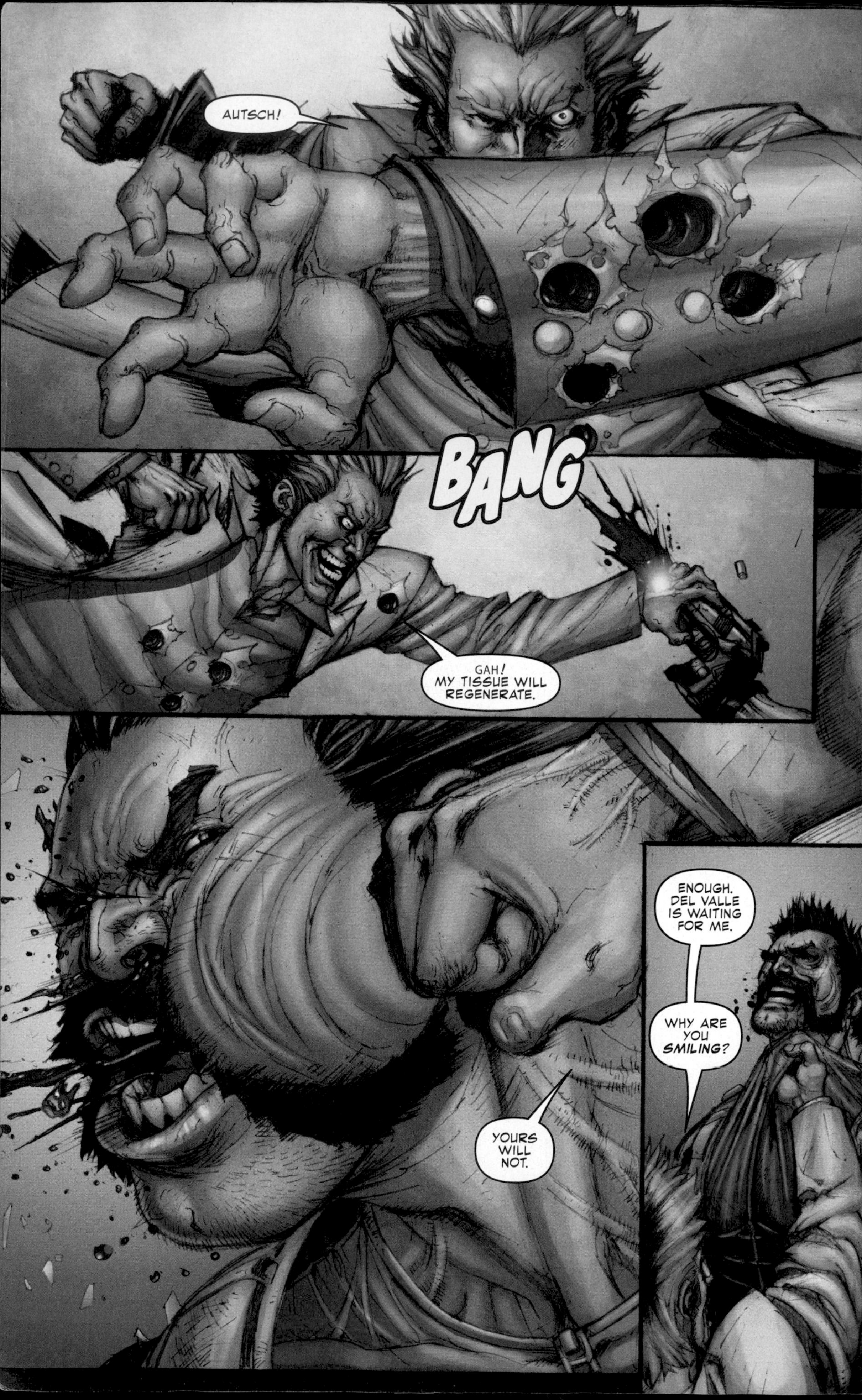
AUTSCH!
BANG
GAH! MY TISSUE WILL REGENERATE.
YOURS WILL NOT.
ENOUGH. DEL VALLE IS WAITING FOR ME.
WHY ARE YOU SMILING?

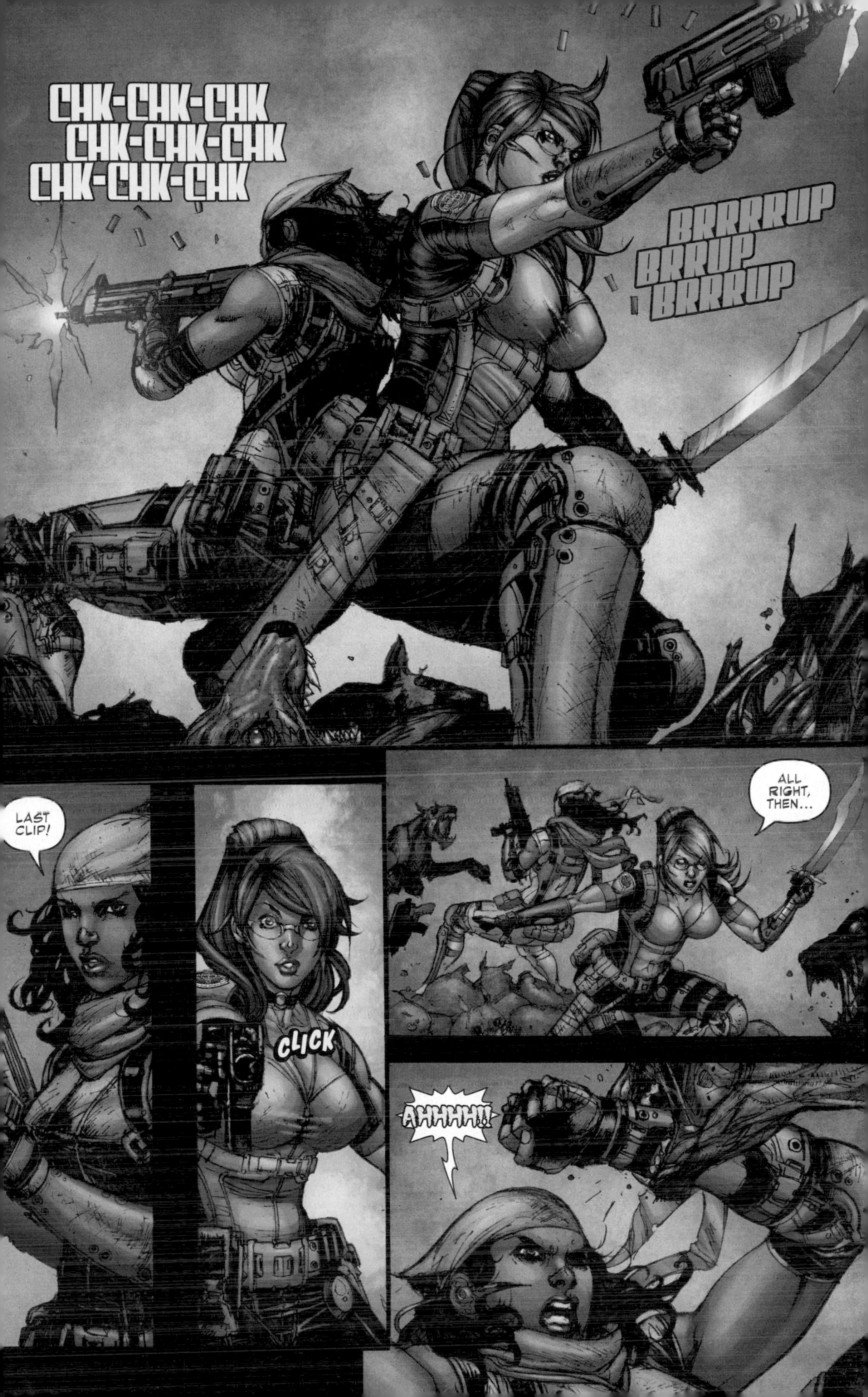
CHK-CHK-CHK
CHK-CHK-CHK
CHK-CHK-CHK
BRRRRUP
BRRUP
BRRRUP
LAST CLIP!
CLICK
ALL RIGHT, THEN...
AHHHHH!!

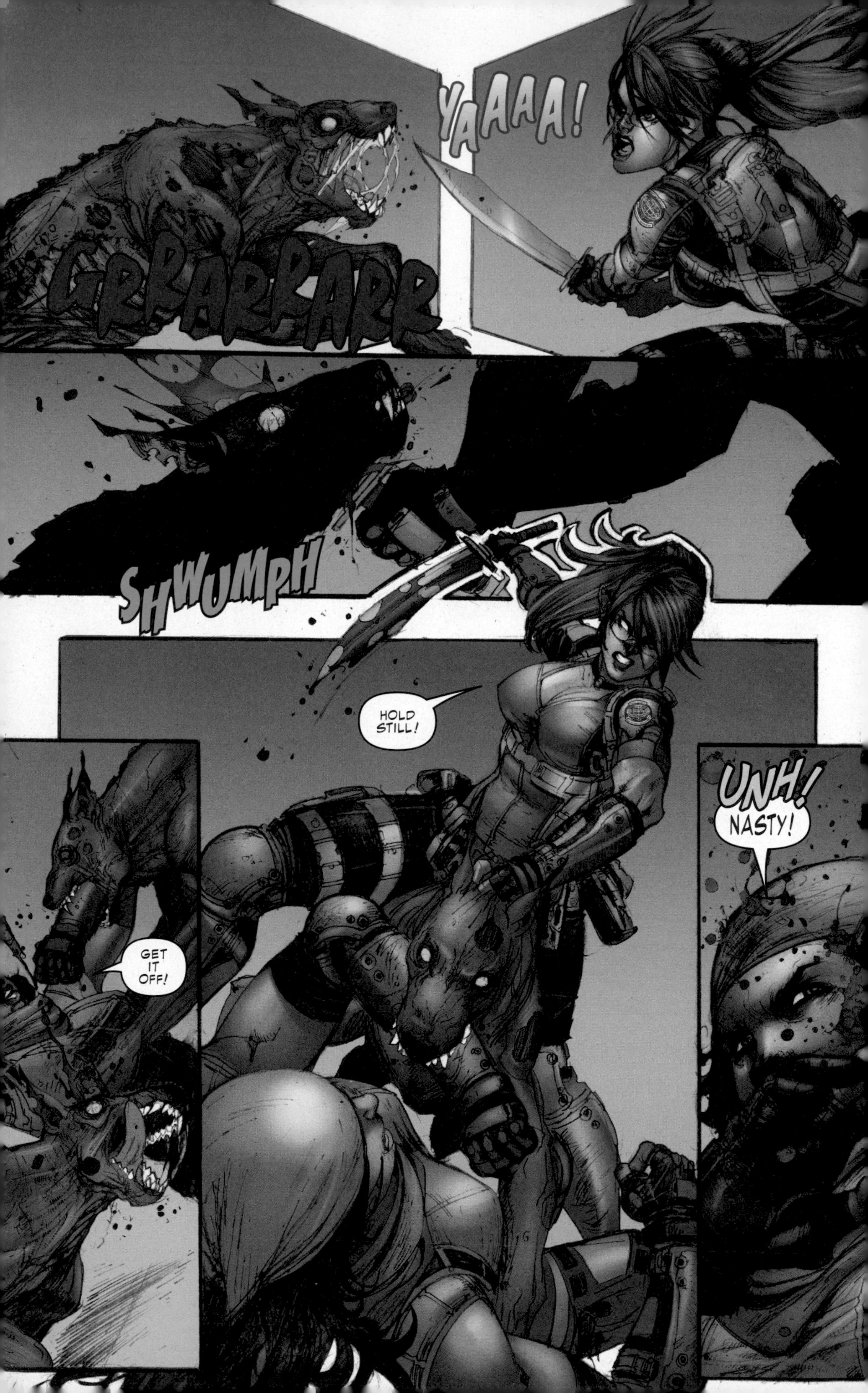
YAAAA!
GRRARRARR
SHWUMPH
HOLD STILL!
GET IT OFF!
UNH!
NASTY!

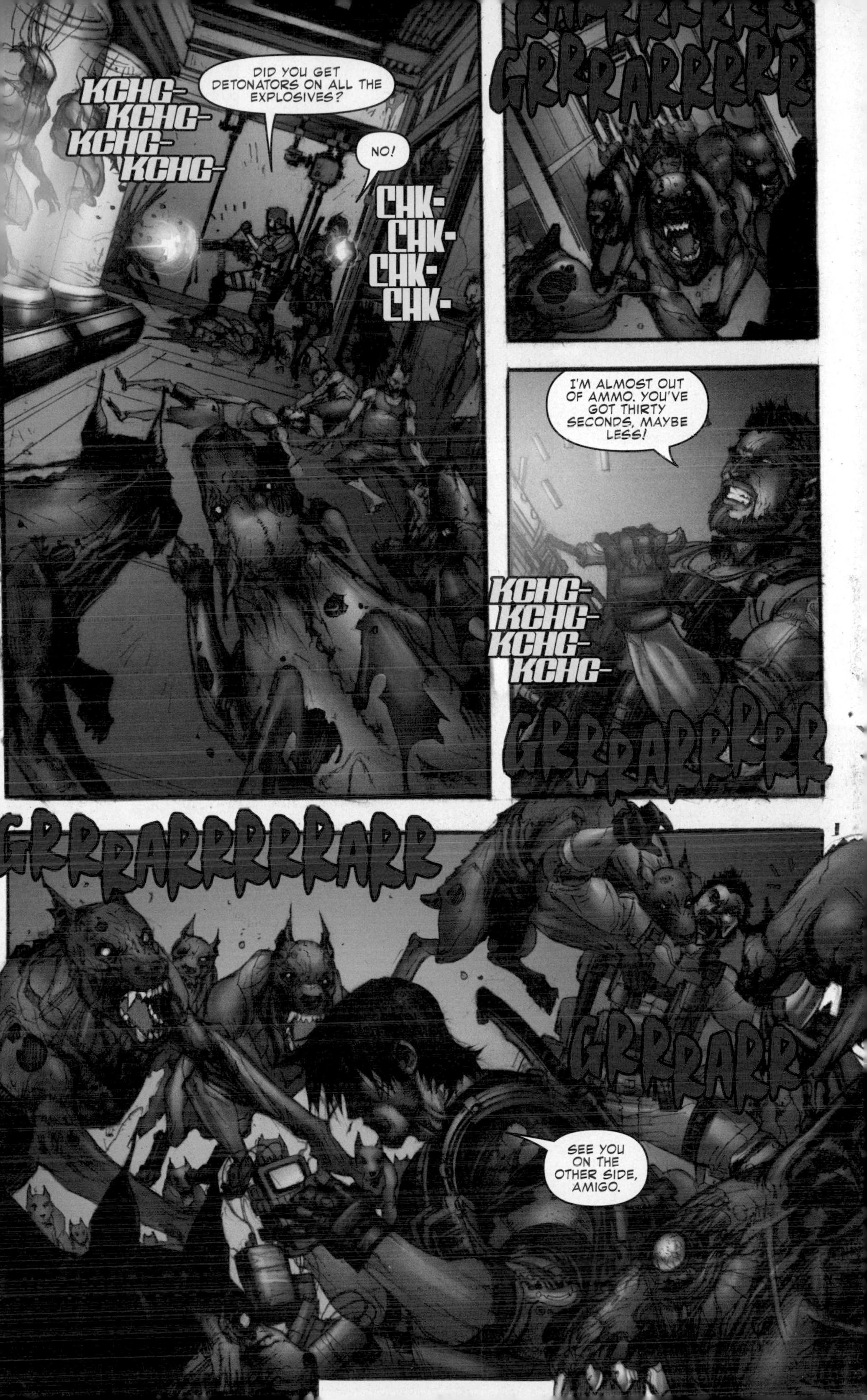
KCHG- KCHG- KCHG- KCHG-
DID YOU GET DETONATORS ON ALL THE EXPLOSIVES?
NO!
CHK- CHK- CHK- CHK-
GRRRARRRRR
I'M ALMOST OUT OF AMMO. YOU'VE GOT THIRTY SECONDS, MAYBE LESS!
KCHG- KCHG- KCHG- KCHG-
GRRRARRRRR
GRRRARRRRRARR
GRRRARR
SEE YOU ON THE OTHER SIDE, AMIGO.

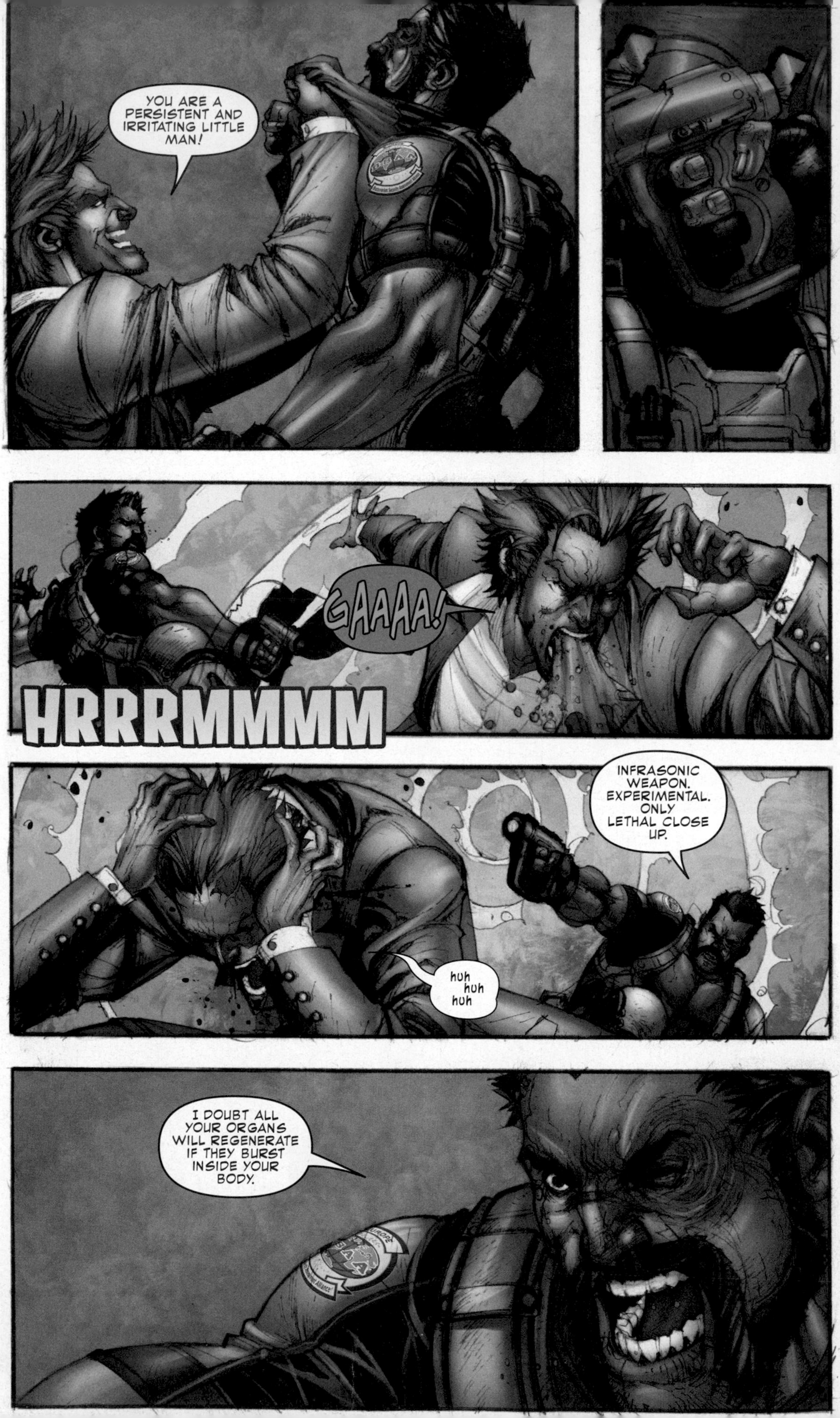

YOU ARE A PERSISTENT AND IRRITATING LITTLE MAN!
GAAAA!
HRRRMMMM
INFRASONIC WEAPON. EXPERIMENTAL. ONLY LETHAL CLOSE UP.
huh huh huh
I DOUBT ALL YOUR ORGANS WILL REGENERATE IF THEY BURST INSIDE YOUR BODY.

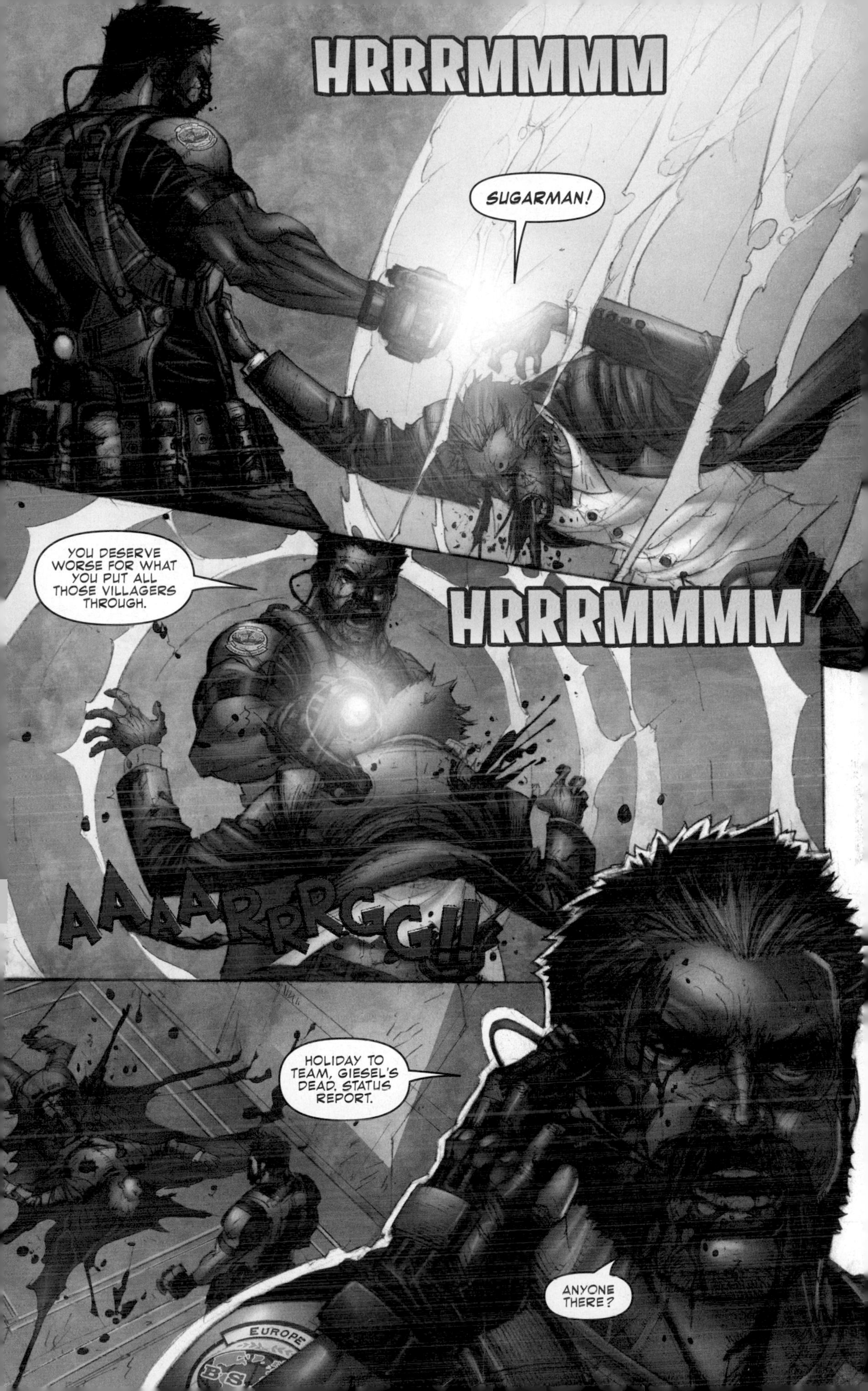

HRRRMMMM
SUGARMAN!
YOU DESERVE WORSE FOR WHAT YOU PUT ALL THOSE VILLAGERS THROUGH.
HRRRMMMM
AAAARRRGG!!
HOLIDAY TO TEAM. GIESEL'S DEAD. STATUS REPORT.
ANYONE THERE?
EUROPE

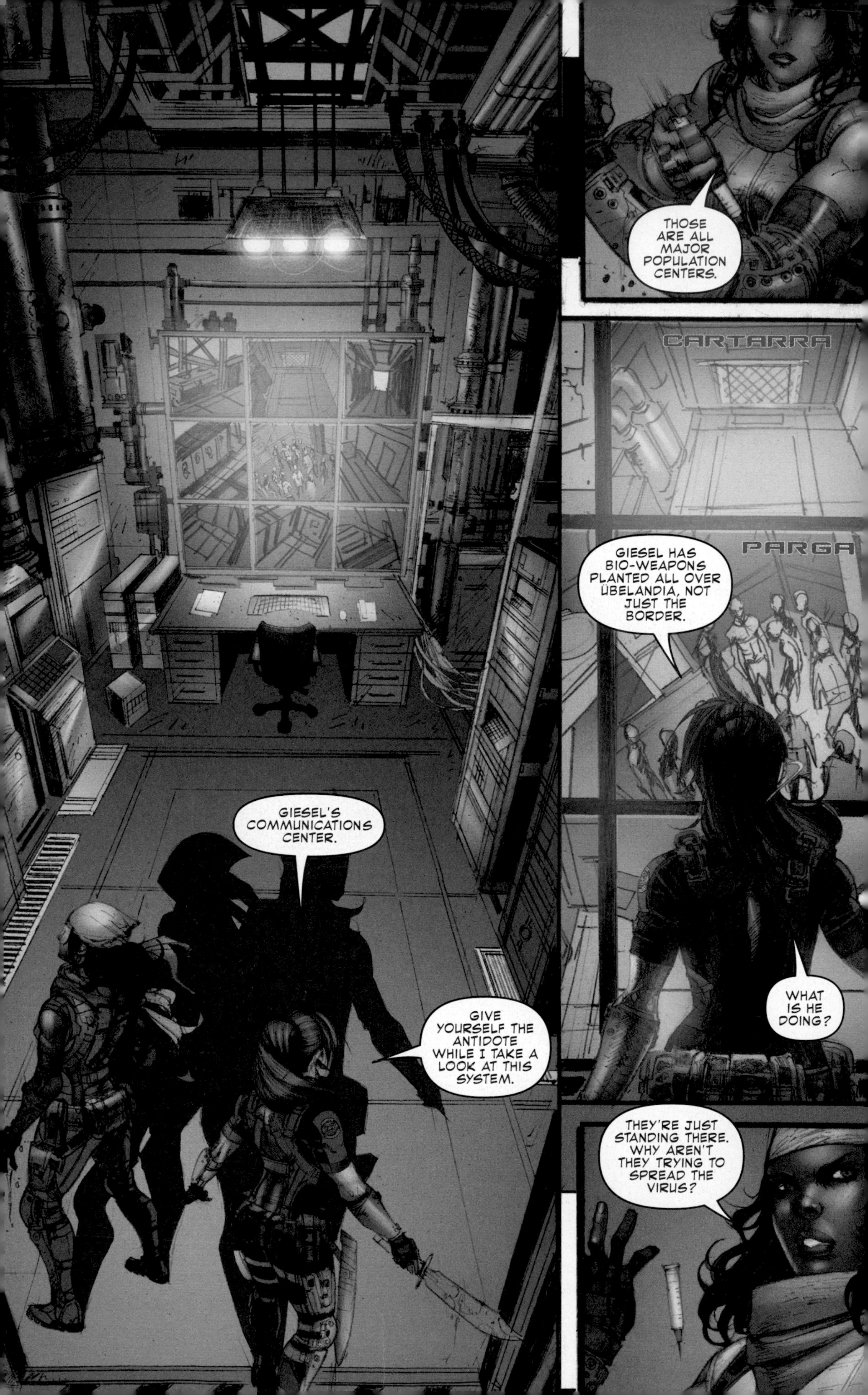
GIESEL'S COMMUNICATIONS CENTER.
GIVE YOURSELF THE ANTIDOTE WHILE I TAKE A LOOK AT THIS SYSTEM.
THOSE ARE ALL MAJOR POPULATION CENTERS.
CARTARRA
PARGA
GIESEL HAS BIO-WEAPONS PLANTED ALL OVER ÜBELANDIA, NOT JUST THE BORDER.
WHAT IS HE DOING?
THEY'RE JUST STANDING THERE. WHY AREN'T THEY TRYING TO SPREAD THE VIRUS?

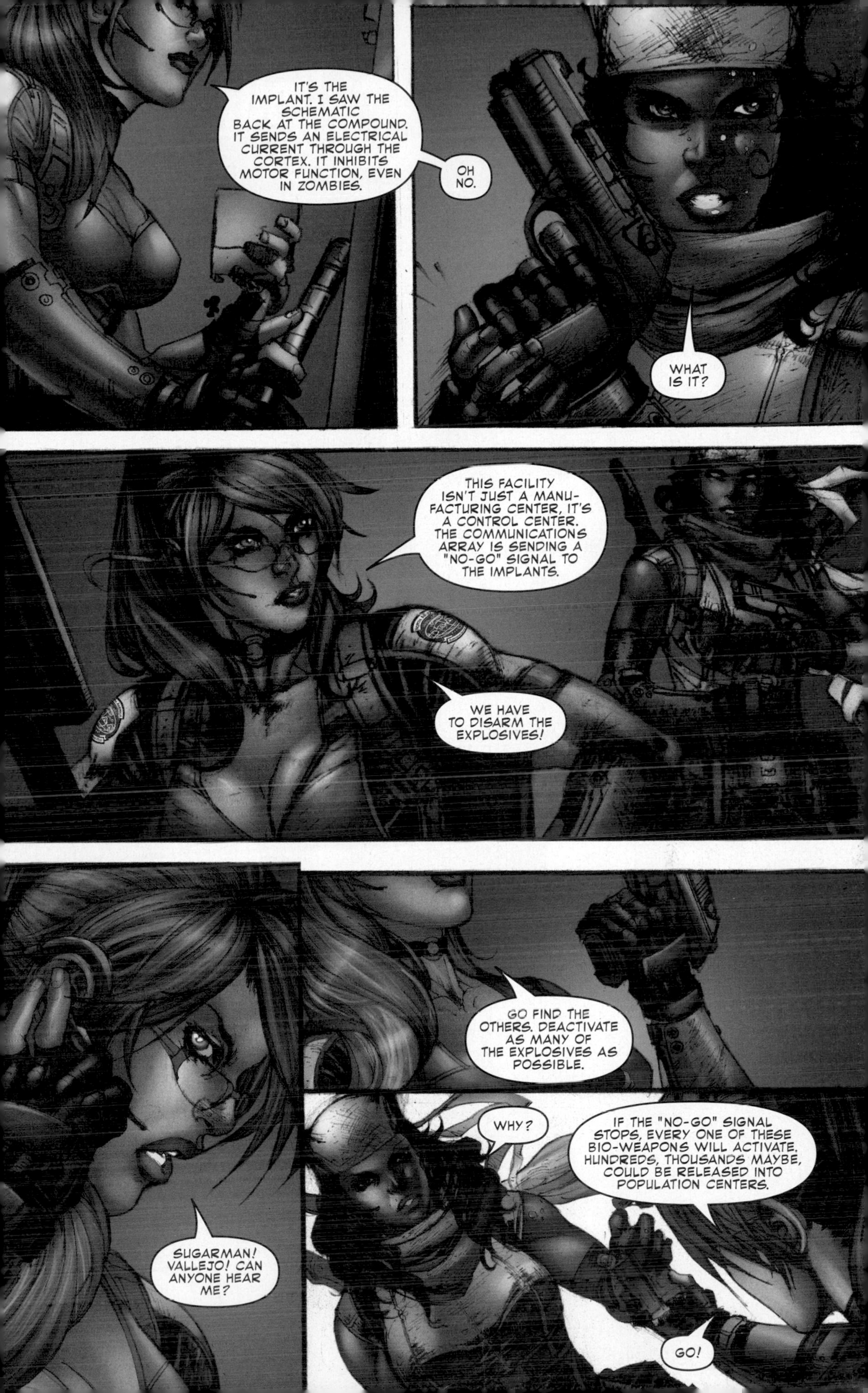

IT'S THE IMPLANT. I SAW THE SCHEMATIC BACK AT THE COMPOUND. IT SENDS AN ELECTRICAL CURRENT THROUGH THE CORTEX. IT INHIBITS MOTOR FUNCTION, EVEN IN ZOMBIES.
OH NO.
WHAT IS IT?
THIS FACILITY ISN'T JUST A MANU-FACTURING CENTER, IT'S A CONTROL CENTER. THE COMMUNICATIONS ARRAY IS SENDING A "NO-GO" SIGNAL TO THE IMPLANTS.
WE HAVE TO DISARM THE EXPLOSIVES!
SUGARMAN! VALLEJO! CAN ANYONE HEAR ME?
GO FIND THE OTHERS. DEACTIVATE AS MANY OF THE EXPLOSIVES AS POSSIBLE.
WHY?
IF THE "NO-GO" SIGNAL STOPS, EVERY ONE OF THESE BIO-WEAPONS WILL ACTIVATE. HUNDREDS, THOUSANDS MAYBE, COULD BE RELEASED INTO POPULATION CENTERS.
GO!

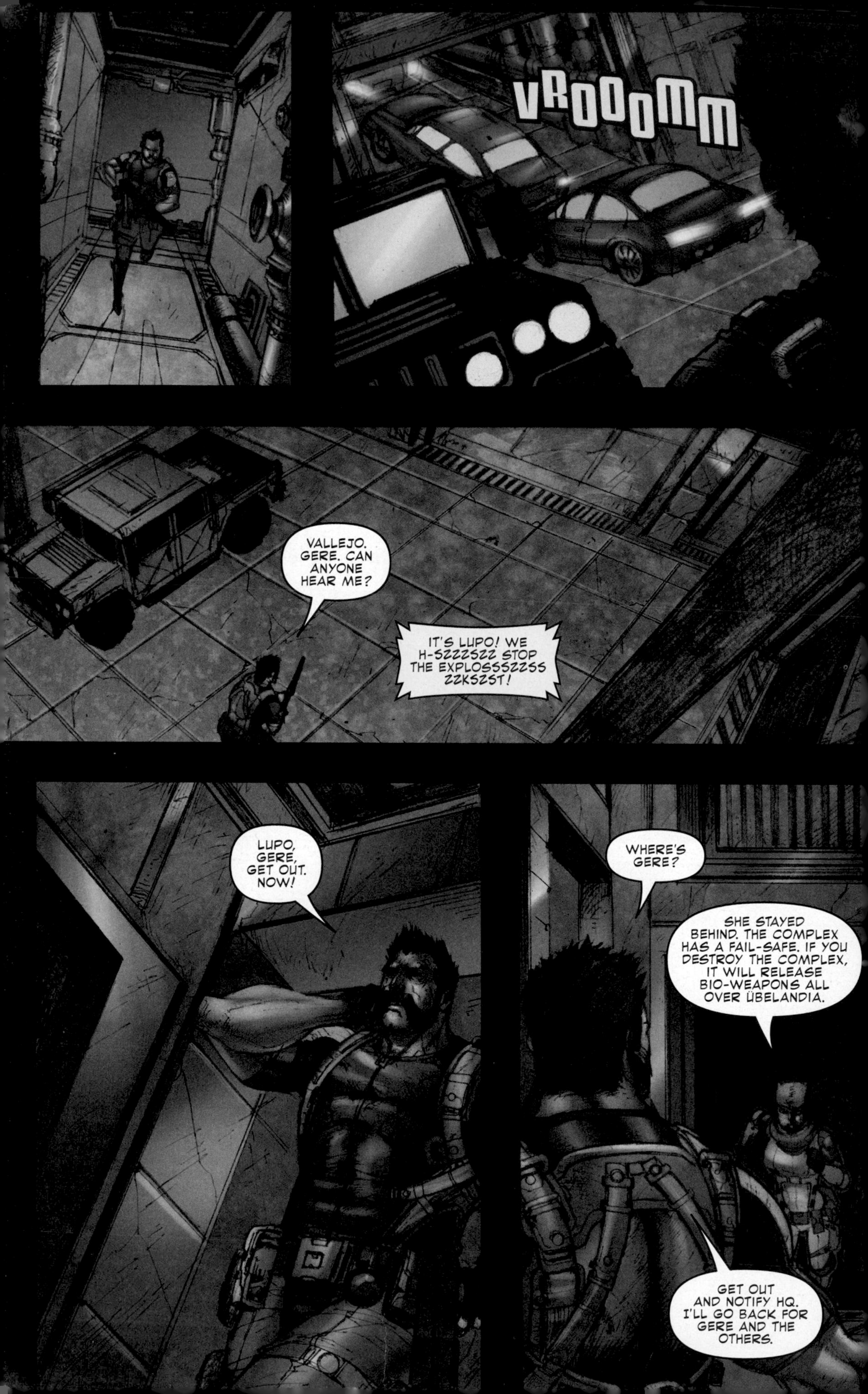
VROOOMM
VALLEJO. GERE. CAN ANYONE HEAR ME?
IT'S LUPO! WE H-SZZZSZZ STOP THE EXPLOSSSZZSS ZZKSZST!
LUPO, GERE, GET OUT. NOW!
WHERE'S GERE?
SHE STAYED BEHIND. THE COMPLEX HAS A FAIL-SAFE. IF YOU DESTROY THE COMPLEX, IT WILL RELEASE BIO-WEAPONS ALL OVER ÜBELANDIA.
GET OUT AND NOTIFY HQ. I'LL GO BACK FOR GERE AND THE OTHERS.

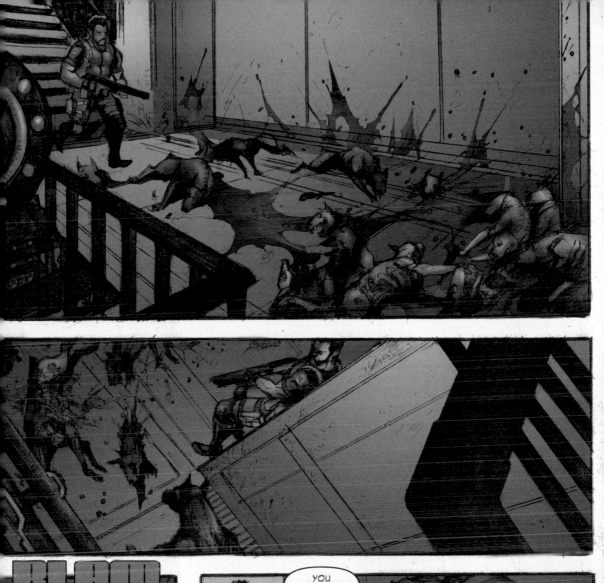

BLAM

YOU SHOULD BE TOPSIDE!

I'M NOT DONE. THE SYSTEM HAS A DEADMAN PROGRAM. I'M TRYING TO CREATE A PERMANENT "NO GO" SIGNAL TO SEND TO THE BIOWEAPONS.

HURRY. I'LL GUARD THE DOOR.

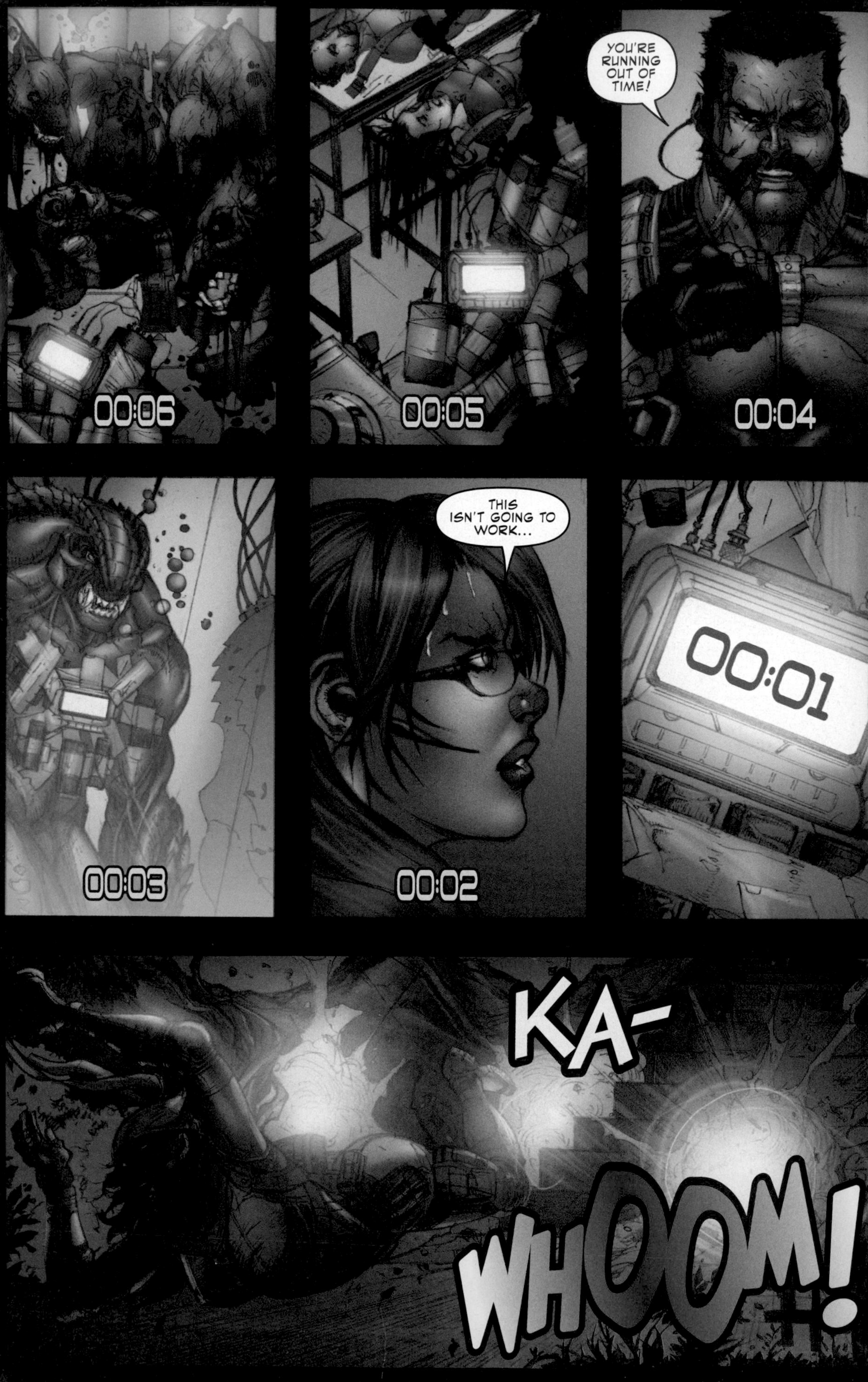
00:06
00:05
YOU'RE RUNNING OUT OF TIME!
00:04
00:03
THIS ISN'T GOING TO WORK...
00:02
00:01
KA-
WHOOM!

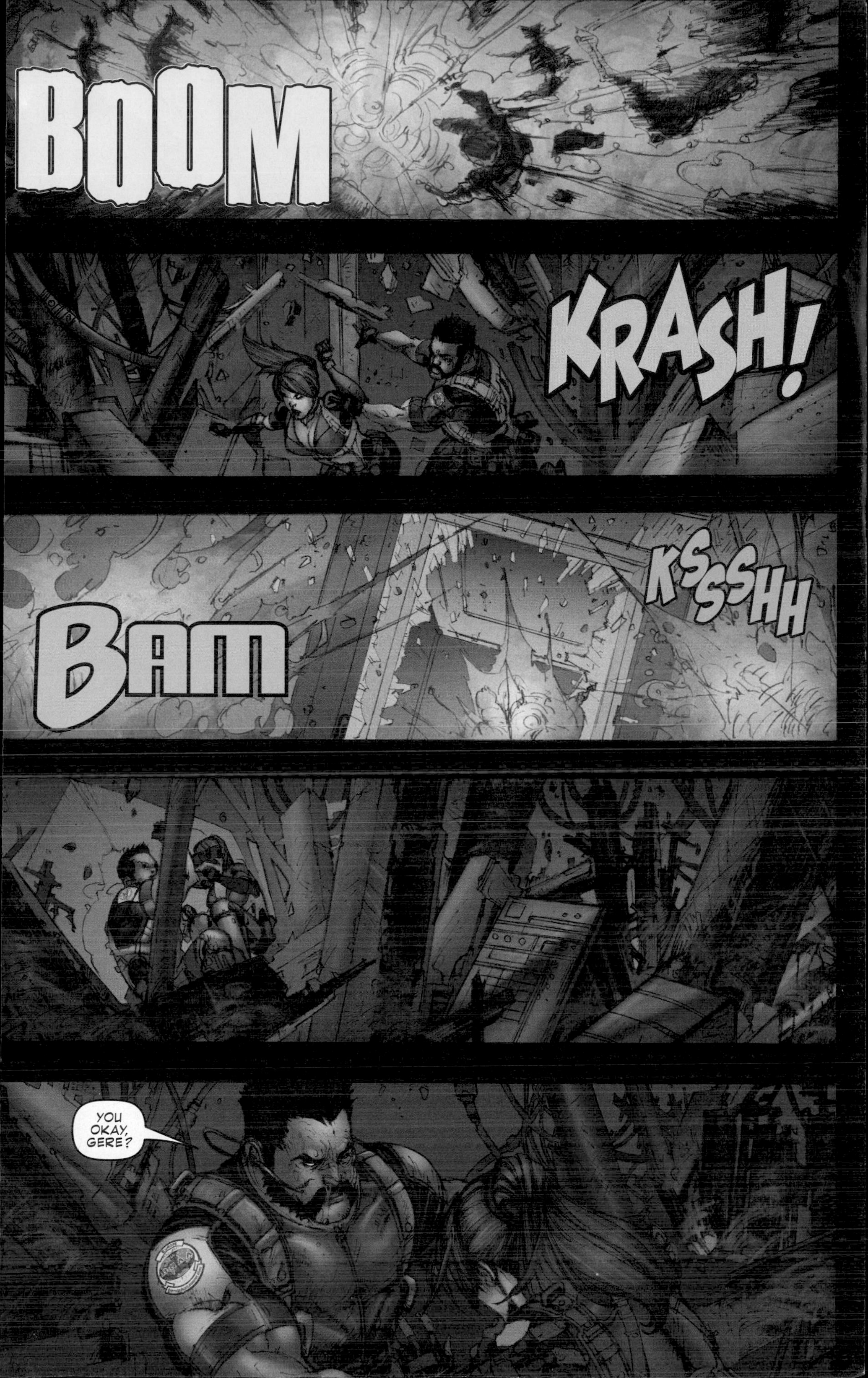
BOOM
KRASH!
BAM
KSSSHH
YOU OKAY, GERE?

GONNA BE A MESS GETTING THROUGH THIS.

UNGH

GERE?

I DID IT.

ROOM IS SPINNING...

YOU CREATED THE NO-GO?

I ACTIVATED THE IMPLANTS. BLEW THE HEAD OFF EACH AND EVERY ONE OF THEM.

HEH. ATTA GIRL. I THINK YOU HAVE A CONCUSSION, BUT YOU'LL LIVE. JUST HAVE TO FIND A WAY OUT OF HERE.

COMMS WON'T WORK. TOO MUCH ROCK.

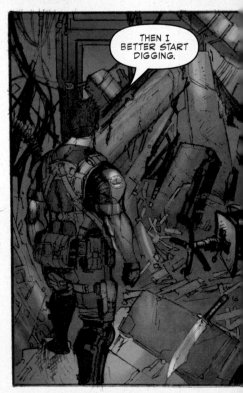

THEN I BETTER START DIGGING.

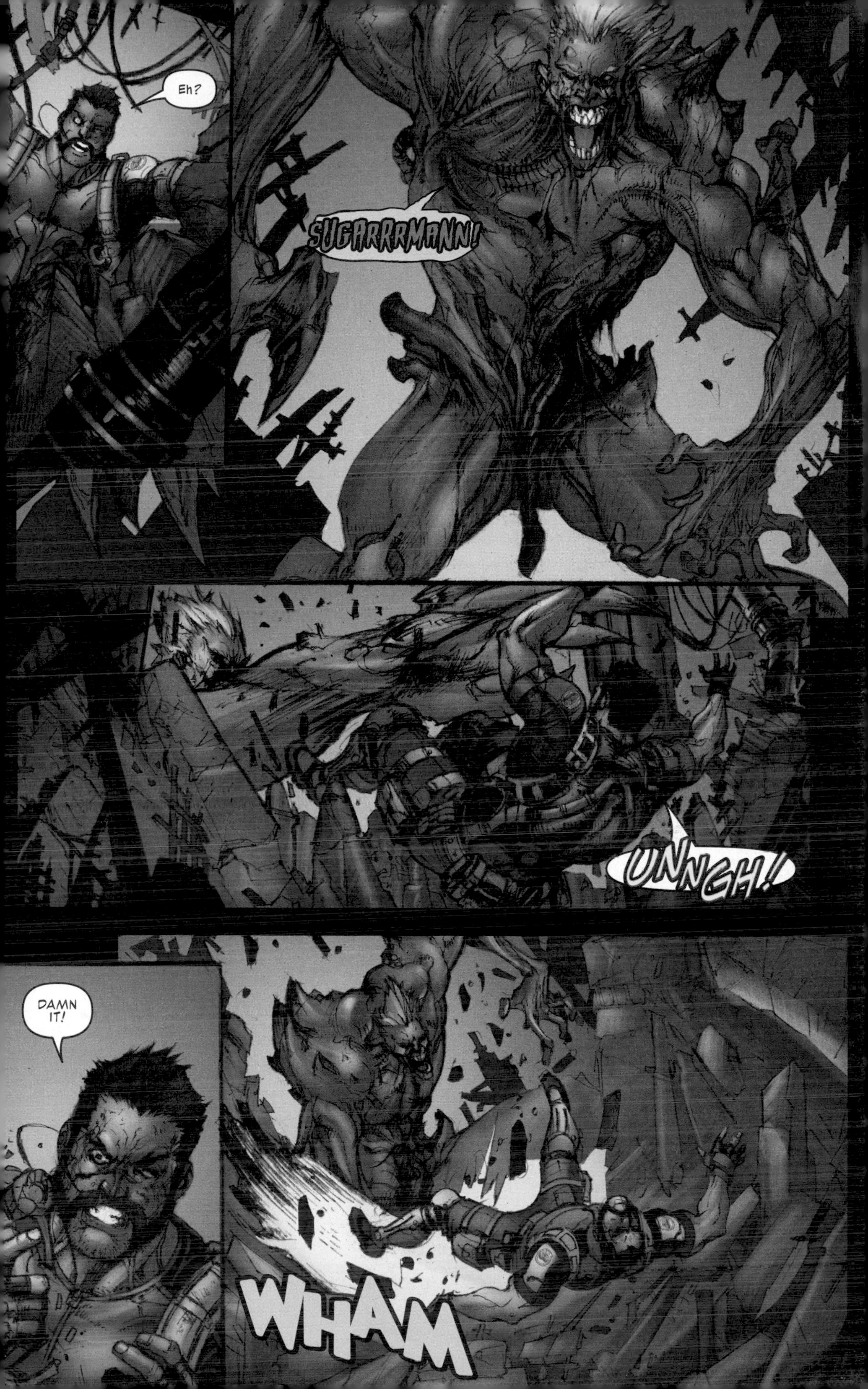
Eh?
SUGARRRMANN!
UNNGH!
DAMN IT!
WHAM

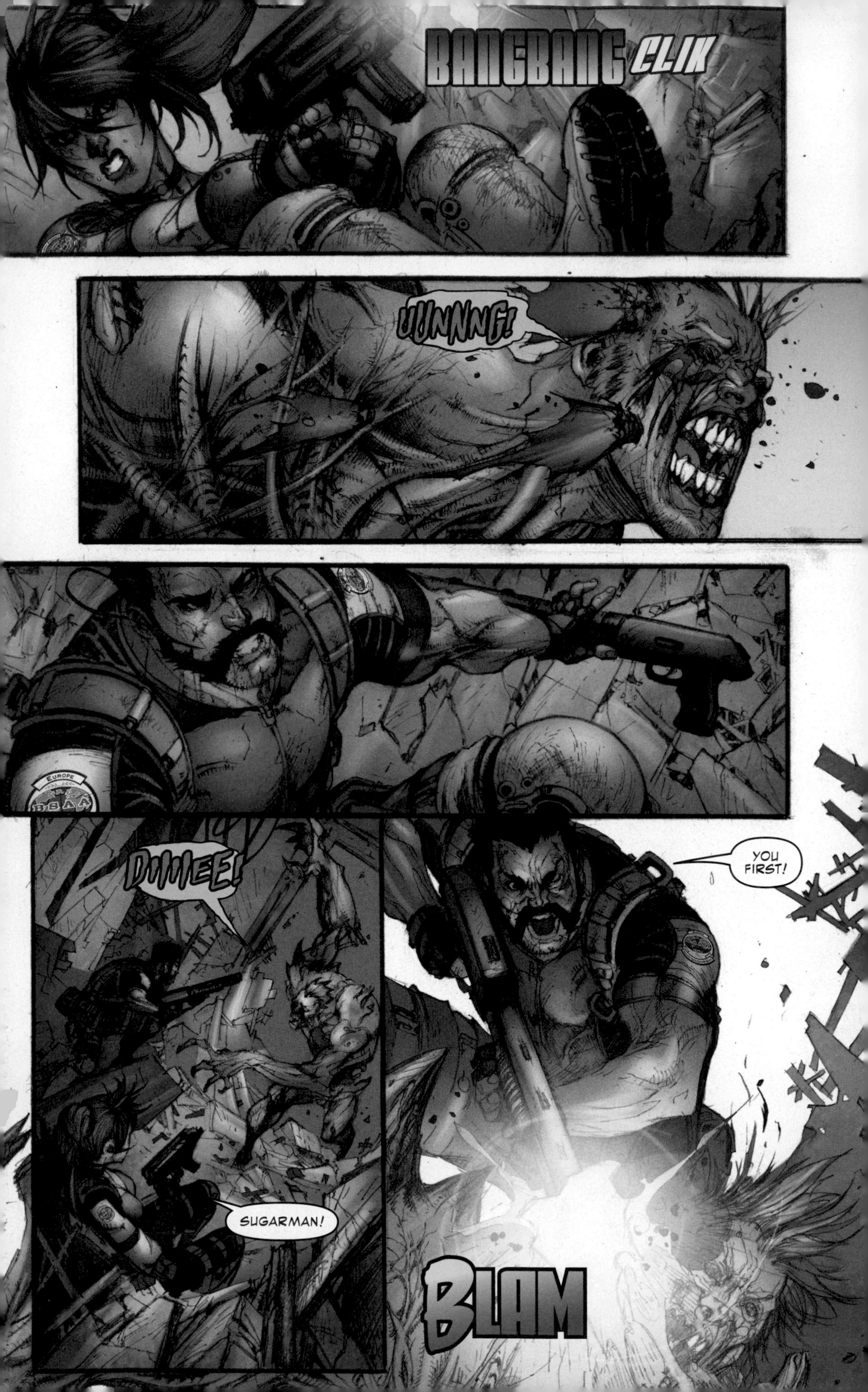
BANGBANG CLIK
UUNNNG!
DIIIEE!
SUGARMAN!
YOU FIRST!
BLAM

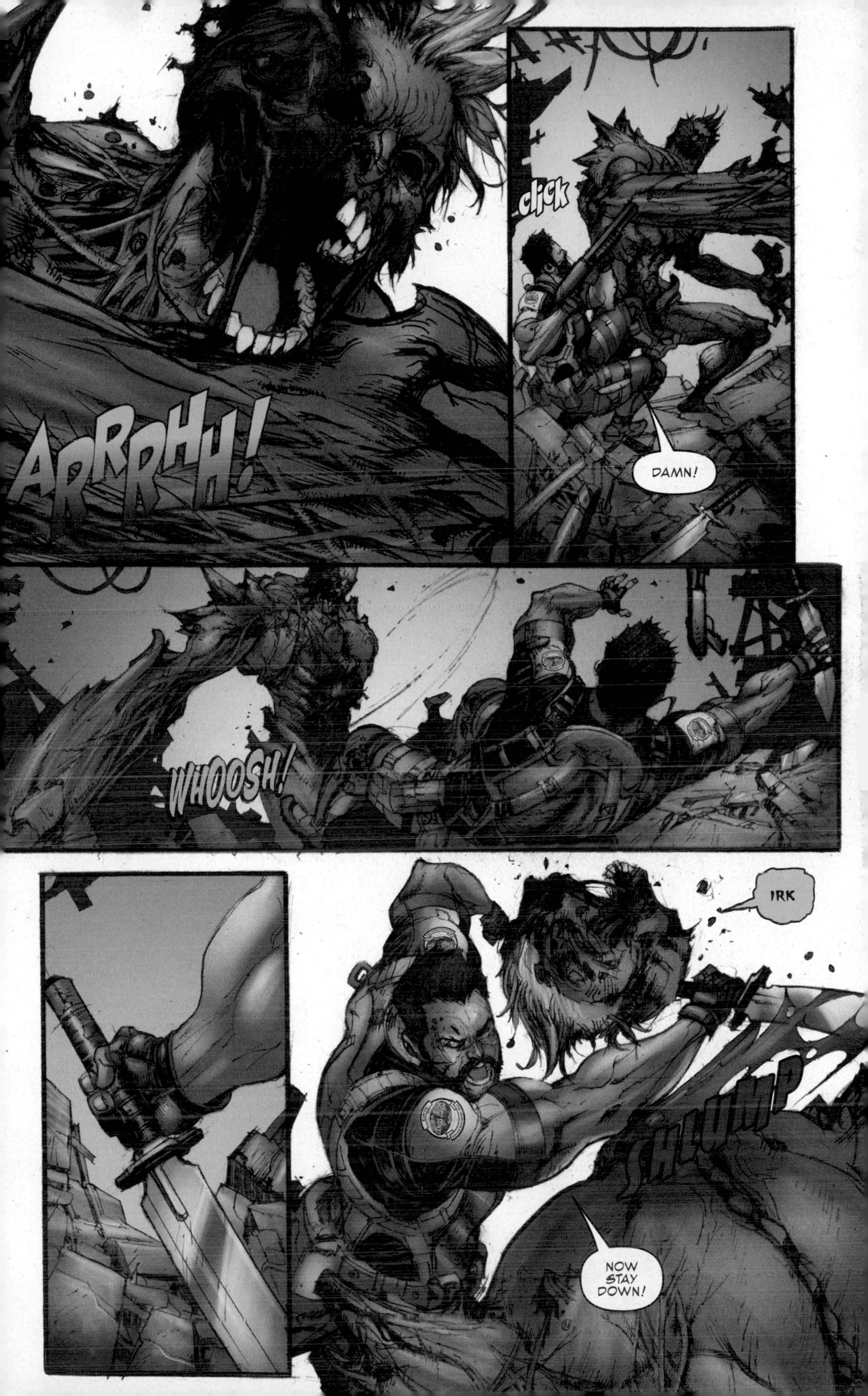

ARRRHH!
click
DAMN!
WHOOSH!
IRK
SHLUMP
NOW STAY DOWN!

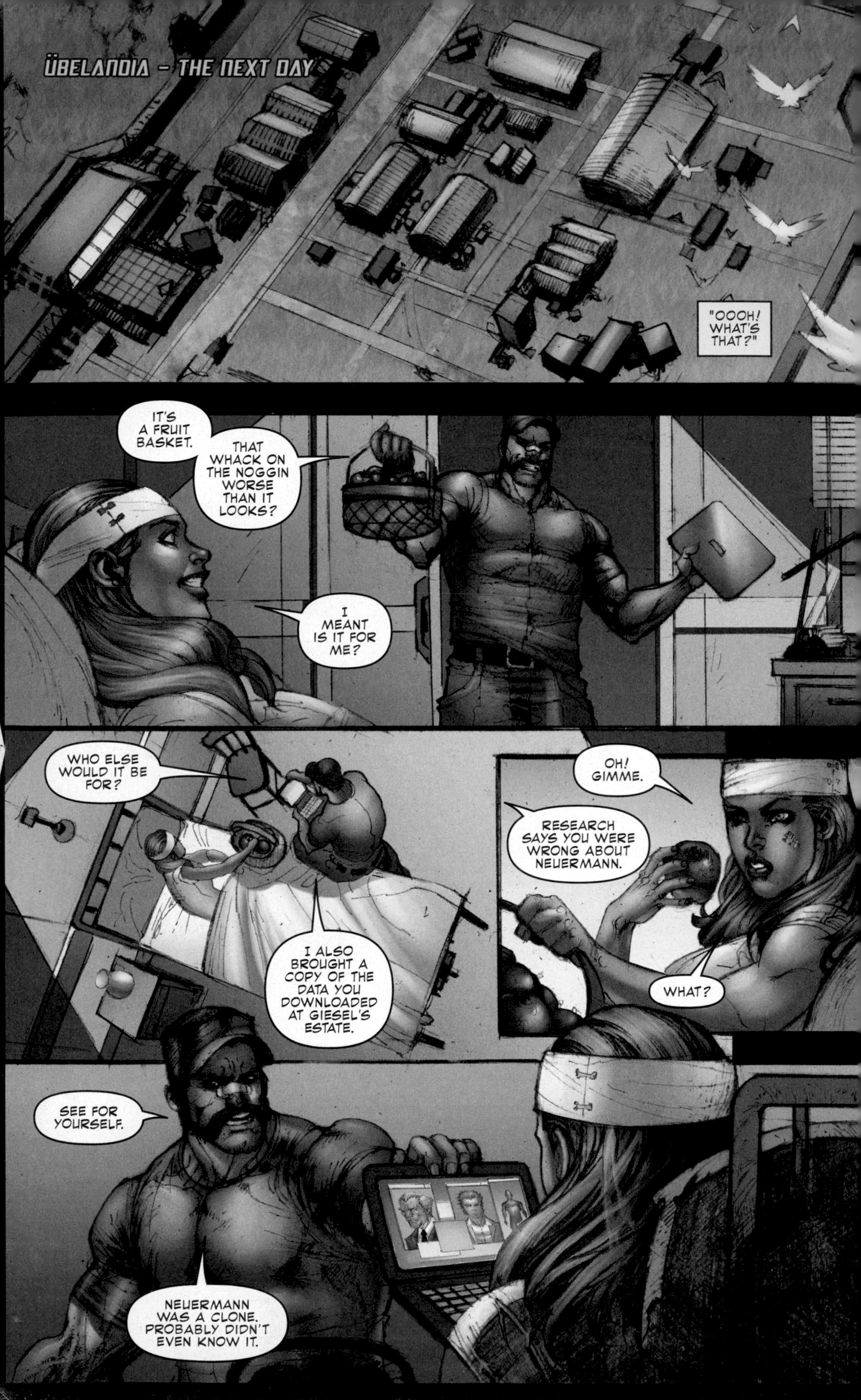
ÜBELANDIA - THE NEXT DAY
"OOOH! WHAT'S THAT?"
IT'S A FRUIT BASKET.
THAT WHACK ON THE NOGGIN WORSE THAN IT LOOKS?
I MEANT IS IT FOR ME?
WHO ELSE WOULD IT BE FOR?
I ALSO BROUGHT A COPY OF THE DATA YOU DOWNLOADED AT GIESEL'S ESTATE.
OH! GIMME.
RESEARCH SAYS YOU WERE WRONG ABOUT NEUERMANN.
WHAT?
SEE FOR YOURSELF.
NEUERMANN WAS A CLONE. PROBABLY DIDN'T EVEN KNOW IT.

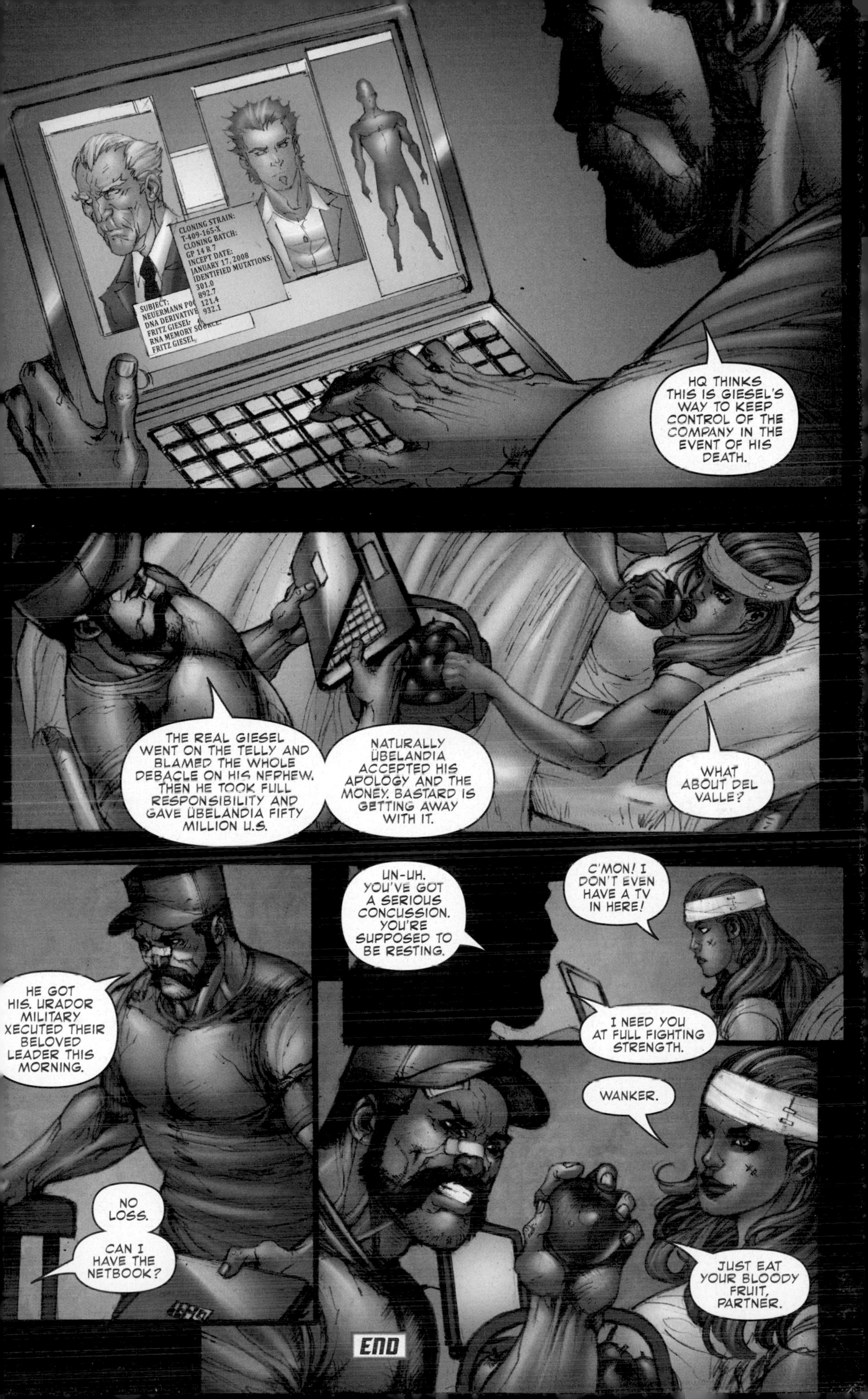
CLONING STRAIN:
T-409-165-X
CLONING BATCH:
GP 14 R 7
INCEPT DATE:
JANUARY 17, 2008
IDENTIFIED MUTATIONS:
301.0
892.7
121.4
932.1
SUBJECT:
NEUERMANN PO
DNA DERIVATIVE
FRITZ GIESEL
RNA MEMORY SOURCE:
FRITZ GIESEL
HQ THINKS THIS IS GIESEL'S WAY TO KEEP CONTROL OF THE COMPANY IN THE EVENT OF HIS DEATH.
THE REAL GIESEL WENT ON THE TELLY AND BLAMED THE WHOLE DEBACLE ON HIS NEPHEW. THEN HE TOOK FULL RESPONSIBILITY AND GAVE ÜBELANDIA FIFTY MILLION U.S.
NATURALLY ÜBELANDIA ACCEPTED HIS APOLOGY AND THE MONEY. BASTARD IS GETTING AWAY WITH IT.
WHAT ABOUT DEL VALLE?
HE GOT HIS. URADOR MILITARY XECUTED THEIR BELOVED LEADER THIS MORNING.
NO LOSS.
CAN I HAVE THE NETBOOK?
UN-UH. YOU'VE GOT A SERIOUS CONCUSSION. YOU'RE SUPPOSED TO BE RESTING.
C'MON! I DON'T EVEN HAVE A TV IN HERE!
I NEED YOU AT FULL FIGHTING STRENGTH.
WANKER.
JUST EAT YOUR BLOODY FRUIT, PARTNER.
END

Variant RESIDENT EVIL 1
Cover by Brandon Badeaux

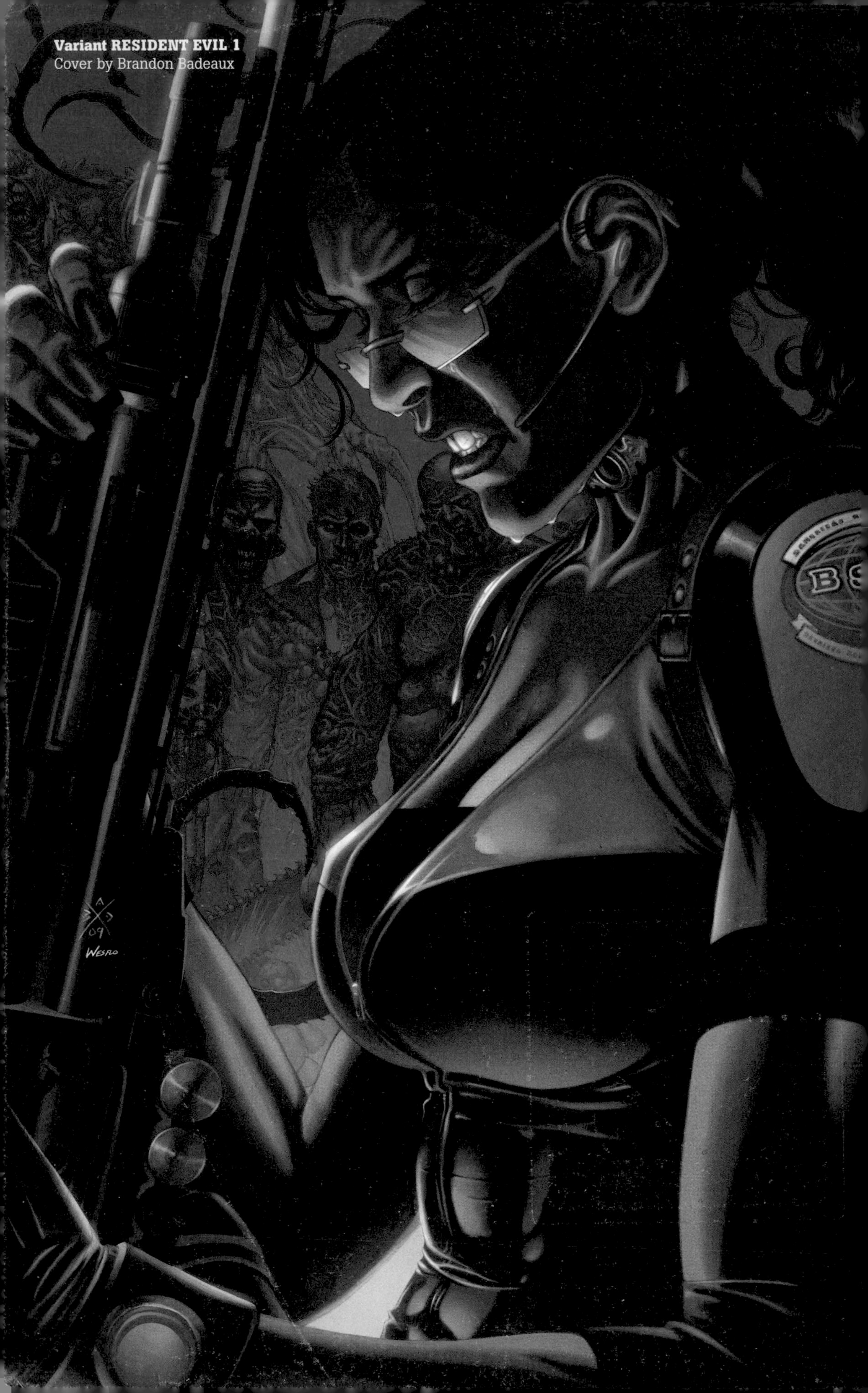